SOCIAL SHAKESPEARE

Also by Peter J. Smith

CHRISTOPHER MARLOWE, *THE JEW OF MALTA*
(editor)

Social Shakespeare

Aspects of Renaissance Dramaturgy and Contemporary Society

Peter J. Smith

First published in Great Britain 1995 by
MACMILLAN PRESS LTD
Houndmills, Basingstoke, Hampshire RG21 6XS
and London
Companies and representatives
throughout the world

A catalogue record for this book is available
from the British Library.

ISBN 0–333–63216–8 hardcover
ISBN 0–333–63217–6 paperback

First published in the United States of America 1995 by
ST. MARTIN'S PRESS, INC.,
Scholarly and Reference Division,
175 Fifth Avenue,
New York, N.Y. 10010

ISBN 0–312–12627–1

Library of Congress Cataloging-in-Publication Data
Smith, Peter J.
Social Shakespeare : aspects of Renaissance dramaturgy and
contemporary society / by Peter J. Smith.
p. cm.
Based on the author's thesis (Ph.D., University of Leicester,
1992).
Includes bibliographical references and index.
ISBN 0–312–12627–1
1. Shakespeare, William, 1564–1616—Political and social views.
2. Shakespeare, William, 1564–1616—Contemporary England.
3. Literature and society—England—History—16th century.
4. Literature and society—England—History—17th century.
5. Social problems in literature. 6. Renaissance—England.
I. Title.
PR3024.S64 1995
822.3'3—dc20   94–2957
                                                CIP

10   9   8   7   6   5   4   3   2   1
04 03 02 01 00 99 98 97 96 95

Printed and bound in Great Britain by
Antony Rowe Ltd, Chippenham, Wiltshire

For Roy and Dorrie

Contents

Acknowledgements

The following have read and provided helpful comments on various chapters, for which I am very grateful: Edward Bond, Richard Dutton, Jean-Marie Maguin, Simon Shepherd, Fiona J. Stafford, Ann Thompson and Roger Warren. Gordon Campbell and Richard Allen Cave read the whole manuscript and provided me with an incisive overview. Tim Luscombe and Sir Ian McKellen supplied me with valuable information, especially in relation to Chapter 8. Jane Marshall caught several articles that might have passed me by and fiddled countless library fines. Catherine Burgass tempered my rhetorical excesses throughout. I began this book as a Research Scholar in the English Department of the University of Leicester and I am grateful to the then heads of English, J. S. Cunningham and W. F. T. Myers, for their humane treatment of a novice. Greg Walker's contribution to the book was incalculable. He was generous with his scholarship, indulgent with his time and unstinting in his enthusiasm.

I am grateful to the following for their assistance with reviews and picture research: Birmingham Rep., Cheek by Jowl, English Shakespeare Company, English Touring Theatre, Leicester Haymarket Theatre, Oxford Stage Company, Renaissance Theatre Company, the RSC Barbican and the Young Vic. Helen Cross of the RSC Stratford deserves a special mention. Hetty Shand guided me through the protocol of professional theatre with patience and good humour. Thanks are due to the staff at the following institutions: the Ashmolean Museum and the Bodleian Library, Oxford; the Shakespeare Centre, Stratford-upon-Avon and Leicester University Library.

The usual admission of authorial responsibility for errors that remain goes without saying.

A Note on the Texts

A number of Renaissance works have been quoted from their original editions. Most of them are unavailable in modern spelling versions and I have chosen not to modernise them. Conversely, Shakespeare, Marlowe, Jonson, etc., have usually been quoted in modern spelling from standard editions. One danger of this inconsistency is that it makes the lesser known writers look arcane and tends to harden canonical prejudice. The reader should be aware of this pitfall and I risk it only for ease of reference.

Unless otherwise stated, all quotations from Shakespeare are from *The Complete Works*, edited by Peter Alexander (London and Glasgow, 1951) and the place of publication of works cited is London.

List of Plates

A. *Much Ado About Nothing*, dir. Alexandru Darie, Oxford Stage Co., 1992. Diane Parish as Hero. (Mark Douet.)

B. Dutch Engraving of Elizabeth I as Europa. (Ashmolean Museum Oxford.)

C. Salt-cellar by Cellini. (Kunsthistorisches Museum, Vienna. Photograph by David Finn.)

D. *The Winter's Tale*, dir. Simon Usher, Leicester Haymarket, 1991. Kevin Costello as Leontes with the statue of Hermione. (Stephen Vaughan.)

E. *Cymbeline*, dir. Bill Alexander, RSC, 1987. Harriet Walter as Innogen and Donald Sumpter as Iachimo. (Ivan Kyncl.)

F. *Romeo and Juliet*, dir. David Leveaux, RSC, 1991. Michael Maloney as Romeo (foreground) and Kevin Doyle as Benvolio. (Richard Mildenhall.)

G. *Romeo and Juliet*, dir. Terry Hands, RSC, 1989. L to R: Patrick Brennan as Benvolio, Mark Rylance as Romeo and David O'Hara as Mercutio. (Shakespeare Centre Library [Joe Cocks Studio].)

H. *The Merchant of Venice*, dir. Tim Luscombe, ESC, 1990. Gary Raymond as Antonio and Hugh Sullivan as the Duke. (Louanne Richard.)

I. *The Merchant of Venice*, dir. David Thacker, RSC, 1993. Designed by Shelagh Keegan. David Calder as Shylock (centre). (Alastair Muir.)

J. *The Jew Of Malta*, dir. Barry Kyle, RSC, 1987. John Carlisle as Machevill. (Shakespeare Centre Library [Joe Cocks Studio].)

K. *The Merchant of Venice*, dir. Bill Alexander, RSC, 1987. Antony Sher as Shylock. (Shakespeare Centre Library [Joe Cocks Studio].)

L. *As You Like It*, dir. Declan Donnellan, Cheek by Jowl, 1991. Adrian Lester as Rosalind and Patrick Toomey as Orlando. (John Haynes.)

M. *Troilus and Cressida*, dir. Sam Mendes, RSC, 1990. Norman
Rodway as Pandarus and Sally Dexter as Helen. (Shakespeare
Centre Library [Joe Cocks Studio].)

N. *Troilus and Cressida*, dir. Sam Mendes, RSC, 1990. Ciaran Hinds
as Achilles. (Shakespeare Centre Library [Joe Cocks Studio].)

O. *Coriolanus*, dir. Tim Supple, Renaissance Theatre Co., 1992.
Kenneth Branagh as Coriolanus and James Simmons as Lartius.
(© Richard H. Smith.)

P. *Coriolanus*, dir. Michael Bogdanov, ESC, 1990. L to R: Vivian
Munn as Roman Senator, Michael Pennington as Coriolanus
and Bernard Lloyd as Menenius Agrippa. (Laurence Burns.)

1

Introduction

I loved to see the Macbeths Jerseys knacking spots of the Plumpduffs Pants.[1]

'Romeo Romeo where for art thou Romeo?' . . . 'Romeo Romeo were four ought though Romeo' . . . 'rome oh rome wher for they romeo.'[2]

I

In 1985 *Political Shakespeare* was published and since then Shakespeare studies have become increasingly politicised.[3] This study is a further contribution to that process but it is one which aims at a distinct refocusing of political criticism upon the Shakespearean text as realised in production. *Social Shakespeare* embraces dramatic production as a site for interpretation rather than prioritising a fixed literary document.

The reasons for the increasingly urgent politicisation of Shakespeare studies in recent years are themselves worthy of analysis. The entrenchment of the Right under Margaret Thatcher and Ronald Reagan in the major English-speaking countries of the world was met by the arrival and establishment, as tertiary lecturers, of those that had been educated during a period of oppositional politics throughout the sixties and seventies. In the United States the oppositional programme took the form of pacific, anti-Vietnam 'hippyism' while in Europe more visibly radical agendas were set by *les Événements* in Paris in the spring of 1968.[4] The students of this period have by now arrived in senior positions within intellectual communities both in Europe and the States and have effected a revolution in the study of cultural forms with obvious consequences for the discipline of English and especially Shakespeare.

The displacement of traditional critics by these 'children of the revolution', is usually greeted by the accusation that the study of artistic forms is being increasingly debased or sullied by the intrusion

1

of politics. In terms of English studies generally, the contention is less pronounced than it was during the last decade. The victimisation of Colin MacCabe at Cambridge and David Craig at Lancaster was perhaps the first intimation of the struggle that was to come as the academy xenophobically resisted the 'immigration' of theoretical ideas from Europe.[5] This struggle was still taking place during the mid-eighties when a number of Higher Education Teachers of English conferences generated particularly acerbic quarrels between the last of a species of English Men of Letters and the champions of the new theory.

Ironically, theory, which is usually perceived to be politically oppositional, has been assured of its place by recent reforms in Higher Education brought about by the Conservative party which has held office ever since its arrival in the late seventies and early eighties. The transformation of polytechnics and colleges of Higher Education into new universities (which took effect from September 1992), puts their socially-informed and progressive predilections on an ostensibly equal footing with the scholarly traditionalism of the 'real' universities. Of course no one who knows anything about HE could possibly believe that parity will result between ancient seats of learning and polys as a result of this cosmetic exercise. Yet John Major's fantasy of a 'classless society' is, we are assured, the reason that over fifty polytechnics have been allowed to alter their letter-heads.[6] Despite their superior position, the traditional universities have been required to embrace theory to keep pace with the polys' penchant for theoretically informed courses such as media studies, film studies, popular culture, communications studies and so on. That one of the most unyielding harbingers of English radicalism, Terry Eagleton, has been transformed into Oxford's major tourist attraction and Warton Professor of English is a symptom of the rapprochement between the bastions of traditional scholasticism and theory. Theory, it seems, is here to stay.

Despite the safe (albeit bumpy) landing of theory within British HE, the struggle over its place in Shakespeare studies is far from over. The juxtaposition of potentially radical theoretical positions with the world's most putatively apolitical writer was bound to be uncomfortable. This discomfort is typified by the public wrangle between Richard Levin, a polemical defender of traditional approaches, and his radical opponents. In *PMLA*, 104 (1989), no fewer than 24 academics signed a letter condemning Levin's paper in the previous number as embodying 'arbitrary selectivity, reductive thematizing, misplaced causality, unexamined and untenable assumptions about intentionality, irresponsible slippage from particulars to abstractions'.[7] The letter concludes with the stinging paragraph:

> We are puzzled and disturbed that Richard Levin has made a successful academic career by using the reductive techniques of this essay to bring the same predictable charges indiscriminately against all varieties of contemporary criticism. We wish to know why ... *PMLA* has chosen to print a tired, muddled, unsophisticated essay that is blind at once to the assumptions of feminist criticism of Shakespeare and to its own.[8]

In the following year, a special number of *New Literary History* published an essay by Levin under the title 'Unthinkable Thoughts in the New Historicizing of English Renaissance Drama'.[9] Catherine Belsey's response followed in the same number, 'Richard Levin and In-different Reading'.[10] In it she accuses Levin of basing part of his argument (about the 'unthinkability' of modern critical concepts in the early modern period) on a misreading of her influential book, *Critical Practice*. She asserts that his deployment of her arguments is 'particularly half-witted' and while 'I should be happy to have the debate ... he prefers to score easier points by inventing a much sillier statement and attributing it to me as a representative of the critical approach he deplores.'[11] For Jonathan Dollimore, Levin is beneath contempt. In the same number of *NLH* he prefixed his essay with the note: 'This essay was prompted by an invitation from Ralph Cohen, editor of *New Literary History*, to reply to a critique of new historicism and cultural materialism by Richard Levin, to be published in the same issue of that journal. Nothing in Levin's article inspired me to take up this generous offer.'[12] Levin is not alone in his condemnation of the new theoretical models, though he may be considered to be a good deal more (foolishly) brave than other less outspoken traditionalists. One less widely known but similarly conservative enemy of theory is Charles R. Forker who reserved his contempt for his review of *Political Shakespeare* itself:

> A monochrome high seriousness virtually annihilates all Shakespearean wit, charm, and sense of humour unless these can be harnessed vulgarly to some ulterior social moralism. Obsessive

class- and gender-consciousness make for a kind of inverse
snobbery. . . . Power and oppression become exclusively and
reductively the theme. Implicit also in this school of academic
discourse is the arrogant assumption that the interpretive act, if
it can be sufficiently startling and revisionist, somehow displaces
and ought to displace the work interpreted, even if (or perhaps
because) it comes from the pen of Western civilization's supreme
literary genius.[13]

Despite the mystification of the humanist assumptions which under-
lie this critique, the charge is a serious one. *Political Shakespeare* is
dourly unabashed about its own ideological agenda. In the fore-
word to the volume its editors sombrely assert that, 'Cultural
materialism . . . registers its commitment to the transformation of a
social order which exploits people on grounds of race, gender and
class.'[14] This formulation looks distinctly jaded and insular alongside the poststructuralist play of Barthes and Hawkes's linguistic
revelry. Robert Weimann draws attention to the risk of sounding
glumly pious or holier-than-thou: 'a politically committed criticism,
would as a matter of course condemn itself to a grim kind of puritanism if the sheer element of fun, release, reckless enjoyment were
ever minimized or, even, by implication, theoretically ostracized'.[15]
While the title of *Social Shakespeare* clearly alludes to that of *Political
Shakespeare*, and while this allusion signifies the similarity of its
political aspirations, it distinguishes itself from the latter study tonally, in its enthusiasm for the Shakespearean works which provide
both its focus and its impetus. In addition, its sustained examination of particular theatrical productions is designed to prevent the
pat resignation of Shakespeare's plays to the 'establishment' and to
forestall the kind of theoretical obfuscation to which 'detheatricalised'
accounts of the plays are prone. Chapter 9, for example, attempts to
clear the plays from the charge of ideological hegemony by distinguishing them from their cultural mediation (which the chapter
theorises as 'Shakemyth'). In this way the notion that any literature
is *a priori* politically partisan is refuted and the plays are shown
potentially to be sites of intervention for a politics of either the Left
or (more commonly) the Right.

The dual project of *Political Shakespeare* is signified in the book's
structure. Part I ('Recovering history') re-reads the plays in the light
of Renaissance history and society. Attention is focused on state-
craft, family life, exploration, colonialism and other areas of debate

current in Renaissance studies; these essays strive to make us Shakespeare's contemporaries. Part II ('Reproductions, interventions') reads Shakespeare in the light of his modern cultural position. In Marxist terminology, Part I is directed towards the moment of production, and Part II to the moment(s) of consumption. The subtitle of *Social Shakespeare* (*Aspects of Renaissance Dramaturgy and Contemporary Society*) is designed to reproduce this double focus but, in addition, there is underpinning the enterprise a stress on the dialogic relationship between past and present; not in terms of a clumsy conflation of the two, erasing the distinctions between Shakespeare's period and our own, but rather in terms of an awareness of a modern historicity which, while it interrogates the ideologies of earlier cultures, acknowledges as inescapable its own ideological position and the historicity of its own insights. The *Contemporary* of my subtitle, then, stands for both the sixteenth and the twentieth centuries, early modern *and* postmodern, and thus refutes the dichotomy of the too-neatly sectionalised *Political Shakespeare*. Don E. Wayne has identified 'a noticeable lag between our ability to recognize the role of power in the plays and poems of Shakespeare . . . and our ability to articulate the forms that power takes in our own historical moment'.[16] *Social Shakespeare* is designed to eradicate this lag.

In spite of the vehemence with which *Political Shakespeare* protests its political aspirations, the volume, as with much apparently oppositional criticism in the area, is frequently, surprisingly defeatist. For example, Sinfield's 'Shakespeare and Education' ends with the humble admission that 'Teaching Shakespeare's plays and writing books about them is unlikely to bring down capitalism, but it is a point for intervention.'[17] Elsewhere, Ivo Kamps timidly confesses, 'The chances that a new reading of a Shakespeare play will noticeably affect our world are negligible.'[18] This submissiveness is the result in part of the recognition that Shakespeare criticism is not usually read outside the academy and that it is (along with all such critical work) the preserve of the elite. It is not likely that cultural perceptions of literature will change significantly due to the publication of another academic volume. This situation is especially true in Shakespeare studies where the sheer number of new publications threatens each of them with overnight obsolescence. This humility seems widely felt at the moment especially in the United States and may be a symptom of the bludgeoning authority of the Right over the last decade. Stephen Greenblatt, for example, who coined the label 'new historicism' and is one of its most influential practitioners, eschews its political authority: 'as far as I can tell (and I should be the one to know) it's no doctrine at all'.[19] But political disengagement is also the inheritance of new criticism with its insistence on textual scrutiny; indeed we might think of new historicism as a continuation of new criticism rather than a departure from old historicism.[20] Greenblatt has pointed out that radical theoretical positions may end up as traditional practices: 'one consequence of the Derridean calling into question of the stability of the sign is to drive you back to a close, nuanced, inflected attention to the text. . . . finally I'm committed to a certain kind of conventional literary criticism'.[21] Walter Cohen attributes this acquiescence to a post-Vietnam disillusionment, noting what he describes as 'the strangely quietist feel of these radical critiques'.[22] *Social Shakespeare* is motivated by a discontent with this kind of political resignation. In part it accepts the pessimistic view of the relative impotence of scholarly books to alter society constructively. However, this study sites the political force of the plays that it explores in the theatre rather than on the printed page, accepting and acting upon a discontent with the shortcomings of much contemporary criticism noted by Jean E. Howard: 'I think it is a mistake to restrict our considerations of the ideological import of Renaissance theatre to an analysis of the scripts. . . . Ideology is enacted through all the theatre's practices, from its pricing structures for admission to the times of its performances.'[23] The impact of theatre extends far beyond the academy and this book's attention to specific productions signifies its acknowledgement that a theatre audience is likely to be both larger and more heterogeneous than the readership of any single academic study.

Despite the fact that recent criticism has examined Renaissance theatre in terms of its materiality, there is still a reluctance to consider the political efficacy of *modern* Shakespearean production. Although *Political Shakespeare* contains an essay on the Royal Shakespeare Company and another on the theatre of Brecht and his rewritings of Shakespeare, there is an unwillingness to consider individual productions and the manner in which they may serve to illustrate or articulate particular political issues.[24] Conversely there is an ever-increasing number of new publications describing and analysing specific performances, but these studies tend too readily to separate the texts (with their 'themes' and dramatic techniques) and the particular performances that they are considering. Most often, the written text takes priority over the performative one. The monographs in the 'Text and Performance' series illustrate the apparent disparity of the titular components with strictly separate sections for each; text of course comes first.[25] This dichotomy overlooks the degree to which the composition of a theatre work is cognisant of the conditions of its performance. The play may well be influenced by the stage, company, theatre, etc. for which it is being composed: 'the written text/performance text relationship is not one of simple priority but a complex of reciprocal constraints constituting a powerful *intertextuality*'.[26] *Social Shakespeare* integrates its understandings of the plays with evidence from actual productions. Of course, this involves the selection of productions which (usually) reinforce its argument, but this is not to say that a particular commentary is in any sense more valid than a contradictory one. Theatrical interpretation is notoriously 'open', and the appropriation of individual theatrical readings to support textual ones needs always to acknowledge its own relativity. This reluctance to read drama in a single or closed way is to infuse Shakespearean criticism with a dialogism appropriate to the unfixity of theatrical production. Moreover, this openness exposes the error (which is frequently overlooked) of ascribing either a reactionary or a subversive motivation to dramatic texts. The vagaries of dramatic performance entirely undermine the supposition of fixed ideological significance. The 'transgression versus containment' division between radical critics and some practitioners of the new historicism obdurately refuses to acknowledge theatrical inconsistency. *Social Shakespeare* regards this as a critical limitation.

Because literary criticism is primarily a written form, it is not surprising that it takes as its object, even in the case of drama, printed versions of text. However, we should remind ourselves of the anachronism of working on editions of plays which, in the playwright's own day, had no sort of textual authority whatsoever. Thomas Healy alerts us to the spurious fixity of the playtexts upon which traditional literary criticism is based: 'Critical discussions may emphasise the drama's popularity within English Renaissance society and examine the conditions of theatrical playing within Elizabethan and Jacobean society, but considerations of plays rarely acknowledge that many possess multiple forms.'[27] I would suggest that this multiplicity of forms does not merely refer to the sometimes extremely divergent textual versions of plays, but also to the infinite variety of their stage manifestations which are augmented every time the play is performed.

This abundance of textual and performative manifestations is partially responsible for one of the most striking features of recent Shakespearean criticism – its frequent contrariety. This lack of a single authority is in part at least the result of the uncertainty that is criticism's poststructuralist inheritance, in which Shakespeare studies inevitably share. Its most obvious symptom is the abundance of anthologies which seem to have outstripped publication of scholarly monographs. The publication of *Political Shakespeare* took place in the same year as *Alternative Shakespeares* and *Shakespeare and the Question of Theory*.[28] These groundbreaking collections have since been followed by a number of revisionist anthologies including within the last few years: *Literary Theory/Renaissance Texts*, *The Shakespeare Myth*, *Shakespeare Reproduced*, *Rewriting the Renaissance*, *The Appropriation of Shakespeare*, *Staging the Renaissance*, *The Matter of Difference*, *Shakespeare Left and Right*, and three anthologies in the Longman Critical Readers series: *Shakespeare's Comedies*, *Shakespearean Tragedy*, and *New Historicism and Renaissance Drama*.[29] Even individual authors are producing collections of essays, comprising the bringing together of articles that have been published in their own right previously in journals and other collections rather than sustained and coherent studies, most obviously Greenblatt's *Shakespearean Negotiations* and *Learning to Curse* (itself the product of more than fifteen years) or the more conservative *Young Hamlet: Essays on Shakespeare's Tragedies* by Barbara Everett.[30] The abundance of anthologies is no doubt a symptom of the institutional pressure upon academics to publish as well as an indication of market forces in relation to the kinds of reading matter which can be afforded by libraries and undergraduates (witness also the number of 'readers' in critical and literary theory which have been published since the mid-eighties). In Renaissance studies this plethora of anthologies is indicative of the plurality of contemporary intellectual positions in relation to the culture of the early modern period and is especially the result of the ambiguities and lack of single ontology inherent in the theatrical experience. The moral and ideological complexities of the plays themselves along with the bewildering multivalency of the theatrical representation have necessitated the abandonment of a single unifying viewpoint. The same play can be constructive of both conservative and radical positions and, moreover, it may be both at the same time. The recent emphasis in Renaissance studies on contradiction rather than cohesion, subversion rather than order, and difference rather than uniformity, is of a piece with the relativisation of both the critical judgements *and* their object of study. Critics now tend to emphasise polyphony and perplexity; Tillyard-ian uniformity is long gone and we fashion the Renaissance in our own fragmented image. In her 'Afterword' to *Shakespeare Repro-duced* (which for obvious reasons could not be called a conclusion), Margaret Ferguson offers a prime example of this rejection of a holistic scheme (or meta-narrative): 'one of the results of working on this volume . . . is that I see more clearly now than I did a year ago the contours of what I don't know, or cannot articulate clearly'.[31] This confusion is not only in the eye of the beholder but in the object itself.

It is in his seminal essay, 'The Circulation of Social Energy' that Greenblatt is most forthright in his call to abandon any single or fixed critical perspective, seeing the Renaissance stage as well as its critical investigation as deeply contradictory:

> the circulation of social energy by and through the stage was not part of a single coherent, totalizing system. Rather it was partial, fragmentary, conflictual; elements were crossed, torn apart, re-combined, set against each other; particular social practices were magnified by the stage, others diminished, exalted, evacuated. What then is the social energy that is being circulated? Power, charisma, sexual excitement, collective dreams, wonder, desire, anxiety, religious awe, free-floating intensities of experience: in a sense the question is absurd, for everything produced by the society can circulate unless it is deliberately excluded from circu-lation. Under such circumstances, there can be no single method, no overall picture, no exhaustive and definitive cultural poetics.[32]

The inherent creative collaboration of drama (and the performance contingent upon it) which is above all other literary forms socially produced, makes the rejection of a single author/authority espe-cially appropriate. *Social Shakespeare* shares this heterogeneity. The choice of plays for detailed study, for example, includes the canoni-cal (*Antony and Cleopatra*) and the marginal (*The Two Gentlemen of Verona*). This project is aware of its own partiality in both senses of being fragmentary, and ordered by its own critical preferences. This partiality is signified by the self-conscious 'inventoriness' of the subtitle, 'Aspects of . . .'.

Greenblatt's rejection of a critical purchase may appear to be (especially in the light of my remarks about the political indifference of the new historicism above) morally irresponsible. *Social Shake-speare*, while it accepts Greenblatt's relativism, prefers not to decode it in terms of a political paralysis or metaphysical chaos which would itself be politically impotent, but rather to see the fragmentation and contradictions of both the plays and their analyses as subversive of an apparently transparent version of Shakespeare which promotes him as the purveyor of eternal human value. Such an unproblematised and essentialist version is inevitably authoritative and prescriptive. *Social Shakespeare* intends to highlight the power of culture and the culture of power which surround the performance of plays that are so deeply implicated in versions of truth and value.

II

Social Shakespeare is divided into three parts. The first sets out the critical agenda and methodology and situates the study in relation to more traditional criticism. Chapter 2 discusses the difficulty of defining Shakespearean comedy and so challenges glib ideas about happiness and festivity. It asserts instead that the plays are both narratively and generically unstable and that in the teeth of this instability they demand a consensual response that guarantees their audience a solidarity which they foreground in their titles. Chapter 3 again focuses on formal and generic qualities, this time those of tragedy. It challenges a critical practice which although it sounds outmoded, is still being taught to students at 'A' and undergraduate level. The idea of the 'fatal flaw' of the tragic hero is deconstructed and demonstrated to be essentialist and ahistorical in its assumptions and reactionary and deterministic in its politics. Chapter 3 goes on to consider the centrality of the acting body and its radical and obvious inconsistency with the abstract 'tragic flaw'. The fourth chapter addresses the issue of gendered geography in the literature and visual arts of the Renaissance and focuses on the manner in which Shakespeare's exploration of the idea is subversive of the norm. The chapter concludes that the collapse of gendered imagery, principally illustrated in *Antony and Cleopatra*, is a dramatic strategy which, as well as being responsible for the play's reputation as one of Shakespeare's most ambiguous works, is itself symptomatic of the epistemological uncertainty which characterises the early modern period.

Part II is an attempt to read specific plays with reference to particular Shakespearean techniques and in the light of the procedural explications of Part I. Chapter 5 explores the notion of drama occurring at the boundaries of the conscious and subconscious mind. But it extends this idea to a consideration of the manner in which private fantasy (particularly that surrounding issues of sexual initiation) is appropriated and anticipated by certain social forces. Ideas set up in Chapter 2, associated with social consensus, are again seen to be at work. The sixth chapter is a demonstration that formal and 'political' criticism are not necessarily different things. It considers how a particular kind of speaking is politically subversive and how the social world needs to censor ambiguous speech in order to reinforce its authority. Linguistic analysis is shown to be inseparable from social analysis, the world of language indistinct from the language of the world. A 'merely' formal criticism, which is so often eschewed by Shakespeare's oppositional critics, is thus shown to have a real political force.

Part III is the most obviously politicised. Chapter 7 considers *The Merchant of Venice* and *The Jew of Malta* alongside Walter Benjamin's remarks about the barbarism that underlies all cultural achievement. It considers specific controversies that the plays raise in the post-Holocaust period and questions the bland assumption of their inherent greatness. A number of recent productions of the plays are discussed in an effort to illustrate the racism or otherwise not just of the texts but of the theatrical establishment that reproduces them. The chapter argues that an awareness of the social conditions of Jews in early modern England will ensure that anti-Semitism (at least in respect of these particular texts) is seen to be historically specific.

No other subject area in Shakespeare studies has generated quite as much vociferous interest as sexuality. Chapter 8 considers the importance of all-male companies in the Renaissance theatre and the implications this may have both for feminist readings of the texts and today's mixed-sex theatre industry. As with Chapter 7, particular historically specific ideas are cited and analysed in an attempt to consider the cultural implications of the various shifts between Renaissance playing and modern theatrical representations. The final chapter concludes by discussing versions of the Bard as he is mythologised by some and deconstructed by others. Shakespeare's apotheosis as a cultural 'deity' has been ratified principally by two agencies, education and the commercial theatre, and this chapter demonstrates their symbiosis in the construction of Shakespeare as a mythological Everyman. The chapter theorises what it calls 'Shakemyth': the complex of cultural ideas surrounding the plays, the social institutions through which they are reproduced and the re-presentation of the mythologised persona of the playwright. Although this might seem an obvious approach in the light of recent work on the cultural construction of Shakespeare by Terence Hawkes, Alan Sinfield, Gary Taylor and others, evidence from the theatre and the National Curriculum illustrates that many of the humanist assumptions about the Bard remain intact.[33] Shakemyth is always ahistorical and asocial and thus exempt from re-reading. *Social Shakespeare* contributes to the exposure of Shakemyth as a dangerous essentialising strategy which amiably protests its own political neutrality while at the same time exercising a deeply reactionary political influence.

The publication of *Political Shakespeare* signalled the arrival of political criticism in Shakespeare studies. *Social Shakespeare* hopes to refine and promote this practice while embarking on a still broader project – the study of Shakespearean drama in its fully social context.

Notes

1. James Joyce, *Finnegans Wake*, third edn (1960), p. 302.
2. Responses of 13-year-old children when asked for ideas about Shakespeare. Cited by Bob Allen, 'A school perspective on Shakespeare teaching', in *Shakespeare in the Changing Curriculum*, ed. Lesley Aers and Nigel Wheale (1991), 40–57, p. 40.
3. *Political Shakespeare: New Essays in Cultural Materialism*, ed. Jonathan Dollimore and Alan Sinfield (Manchester, 1985).
4. For the effects of Vietnam especially on gender issues in the American academy, see Linda E. Boose, 'The Family in Shakespeare Studies; or – Studies in the Family of Shakespeareans; or – The Politics of Politics', *Renaissance Drama*, 40 (1987), 707–42, pp. 738–40.
5. For Colin MacCabe, see Bernard Bergonzi, *Exploding English: Criticism, Theory, Culture* (Oxford, 1990), pp. 10–17; for David Craig, see *Rewriting English: Cultural Politics of Gender and Class*, ed. Janet Batsleer et al. (1985), p. 26.
6. It seems that employers are already worried about the 'new' universities. In the month that their new status came into effect, an advertisement asked for 'Graduates with excellent degrees from good universities' (*Cosmopolitan*, September 1992).
7. *PMLA*, 104 (1989), 77–8, p. 77.

8. Ibid., p. 78.
9. *New Literary History*, 21 (1990), 433–47.
10. Ibid., 449–56. Belsey was among the signatories of the *PMLA* letter the previous year.
11. Ibid., p. 455.
12. Jonathan Dollimore, 'Shakespeare, Cultural Materialism, Feminism and Marxist Humanism', *New Literary History*, 21 (1990), 471–93, p. 471. The latest addition to the Levin controversy is *Shakespeare Left and Right*, ed. Ivo Kamps (1991), in which Levin is uncomfortably bound with his main detractors.
13. Cited in *New Historicism and Renaissance Drama*, ed. Richard Wilson and Richard Dutton (1992), p. 219.
14. Dollimore and Sinfield, *Political Shakespeare*, p. viii.
15. Robert Weimann, 'Towards a literary theory of ideology: mimesis, representation, authority', in *Shakespeare Reproduced*, ed. Jean E. Howard and Marion F. O'Connor (1990), first published 1987, 265–72, p. 272. What Weimann identifies as 'puritanism' is perhaps best illustrated in Sinfield's suggestion that the National Curriculum's compulsory inclusion of Shakespeare is designed to reproduce 'a prole class where some people will know that they don't really count because they didn't quite make it through. . . . They know really that their destiny is to move . . . boxes from one side of the warehouse to the other. And that's what the Government wants and that's what it's really about' ('Shakespeare in the Curriculum', The *Times Educational Supplement* / English Shakespeare Company Debate, 1 December 1992, p. 22).
16. Don E. Wayne, 'Power, Politics and the Shakespearean text: recent criticism in England and the United States', in *Shakespeare Reproduced*, 47–67, p. 58.
17. Dollimore and Sinfield, *Political Shakespeare*, p. 154.
18. Kamps, *Shakespeare Left and Right*, p. 8.
19. Stephen J. Greenblatt, *Learning to Curse: Essays in Early Modern Culture* (1990), p. 146.
20. According to Hugh Grady, new criticism became 'instrumentalized, depleted, and irrelevant' as it settled into the academy (*The Modernist Shakespeare* (Oxford, 1991), p. 123).
21. '"Intensifying the surprise as well as the school": Stephen Greenblatt interviewed by Noel King', *Textual Practice*, 8 (1994), 114–27, pp. 115, 124.
22. Walter Cohen, 'Political Criticism of Shakespeare', in *Shakespeare Reproduced*, 18–46, p. 37. H. Aram Veeser shrugs off Eagleton's attack on new historicism's 'Sub-Nietzschean defeatism' with the concise but not altogether persuasive rejoinder, 'N[ew] H[istoricist]s consider Eagleton an old fart' (*The New Historicism: A Reader* (1994), p. 12).
23. Jean E. Howard, 'Crossdressing, The Theatre, and Gender Struggle in Early Modern England', *Shakespeare Quarterly*, 39 (1988), 418–40, p. 439.
24. The theatre is in an unrivalled position to respond to current affairs.

In August 1992, David Thacker's production of *The Merry Wives of Windsor* illustrated this kind of topicality. As Falstaff seduced Mistress Ford, he tore off her shoe and put her toe in his mouth. The allusions to the David Mellor affair and similar accusations involving the Duchess of York made the moment especially redolent. As John Peter slyly wrote, 'Nice to see someone at Windsor enjoying themselves' (*The Sunday Times*, 6 September 1992). Further accusations of sexual misconduct levelled against the Minister for Fun included the charge that he 'recit[ed] Shakespeare in the nude' (*The Guardian*, 23 September 1992). No wonder the Tories want the Bard to be a compulsory part of the National Curriculum.

25. Examples of titles in this series include Pamela Mason, *Much Ado About Nothing* (1992); Lois Potter, *Twelfth Night* (1985); Roger Warren, *A Midsummer Night's Dream* (1983).

26. Keir Elam, *The Semiotics of Theatre and Drama* (1991), first published 1980, p. 209.

27. Thomas Healy, *New Latitudes: Theory and English Renaissance Literature* (1992), p. 123.

28. *Alternative Shakespeares*, ed. John Drakakis (1985); *Shakespeare and the Question of Theory*, ed. Patricia Parker and Geoffrey Hartman (1991), first published 1985.

29. *Literary Theory/Renaissance Texts*, ed. Patricia Parker and David Quint (1986); *The Shakespeare Myth*, ed. Graham Holderness (Manchester, 1988); *Rewriting the Renaissance*, ed. Margaret W. Ferguson, Maureen Quilligan, and Nancy J. Vickers (1986); *The Appropriation of Shakespeare*, ed. Jean I. Marsden (Hemel Hempstead, 1991); *Staging the Renaissance*, ed. David Scott Kastan and Peter Stallybrass (1991); *The Matter of Difference*, ed. Valerie Wayne (Hemel Hempstead, 1991); *Shakespeare's Comedies*, ed. Garry Waller (1991); *Shakespearean Tragedy*, ed. John Drakakis (1992).

30. Stephen Greenblatt, *Shakespearean Negotiations* (Oxford, 1988); Barbara Everett, *Young Hamlet: Essays on Shakespeare's Tragedies* (Oxford, 1989).

31. Margaret Ferguson, 'Afterword' to *Shakespeare Reproduced*, 273–83, p. 273.

32. Greenblatt, *Shakespearean Negotiations*, p. 19.

33. See, for example, Terence Hawkes, *That Shakespeherian Rag: Essays on a Critical Process* (1986); Alan Sinfield, *Faultlines: Cultural Materialism and the Politics of Dissident Reading* (Oxford, 1992); Gary Taylor, *Reinventing Shakespeare* (1990).

Part I
Genre and Imagery

2

Shakespeare's Comedy of Consensus

For poetry makes nothing happen.[1]

I

On Valentine's Day 1989 Salman Rushdie was sentenced to death. In July 1991 the Japanese translator of *The Satanic Verses* was fatally stabbed and two years later 40 people were killed in Turkey as the hotel in which Aziz Nesin, translator and publisher of parts of the novel, was attacked by rioters. In November 1993 Rushdie's Norwegian publisher was shot dead.[2] The last few years of murders, death threats, intimidation and political disturbance surrounding the publication and reception of *The Satanic Verses*, serve as a perfect illustration of just how wrong Auden is. In one sense though, paradoxically, Auden *is* correct: poetry (or literature) does make nothing *happen*: literature can and does question the apparently commonsensical notions which have ceased to be important to us, unquestioned orthodoxies which have hardened into unnoticeable realities, into, so to speak, nothings. Literature, then, makes these nothings happen. We are examining Islam, Iranian politics, the issues of censorship and racism afresh in the light of a novel. Literature can bring about social and political change, or more likely in the case of Rushdie's book, serve as a channel to direct the flow of religious or political feelings which will effect change for good or ill. What we are doing when we meet in any classroom is discussing texts that really have the power to change people's lives. Those who think this assertion grandiose need only ask themselves why Rushdie's book has been burned, and its author sentenced to death; the answer must be because the work is important enough to somebody.

Could a discussion of Shakespearean comedy be anywhere near

as contentious? We are all supposed to know what Shakespearean comedy is. We have read or seen at least one example, and we certainly all recognise that *As You Like It* is a comedy while *King Lear* is something else. Unfortunately, though, a familiarity with the plays and even an intuitive grasp of the kind of drama constituted by Shakespearean comedy does not enable us to define the genre. The fact that we share a consensus about the sort of thing that Shakespearean comedy is, does little to change the fact that Shakespearean comedy, in itself, is nothing specific. The ironies of setting and marking examination questions on Shakespearean comedy are thus brought sharply into focus. While such questions ask students to negotiate the terrain of Shakespearean comedy, no one can really tell them precisely where to go. Teachers and lecturers can point students in the right direction but there are no accurate maps, no single objective and correct account of the subject. Even the *OED* fails to capture the infinite variety of Shakespearean comedy. It offers, 'A light and amusing stage play with a happy conclusion to its plot.' But are Malvolio's final 'I'll be reveng'd on the whole pack of you' (V. i. 364), or a tired old fool singing about the rain and the impotence of old age, the signs of a happy conclusion? The *OED* continues: 'That branch of the drama which . . . depicts laughable characters and incidents.' But try telling that to the wedding guests in *Much Ado* after the 'death' of the bride, or explaining to Phoebe that the man she so desperately wants to marry (at the end of *As You Like It*) and who has theoretically promised himself to her is actually a woman. Shakespearean comedy accommodates the unjust incarceration and taunting of Malvolio, the vicious and humiliating slander of Hero at her own wedding, the marginalisation and ultimate rejection of Jaques, Feste and Antonio (the sea captain). Shakespearean comedy can even encompass, in the demise of the withered old Adam, death; not counterfeit death, like Hero's or Hermione's, nor even death which is threatened but unrealised (as with the snake about to entwine itself around the neck of Oliver), but the final complete disappearance which looks back to the first capital offence: eating a piece of forbidden fruit. This Adam, like his namesake, and ultimately like all of us, must return to ashes – hardly a cheery thought for a comic play, 'Dear master, I can go no further. O, I die for food! Here lie I down, and measure out my grave. Farewell, kind master' (II. vi. 1–3). Adam has no more to say after this moment. That Shakespeare gave him no further lines suggests that his death, after the camp-fire scene (II. vii), is a dramatic possibility.

When Dr Johnson published his edition of Shakespeare's works in 1765, he rightly recognised the tensions within single plays between the comic and the uncomic: 'Shakespeare has united the powers of exciting laughter and sorrow not only in one mind but in one composition. Almost all his plays are divided between serious and ludicrous characters, and, in the successive evolutions of the design, sometimes produce seriousness and sorrow, and sometimes levity and laughter.'[3] We only have to think of the co-existence in a single play of characters as diverse as Don John and Dogberry, Angelo and Elbow, or Touchstone and Jaques to see what Johnson means. The question remains, though, how are we as literary critics to cope with this diversity?

II

As the players approach the court of Elsinore, Polonius introduces them to their patron, Hamlet, in terms of a banal catalogue of literary genres as: 'The best actors in the world, either for tragedy, comedy, history, pastoral, pastoral-comical, historical-pastoral, tragical-historical, tragical-comical-historical-pastoral, scene individable, or poem unlimited' (II. ii. 392–5). It is tempting to see our desire to objectify, to delimit fully Shakespearean comedy, as this kind of pedantic scholasticism. Even Polonius has to form compounds to describe usefully the ambiguity of the players' work. His own critical discourse stretches itself implausibly around the multivalent possibilities of the acting. In so doing, he is pre-empting every one of the literary commentators who, in the last four hundred years, has attempted to define Shakespearean comedy. But unlike a good many of them, he realises, albeit uncomfortably, that the subject calls into question the actual processes, even the very language through which he articulates it. Shakespearean comedy seems to be trying to resist descriptive accounts of itself, shirking the bridle of critical control, and this unwillingness to serve makes it what it is. We apprehend the nature of the beast in terms of its resistance. Shakespearean comedy takes us along with it into its own world of uncertainty and bewilderment, a world where Bottom is transformed into an animal and couples with a fairy queen, a world where boy actors dress as girls and then become boys to woo other boys that they want for their female selves, a world where sad and merry madness coexist, servants become masters and masters slaves. It is a labyrinthine world with no fixed signposts; a world where the

dense thickets of the forest conspire to exclude the cold light of
reason, a place that abounds in the mystery of language and identity with statements like Feste's 'Nothing that is so is so' (IV. i. 8),
or Viola's 'I am not what I am' (III. i. 138). Sebastian, finding himself suddenly propositioned by a rich and beautiful woman, ration-
alises his good fortune by looking for a certainty beyond the craziness
of Illyria:

> This is the air; that is the glorious sun;
> This pearl she gave me, I do feel't, and see't;
> And though 'tis wonder that enwraps me thus,
> Yet 'tis not madness.
>
>   (IV. iii. 1–4)

If the warm light of day shines here, the black hole of Malvolio's
prison cell acts as a focus both for the deprivation of light (standing
for reason) and accordingly the opacity of language:

> *Fest.*: Say'st thou that house is dark?
> *Malv.*: As hell, Sir Topas.
> *Fest.*: Why, it hath bay windows transparent as barricadoes, and
>   the clerestories toward the south north are as lustrous as ebony;
>   and yet complainest thou of obstruction?
>
>   (IV. ii. 34–9)

If the signposts of Illyria can point only south north, how are we to
find our way in the world of literary criticism generally and of
Shakespearean comedy in particular?

Raymond Williams recounts his early bewilderment at this in-
conclusiveness of Shakespeare studies. In the autumn of 1939, he
found himself as a student in Cambridge University Library:

> I was there to pick up a couple of books on Shakespeare for an
> essay. My first impression of those hundreds of volumes, tightly
> stacked in what looked like an industrial warehouse, can be best
> understood if I add that this was the first time I had been in any
> library larger than a living room. Wandering in and out, trying
> to decipher (as still today) the complicated system of classifica-
> tion, I came across a section which induced a kind of vertigo. I
> don't, fortunately, remember all the actual titles, but a quick scan
> showed me Shakespeare as royalist, democrat, catholic, puritan,

feudalist, progressive, humanist, racist, Englishman, homosexual, Marlowe, Bacon and so on round the bay. I flicked the pages of some of the more improbable ascriptions. The compounded smell of disuse and of evidence rose to my nostrils. I got out and went for a walk.[4]

The similarity between Williams's and Polonius's taxonomic struggles points up the fact that Shakespeare's comedy, just like that of Hamlet's players, lies beyond an easy classification. The traditional idea of literary criticism as one which answers questions about the play, which seeks to lay bare certain embedded truths within it, which, in the words of Tony Bennett, 'sets out to deliver the text from its own silences by coaxing it into giving up its true, latent or hidden meaning' – this idea of literary criticism is one which cannot cope with Shakespeare's comic plays.[5]

If classification is beyond us and all our readings are unique and different, how can we begin to discuss *Much Ado* or *Twelfth Night* at all? We have seen that although none of us could come up with a dictionary definition of comedy – indeed even the dictionary couldn't manage that – we all have a more or less rough idea of what Shakespearean comedy is like. This expectation is generated by the plays' titles. What the plays seem to be about and the ways in which we understand them are in fact identical: the watchword is *consensus*. The plays are insistent that we must share values with them, that we can only make sense of their chaotic world if we recognise that we are implicated in a conspiratorial relationship with them. Titles like *Measure for Measure, Much Ado About Nothing* and *All's Well That Ends Well* assure us that these plays unfold in a comic universe, that we can rely upon a sense of balance (measure for measure) or providence to sort things out. Angelo's vicious manipulation of Isabella, Hero's death, Helena's separation from her husband *are* urgent and threatening but at the same time we know that they are problems that have been raised only to be solved. It is no accident that at its most anarchic moment Shakespeare's most indulgent comedy, *A Midsummer Night's Dream*, draws attention to its own harmlessness. Puck assures us, 'Jack shall have Jill; / Nought shall go ill; / The man shall have his mare again, and all shall be well' (III. ii. 461–3). Viola in *Twelfth Night* is prepared to trust the comic spirit too: 'O Time, thou must untangle this, not I; / It is too hard a knot for me t' untie' (II. ii. 38–9). These plays are comedies precisely because their knots *are* eventually untied and

our enjoyment is in watching *how* the solutions will come about
rather than wondering whether or not they will.

Other play-titles are even more eager to make explicit the contract that they share with the audience: *The Comedy of Errors, Twelfth
Night or What You Will* and perhaps most obviously *As You Like It*.
These plays either announce their own comic status for us and
thereby indicate that nothing can go wrong, or simply project their
openness on to us. These plays mean whatever we want them
to mean, they are in that sense vehicles for our own wish-fulfilment. But if our enjoyment of the plays depends upon their willing-
ness to rely upon our judgements, they also implicitly demand that
we share *their* moral strategies, that the consensus which allows us
to decode them and approve of them *is actually set up by them* and
moreover is, as we shall see, constructed deliberately to exclude
certain social groups. Linda E. Boose contextualises this 'comic
contract' against the social circumstances of Renaissance dramatic
practice, attributing it to 'the new commercial enterprise of public
theatre'.[6] She writes, 'With its emphasis on social bonds, comedy
inherently proposes a structure that is peculiarly dependent on
audience gratification.'[7]

Shakespearean comedy works by exclusion. Different levels of
knowledge are exposed in front of an audience that is privy to all
the secrets. We know that the letter that Malvolio postures with is
actually a fraud, we know that Sir Topas is really Feste, we know
that Ganymede is really Rosalind, that Cesario is really Viola, that
Hero's death is an elaborate hoax and that Benedick and Beatrice
are playing 'hard to get'. We are consistently shown the shortfalls
in the various readings of the world that abound in places like
Messina, Arden and Illyria. Ours is the position of looker-on, just
like the three crouched behind the box-tree, aware of the disparity
in the relative amounts of knowledge that the characters possess
regarding their place in the world and their relationships to others.
No one in the plays knows as much as we do – even Feste mistakes
Sebastian for Viola. We are omniscient precisely because the plays'
characters are not. Excluded from the social know-how and ultimately from self-knowledge, Shakespeare's comic figures struggle
laughably to make sense of fragments of evidence. We cannot shout
'Look behind you' to Malvolio, although Fabian nearly does: 'Ay,
an you had any eye behind you, you might see more detraction at
your heels than fortunes before you' (II. v. 124). We cannot tell
Orlando or Orsino who these young lads actually are, because the

essential ingredient of Shakespeare's comic construction is our recognition that we are in a more complete condition of knowledge
and this is, as I have suggested, the prerequisite of the plays' titles.

The phrase 'what you will' appears several times in Shakespearean drama. In *As You Like It*, Jaques asks Amiens to sing another
stanza: '*Jaques*: Call you 'em stanzos? *Amiens*: What you will, Monsieur Jaques' (II. v. 17–18). In *Twelfth Night*, Olivia instructs Malvolio
to get rid of the young man calling at her door: 'if it be a suit from
the Count, I am sick, or not at home – what you will to dismiss it'
(I. v. 102). Other instances (in *Two Gentlemen*, *A Midsummer Night's
Dream*, *Othello*) accord with this use of the phrase – what amounts
really to a delegation of responsibility. You can call the verses of
my song whatever you want to call them, says Amiens, while Olivia
gives Malvolio free rein to decide on the excuse to repulse the
suitor. When the phrase is used as a subtitle to one of Shakespeare's
plays (*Twelfth Night*), it has the same effect. Ours is the responsibility, ours the judgement that will liberate or indict the characters
and finally the play itself. Feste tells us that the players will strive
to please us every day but ultimately they can do no more than
strive.

What is at stake, then, in these kinds of titles is an appeal for
audience participation.[8] We are asked to ally ourselves with the structures of comic values in place and to embrace them. As Olivia tells
us, it is a system of values to which Malvolio refuses to subscribe:
'O, you are sick of self-love, Malvolio, and taste with a distemper'd
appetite. To be generous, guiltless, and of free disposition, is to take
those things for bird-bolts that you deem cannon bullets' (I. v. 85–
6). Along with Malvolio, it is we who are being asked not to make
mountains out of molehills, not to take this Shakespearean illusion
too seriously. Puck offers a solution to those in the audience who
have been upset by *A Midsummer Night's Dream*:

If we shadows have offended,
Think but this, and all is mended,
That you have but slumb'red here
While these visions did appear.
And this weak and idle theme,
No more yielding but a dream,
Gentles, do not reprehend.
If you pardon, we will mend.
(V. i. 412–19)

By pretending the play is no more than a dream, we can in effect make it part of our own mental process; we can forgive it.

The comedies attempt to assert the existence of what we might usefully think of as an ideal interpretative community, not merely in terms of the way in which their own social fabrics are reordered after a period of anarchy (Senior returns to his dukedom, Hero and Claudio are reconciled, Orsino and Olivia are successfully united, though of course, only as in-laws) – not simply in terms of the formulation of a stable and secure society in the plays, but also in their usually successful attempts to elicit the audience's corroboration. We *do* agree to befriend Puck, we *do* wish Rosalind a kind farewell, and even the bitter-sweet ending of *Twelfth Night* will generally satisfy. This idea of community, of what I called earlier 'consensus', is latent in the titles of the plays. Our approval is sought before the plays even begin. The final harmonious ending of comedy brought about by audience assent has long been recognised as the feature which distinguishes the genre from tragedy. We find the assumption voiced in Shakespeare's own time in the platitude of Thomas Heywood, 'Comedies begin in trouble, and end in peace; Tragedies begin in calmes, and end in tempest.'[9]

III

I have not tried to offer a solution to the problem of defining Shakespearean comedy but rather to account for the broad differences in interpretative strategies between comedy and other sorts of play and to illustrate that the comedies require the vindication of their audience not merely in terms of their epilogues but also, more obviously, in terms of their titles. I said earlier that, what the plays seem to be about and the ways in which we understand them are in fact identical. Having attempted to show that we understand them in terms of a consensus that we share with them, I now want to consider how the plays actually deal with the notion of consensus.

In his history of youth subcultures, Dick Hebdige analyses teds, mods, rockers, skinheads and punks in terms of their rejection of a single cultural identity: 'the emergence of such groups', he writes, 'has signalled in spectacular fashion the breakdown of consensus in the post-war period'.[10] In other words, the multitude of youth styles indicates a profound dissatisfaction with the prevailing social consensus. Fashion (or in the case of punk, anti-fashion – which is itself a fashion) is a means of signifying an attitude, a kind of consensus to a larger social group (other punks). Fashion is a signal both of dissatisfaction and nonconformity and paradoxically of satisfaction and conformity.

The Messina of *Much Ado* is an inescapably fashion-conscious place. We hear about rabatos and slops (ruffs and baggy breeches), about gloves, doublets, masks, and even Dogberry insists that he owns two gowns. Pedro and Claudio debate going to the barber's to have beards trimmed and Beatrice tells the messenger of Benedick's inconstancy in terms of his impressionable dress-sense: 'he wears his faith but as the fashion of his hat; it ever changes with the next block' (I. i. 63). Margaret and Hero discuss 'the Duchess of Milan's gown that they praise so' (III. iv. 15) and the maid tactfully attempts to reassure the bride that 'yours is worth ten on't' (l. 21). Oxford Stage Company's 1992 production, designed by Maira Miu, emphasised the importance of the ill-fated bridal gown by dressing Hero in a magnificently ornate dress and head-dress (see Plate A). In III. iii Conrade and Borachio discuss the importance of looking like the times:

Bora.: Thou knowest that the fashion of a doublet, or a hat, or a cloak, is nothing to a man.
Conr.: Yes, it is apparel.
Bora.: I mean, the fashion.
Conr.: Yes, the fashion is the fashion. . . .
Bora.: Seest thou not, I say, what a deformed thief this fashion is, how giddily 'a turns about all the hot bloods between fourteen and five and thirty, sometimes fashioning them like Pharaoh's soldiers in the reechy painting, sometime like god Bel's priests in the old church-window, sometime like the shaven Hercules in the smirch'd worm-eaten tapestry, where his codpiece seems as massy as his club?
Conr.: All this I see; and I see that the fashion wears out more apparel than the man. But art not thou thyself giddy with the fashion too, that thou hast shifted out of thy tale into telling me of the fashion?

(ll. 108–31)

In Messina, it is even fashionable to talk about the fashion and Conrade's contempt for it and his allegation that Borachio has become side-tracked by this irrelevant topic (note his pun on *shift*

meaning 'a shirt') indicate that he does not belong in this Voguish
world. The word 'fashion' appears eighteen times in this play, more
than in any other of Shakespeare's works.[11] Fashion is significant
because we are able to measure by their attitude towards it the
relative loyalties of individuals to the dominant social consensus.
It is no accident that the play's thugs are so unfashionable. Even
Benedick realises that Claudio's new obsession with fashion indicates a recently formed social relationship: 'I have known when he
would have walk'd ten mile afoot to see a good armour, and now
will he lie ten nights awake carving the fashion of a new doublet'
(II. iii. 17). When Ursula and Hero are overheard accidentally-on-
purpose in an effort to matchmake the two Bs, they dwell on
Beatrice's dissent from fashionable behaviour:

> *Ursu.:* Sure, sure, such carping is not commendable.
> *Hero.:* No; not to be so odd and from all fashions,
>   As Beatrice is, cannot be commendable;
>   But who dare tell her so?
>
> (III. i. 71–4)

Fashion corresponds, as Hebdige shows, directly to social unanim-
ity, mutual sympathy and likemindedness, in short to consensus. In
Twelfth Night, Toby tells Maria that 'I'll confine myself no finer than
I am' (I. iii. 9), in other words, he will dress according to his station.
'These clothes be good enough to drink in, and so be these boots
too', he continues. Aguecheek is concerned about his hairstyle ('But
it becomes me well enough, does't not?' (I. iii. 95)), while Viola
recognises the impropriety of hugging her brother in her 'masculine usurp'd attire' (V. i. 242). Feste points out that his loud check
conceals a socially incisive sense of humour: 'I wear not motley in
my brain' (I. v. 52).

The assertion that the obsession with fashion marks a concern
with social relationships echoes the often vituperative writings of
the early modern period on the question of dress. As Lisa Jardine
has shown, sumptuary law was an important consideration in a
society determined to discourage social mobility.[12] Contemporary
sources insist upon the propriety of dressing according to rank, and
scorn is reserved for those who confine themselves finer than they
are. Ideas of social and class 'consensus' are implicit in sumptuary
regulation for confusion of dress leads directly to the erosion of the
social order:

as for the priuat subiects, it is not at any hand lawful that they should wear silks, veluets, satens, damasks, gould, siluer and what they list (though they be neuer so able to maintain it) except they being in some kinde of office in the common wealth, do vse it for the dignifying and innobling of the same. But now there is such a confuse mingle mangle of apparel in *Ailgna*, and such preposterous excess thereof as eueryone is permitted to flaunt it out, in what apparell he lust himselfe, or can get by any meanes. So that it is verie hard to knowe, who is noble, who is worshipfull, who is a gentleman, who is not: for you shall haue those, which are neither of the nobilitie, nor yeomanry, no, nor yet anie Magistrat or Officer in the common welth, go daylie in silkes, veluets, satens, damasks, taffeties, and such like, not withstanding that they be both base by byrthe, meane by estate, & seruyle by calling. This is a great confusion & a general disorder, God be mercyfull vnto vs.[13]

Wealthy costume was thus a responsibility of office. John Williams, preaching before the king in 1619, is circumspect about condemning all luxurious garments; indeed, he argues that lavish costume is an onus upon the nobility who dress 'not for the cockering and cherishing of their bodie, but for the credit and countenance of their *place* and dignitie. . . . God that hath thus blest thee, hath thus cloathed thee: God, that hath brought thee to Kings houses, hath thus apparelled thee for Kings houses.'[14] For Sir John Harington, dressing beyond one's station was part of a larger vice of human affectation designed not simply to deceive others but ultimately to delude the self:

wee goe brave in apparell that wee may be taken for better men than wee bee; we use much bumbastings and quiltings to seem better formed, better showldered, smaller wasted, and fuller thyght, then wee are; we barbe and shave ofte, so seeme yownger than wee are; we use perfumes both inward and outward to seeme sweeter then wee bee; corkt shooes to seeme taller then wee bee; wee use cowrtuows salutations to seem kinder then wee bee; lowly obaysances to seeme humbler then we bee; and sometyme grave and godly communication to seem wyser or devowter then wee bee.[15]

Such assaults on sartorial superficiality are predicated upon a deeply conservative sense of social place. Williams describes sumptuous costume in terms of a travesty of land-ownership – the most obvious indicator of social standing:

> To see a man (who is but a *Steward* of what hee possesseth, and to render a fearefull account of the same) to haue a *Farme* clapt vpon his feete, a *Coppy holde* dangling vp and downe his legges, a *Manor* wrapt about his body, a *Lordship* hanging vpon his shoulders, nay (peraduenture) the *Tythes* (*Christs patrymonie*) turn'd to a Cap, and the *bread* of the poore to a plume of feathers: and all this waste to no *ende* then this, that people might come out and see, *this man cloathed in soft rayments.*[16]

Thomas Lodge was convinced, however, that true nobility would not be taken in by appearances: 'think you that the gracious *Elizabeth* cannot ... finde out a vain head vnder a wauing feather, a dissolute minde vnder a codpéece dublet, a wanton thought vnder a straunge habite. ... the eye fixed on heauenlye contemplations, gazeth not on earthlye beautie.'[17] The vice of extravagant self-fashioning was personified in the caricature of the gallant whose frequent mockery often included a sense of the theatrical nature of his modish performance. Henry Hutton's satire on 'Monsier *Brauado*' is typical:

> The Globe to morrow acts a pleasant play,
> In hearing it consume the irkesome day.
> Goe take a pipe of To[bacco]. the crowded stage
> Must need be graced with you and your page.[18]

Williams too cites the theatre as a place of sartorial intemperance when he notes that church-going provides an opportunity to show off the latest fashions: 'thou cõmest thus rigged to the house of God, for that's now adaies the *Theatre* of all this vanitie' and he adds later that those who overdress for church 'enter Gods house, as if it were a Playhouse'.[19] John Earle attacks the thespian affectation of the gallant, describing him as one who 'is neuer serious but with his Taylor, when hee is in conspiracie for the next deuice. ... He is a kind of walking Mercers Shop, and shewes you one Stuffe to day, and another to morrow.'[20] One of the standard objections was financial: 'He is a gull, whose indiscretion, / Cracks his purse strings to be in fashion.'[21] Stubbes is contemptuous of such foppish extravagance: 'now it is small matter to bestowe twentie nobles, ten pound, twentie pound, fortie pound, yea a hundred pound of one paire of Breeches (God be mercifull vnto vs)' and he later refers to the starching houses (in which the ruffs were laundered) as 'brothell houses' and 'farting houses'. [22] Robert Tofte brings together the sartorial and financial imprudence of the Aguecheek-like gallant as he is personified in the figure of Midas:

> Wearing a siluer sword for fashion sake
> And yet disgracefull Blowes and words will take:
> Whose Speech and Ruffe seeme Both, as One to be,
> Of the new Set, (Twins in Formalitie,)
> Where if you barre him from his Common places,
> He is tongue-tide then, for therein his chiefe grace is,
> Whose Apish Trickes and Nods, with ducking low,
> The perfect Type of Vanitie doth show,
> Whilst (capring for the nonce) his Coyne must iingle,
> His sole Attendance being his loathsome Ingle [young male prostitute]:
> Thinking he should be prais'd for his pyde cloathes,
> (For he no better parts (than these are) shows). [23]

Midas is complete with all the requisite trappings: a sword he cannot use, a ruff that matches his rhetoric in its foppishness, a foolish bow, more money than sense, a young page and a loud suit. The final parenthetical line undercuts the whole display: Midas is no more than the sum of his fashion accessories. With characteristic temperance, Thomas Heywood, defender of things theatrical, attempts to exculpate the sin of overdressing: 'God hath not enioyned vs to weare all our apparrell solely to defend the cold. Some garments we weare for warmth, others for ornament. So did the children of Israel hang eare-rings in their eares, nor was it by the law forbidden them.'[24]

In spite of this cautioning against their deceptive nature, clothes for Malvolio maketh the man. Supposing that his mistress is especially taken with smiling, yellow socks and elaborately crossed garters, he affects the lot in an effort to elicit her approval. Maria has of course constructed the list in terms of her lady's pet hates. Smiling will be utterly inappropriate to Olivia's period of mourning, yellow is a colour that she has always loathed and as for cross-gartering it is, we are assured, 'a fashion she detests' (II. v. 181). Malvolio's inability to dress according to the fashions labels him visually as an outsider, not simply a fuddy-duddy. He is not old-fashioned, he is completely out of fashion. His shocking outfit is symbolic of a deeper misalliance with prevailing codes of behaviour and this is best illustrated in his interruption and banning of the comic revels enjoyed by Toby and 'the lighter people' (V. i. 326). Monsieur Melancholy (Jaques in *As You Like It*) is another example of an unfashionable person although this is by choice rather than through error. In his famous 'All the world's a stage' speech (II. vii. 139–66), Jaques does recognise the importance of fashion to archetypal man. The soldier is 'bearded like the pard', the judge has knowing eyes and 'beard of formal cut', and even senility has its own pathetic fashion: 'lean and slipper'd pantaloon, / With spectacles on nose and pouch on side'. Clothing, in these instances, serves to define the self in accordance with a sartorial norm. Elsewhere, even rituals which suggest the *revelation* of self in fact symbolise a similar capitulation to larger social conventions.

Hero, Olivia and Rosalind all have the chance in these plays to unveil themselves (the latter metaphorically). Symbolising as it does the revelation of their true selves, the removal of the veil also signifies a preparedness to submit the self to another. (The marriage veil is a fine example of this; indeed Hero's is just such a veil.) So this comic consensus, which fashion signifies, has ultimately to do with the formation of social structures from which the unfashionable are banned. There is no place for Jaques, Frederick, Antonio, Aguecheek, Malvolio, Don John, Shylock, (the other) Antonio, etc. Consensus, like fashion, needs to be defined against dissent and disarray. It needs to determine who the outsiders are and rid itself of them. Finally it needs to reassure us that we are not one of them. Fashion implies a knowing assent to social and cultural structures and the heroes and heroines of Shakespearean comedies are, for this very reason, natty dressers.

IV

As regards structure, comedy has come a long way since Shakespeare, who in his festive conclusions could pair off any old shit and any old fudge-brained slag (see Claudio and Hero in *Much Ado*) and get away with it. [25]

Shakespearean comedy is almost universally recognised as being comedy about love and marriage. In other words it dramatises a move towards a common structure which binds individual women and men and also admits these new partnerships to the institution of marriage itself. Throughout the course of Shakespeare's comic plays, youngsters (although as the example of Benedick and Beatrice suggests, not exclusively so) are encouraged to move away from their own self-definition to share themselves firstly with another person and secondly, but as a direct consequence, with a universal social structure. Consensus is again in operation. The critical commonplace that the comedies are about youthful rebellion and self-discovery may be true but such rebellion is only ever temporary. A reversion to social order is the ultimate destination of all these plays. Orlando, Orsino, Sebastian and Claudio are required in the course of the plays to revalue their own selves and to redefine their personalities in relation to a larger social institution. Moreover, Shakespeare's comedies assure us that it is really the men who are in need of this redefinition. Orlando with his sonnets and Orsino with his self-indulgent and cloying rhetoric illustrate the immaturity of male Narcissism. Against this Rosalind and Viola reject male romantic exaggeration and assert pragmatic and fundamental truths about the nature of relationships: 'men have died from time to time, and worms have eaten them, but not for love' (IV. i. 95).

In *Twelfth Night* and *As You Like It* the sexual roles are never challenged. Although Viola and Rosalind dress up as boys, what the plays take to be their feminine intuitiveness is allowed to shine through their disguises. This is, if not a mother wit, certainly a female one. The situation in *Much Ado* is different. Marriage is explicitly conceptualised in terms of an external sociality, in terms of social responsibility rather than individual maturation. The play is set solely in Messina unlike *As You Like It* which moves away from court to pursue its themes in the forest of Arden or *Twelfth Night* which oscillates between Orsino's and Olivia's households. This concentration in terms of setting is related to the increased social stress on the institution of marriage. In *Much Ado* love is defined in terms of society not thought up and worked out in the forest and then taken back to town (as is the case in *A Midsummer Night's Dream*, for example). As we might expect, for the characters of *Much Ado* even love is merely a fashion. Discussing the joining of Benedick and Beatrice, Pedro insists: 'I would fain have it a match; and I doubt not but to fashion it' (II. i. 331). Even the friar's proposition of his plan is tainted by this unfortunate pun: 'doubt not but success / Will fashion the event in better shape / Than I can lay it down in likelihood' (IV. i. 234–6). Messinian love pretends to be no more than it is: a mechanism for exchanging and sharing political power. When it appears that Hero is dishonest, Pedro makes the political consequences of her transgression clear: 'I stand dishonour'd that have gone about / To link my dear friend to a common stale' (IV. i. 63–4). Claudio's initial infatuation with Hero fades with her reputation, as his own political integrity is compromised.[26] Leonato is heartbroken, not that his daughter has been publicly defamed, but rather that his own reputation has been sullied. He wishes that he had nurtured a beggar so that if 'smirched thus and mir'd with infamy, / I might have said "No part of it is mine; / This shame derives itself from unknown loins"' (IV. i. 133–5). As has often been remarked upon, Hero is pretty well out of it. Shirley Nelson Garner calls her 'the most silent of Shakespeare's female figures. . . . Just as she is without speech, so she is without defences.'[27] The marriage of which she is half, does not seem to involve her at all. All important is male reputation, her father's and her husband's. Marriage in *Much Ado* clearly functions to structure the social fabric rather than to give expression to anything as fanciful as love. Hero's passivity is typical of the mildness of the Shakespearean comic heroine when dressed in the clothes of her own sex. There is no room in Messina for Illyrian fantasy or Arden-like immaturity. Marriage is a hard political reality and reputations, male reputations, are at stake.

Even though *As You Like It* and *Twelfth Night* dally with the innocence of love, finally we are assured that marriage is necessary in terms of male benefit. The plays are determined to ensure that marriage has paternal consent and that it will replicate familial structures. The second scene of *Twelfth Night* assures us that Orsino is a suitable partner for the play's heroine, he is a bachelor and moreover, as if we did not already know having seen him in I. i, he is noble 'in nature as in name' (I. ii. 25). Finally we are told that Viola's father knows him: 'I have heard my father name him' (l. 28). Similarly in *As You Like It*, Rosalind assures us that her and Orlando's fathers were on the best of terms: 'My father lov'd Sir Rowland as his soul' (I. ii. 214), a sentiment that Senior is allowed to confirm when he greets Orlando at the feast in II. vii: 'If that you were the good Sir Rowland's son . . . / Be truly welcome hither' (ll. 191–5). Orlando's flight into the forest follows his proud declaration of his lineage to Frederick who responds menacingly, 'I would thou hadst told me of another father' (I. ii. 209). Wooing Ganymede takes place in the course of his exile. Family and marriage are, like fashion, indicators of consensus. Until his 'conversion' at the play's conclusion, which is marked by his marriage to Celia, Oliver has done his best to negate fraternal responsibility, even to the extent of inciting Charles the wrestler to 'break his [brother's] neck' (I. i. 130). The plays' outsiders have no time for familial or marital responsibilities. Don John feels towards his brother exactly as Oliver to his: 'I had rather be a canker in a hedge than a rose in his grace' (I. iii. 22) and as for marriage, when he is informed of Claudio's intended match, he responds bluntly: 'Will it serve for any model to build mischief on? What is he for a fool that betroths himself to unquietness?' (I. iii. 41). This impression of marriage in relation to maleness goes a long way to explain the absence of mothers in Shakespeare's drama. Although we hear of Viola's father, and although she introduces herself to her estranged brother via him ('My father had a mole upon his brow' (V. i. 234)), we never hear of her mother. Hero's mother is briefly alluded to as a potentially unfaithful woman: '*Pedro*: I think this is your daughter. *Leonato*: Her mother hath many times told me so' (I. i. 87–8). This sole mention of the mother-figure, coupled with the possibility of infidelity, is repeated in *King Lear* and *The Tempest*. Elsewhere mothers are not mentioned at all (*As You Like It*, *A Midsummer Night's Dream*, and so on). Marriage is a male institution wherein women are censored into nothing. The function of marriage at the conclusion of these plays is to render harmless the manipulative skills of Shakespeare's females. Paulina, Isabella, Viola, Rosalind and Beatrice are hurriedly married off to effect their ineffectiveness.[28] These women are required to cooperate with and to submit themselves to a society ruled by men. At the same time as the plays celebrate the resourcefulness of their heroines, they continually point up the fragility of woman. Hero swoons, Innogen sickens, Rosalind passes out at the sight of the bloody handkerchief and Viola tells us quite frankly that she is terrified of the foppish Sir Andrew. The categories of sexual definition remain fundamentally unchallenged; Viola and Rosalind affect an exterior maleness but this emphasises rather than challenges their interior femaleness. Rosalind, for example, remarks that in spite of her 'swashing and . . . martial outside', her heart will contain 'what hidden woman's fear there will' (I. iii. 115).

Ultimately, the movement from solipsism to society effects a transference of power from the female, where the power lies during courtship, to the male where power, both institutionally and socially, lies within marriage. Moreover, while marriage functions to bring men together, it serves to separate women. Leonato forgives and is reconciled to Claudio and Pedro, Benedick who promised earlier to kill Claudio takes him, through their mutual marriage, as a relative: 'For thy part, Claudio, I did think to have beaten thee; but in that thou art like to be my kinsman, live unbruis'd, and love my cousin' (V. iv. 108). Marriage separates Desdemona and Emilia, Hermia and Helena, and Rosalind and Celia. One of the most moving descriptions of same-sex attachment in Shakespeare's drama comes in Helena's nostalgia for her and Hermia's childhood days:

> We, Hermia, like two artificial gods,
> Have with our needles created both *one* flower,
> Both on *one* sampler, sitting on *one* cushion,
> Both warbling of *one* song, both in *one* key;
> As if our hands, our sides, voices, and minds,
> Had been incorporate. So we grew together,
> Like to a double cherry, seeming parted,
> But yet an union in partition,
> Two lovely berries moulded on *one* stem;
> So, with two seeming bodies, but *one* heart;
> Two of the first, like coats in heraldry,
> Due but to *one*, and crowned with *one* crest.
>   (III. ii. 203–14, my emphases)

The emphasis on oneness reinforces the physical and emotional intimacy of the girls. This, as Helena goes on to say, is ruptured by male interference, 'And will you rent our ancient love asunder, / To join with men in scorning your poor friend?' (ll. 215–16). Similarly female empathy is destroyed in the course of *As You Like It*. Celia protests to her father near the beginning of the play that Rosalind is innocent of conspiracy against him:

> If she be a traitor,
> Why so am I: we still have slept together,
> Rose at an instant, learn'd, play'd, eat together;
> And wheresoe'er we went, like Juno's swans,
> Still we went coupled and inseparable.
>   (I. iii. 68–72)

Even the brutal Charles and the wily Le Beau acknowledge the strength of their bond. The wrestler notes that 'never two ladies loved as they do' (I. i. 103) and the courtier asserts that their 'loves /

Are dearer than the natural bond of sisters' (I. ii. 254–5). Such touching intimacy can never survive the presence of two husbands. When Rosalind tells her father and husband, 'To you I give myself, for I am yours. / To you I give myself, for I am yours' (V. iv. 110–11), Celia is nowhere to be seen. Rosalind exists now solely in terms of her subordination to father and husband who are themselves united through their mutual relationship with her. Marriage, therefore, functions to reinforce the hegemony of patriarchy: 'The atonement of earthly things celebrated in Hymen's wedding song incorporates man and woman within a process that reunites man with man.'[29]

The French feminist Simone de Beauvoir points out in *The Second Sex* that, in a patriarchal society, women exist only in relation to men. We must, she says, 'face the question: what is a woman?':

> To state the question is, to me, to suggest, at once, a preliminary answer. The fact that I ask it is in itself significant. A man would never set out to write a book on the peculiar situation of the human male. But if I wish to define myself, I must first of all say: 'I am a woman'; on this truth must be based all further discussion. A man never begins by presenting himself as an individual of a certain sex; it goes without saying that he is a man.[30]

I have shown how the idea of consensus, operating via behavioural patterns, like style and fashion, and social institutions, like love and marriage, serves to centralise power in the plays and also to exclude what I called 'outsiders'. I have also attempted to show how Shakespeare's comedy inscribes its audience within these power structures; that is, how the plays themselves communicate via an unspoken covenant with their audience and how both in and outside the plays, this covenant is quite literally a gentleman's agreement. Such a blatantly inequitable arrangement has unsurprisingly caused some critics to reject the opportune marriages as unsatisfactory conclusions. Norman N. Holland, writing of *A Midsummer Night's Dream* typifies this critical anxiety: 'I want these couples married at the end, but I don't see – I don't trust, really – the way the comedy gets them together. Out of infidelity comes fidelity – but how?'[31]

V

At the end of *As You Like It*, Rosalind steps forward and modestly asserts the impropriety of a female being in such a position of authority as to have the last word: 'It is not the fashion to see the lady the epilogue' (Epilogue. 1). It certainly is not the fashion because as we have seen, fashion in Shakespearean comedy is a loaded word. She asks us how she might compel us to like the play:

> My way is to conjure you; and I'll begin with the women. I charge you, O women, for the love you bear to men, to like as much of this play as please you; and I charge you, O men, for the love you bear to women – as I perceive by your simp'ring none of you hates them – that between you and the women the play may please.
>
> (Epilogue. 11)

Rosalind celebrates the play as an event that unifies the two sexes. Women and men are exhorted by the love they bear to each other to love the play equally. We have seen that the love and especially the marriage that the play(s) feature, while it may be a marriage of true minds, is certainly not a true marriage of minds. Nevertheless Rosalind assures us that the values we share with each other are the values of the play. We may not approve of them, but we are expected to shoulder them in deference to the play's comic demands. Then, just when we thought we knew where we were, Rosalind continues:

> If I were a woman, I would kiss as many of you as had beards that pleas'd me, complexions that lik'd me, and breaths that I defied not; and, I am sure, as many as have good beards, or good faces, or sweet breaths, will, for my kind offer, when I make curtsy, bid me farewell.
>
> (Epilogue. 17)

Who is speaking this – Ganymede ('If I were a woman . . . '), Rosalind ('when I make curtsy'), or a boy actor, playing a girl, playing a boy? The epilogue, separated from the required suspension of disbelief which the rest of the play demands, is a suitable place to talk self-consciously about the play itself, and also to challenge the sexual categories which the drama assumes.[32] The speaker of the epilogue confuses the definable sexual roles according to which the whole play has structured itself. While we can argue that the epilogue foregrounds the maleness that, as de Beauvoir suggested, defines femaleness, and thus turns the drama itself (with its all-male cast) into a male preserve, this would overlook the attention that the speaker pays to the judgement of the women (s/he starts with them) as well as the necessity for men to take this female verdict into account ('I charge you, O men, for the love you bear to women . . .'). This challenging of sexual categorisation coincides with what we would expect to be the formal point of closure and so *As You Like It* disturbs gender through its revisionist attitude to genre. In *Much Ado* and *Twelfth Night*, the plays end in a comparatively straightforward way: marriage confirms the consensus of patriarchy. But in *As You Like It*, the epilogue fractures the confidence of consensus, implying 'that the marriages in the play are a great deal more iffy than is usually supposed'.[33] The consequent insecurity challenges us to decide the fate not only of the play itself, but because we are implicated within it, of the categories of female/male by which we judge the play and, more crucially, by which we live.

'A poet's work [is] To name the unnameable, to point at frauds, to take sides, start arguments, shape the world and stop it from going to sleep.'[34] The prophet/poet of *The Satanic Verses* clamouring to keep the world awake reformulates Auden's assertion with which we started: 'poetry makes nothing happen'. *As You Like It* is, in this sense, truly poetry, for the nothing that it makes happen, the unnameable with which it keeps us awake, is nothing less than our relationships to one another as women and men.

Notes

1. W. H. Auden, 'In Memory of W. B. Yeats', in *Collected Shorter Poems 1927–1957* (1969), p. 142.
2. The *fatwa* was endorsed approvingly by Dr Kalim Saddiqui (chair of the British Parliament of Muslims) in an interview, *Beyond Belief*, with Ludovic Kennedy broadcast on Radio 4 on 5 September 1992.
3. Samuel Johnson, *The Yale Edition of the Works of Samuel Johnson*, ed. Allen T. Hazen *et al.*, 14 vols (1958–78), VII, 66–7.
4. Raymond Williams, 'Afterword' to *Political Shakespeare: New Essays in Cultural Materialism*, ed. Jonathan Dollimore and Alan Sinfield (Manchester, 1985), 231–9, p. 231.
5. Tony Bennett, *Formalism and Marxism* (1979), p. 107.
6. Linda E. Boose, 'The Comic Contract and Portia's Golden Ring', *Shakespeare Studies*, 20 (1988), 241–54, p. 241.
7. Ibid., p. 241.
8. For a slightly more trenchant reading of these titles, see Richard

Dutton who believes that they challenge as much as embrace their audience: 'the titles of his later romantic comedies . . . followed a vogue in the late 1590s for off-handed flippancy. . . . *All's Well that Ends Well* . . . is balanced on a provocative edge between complacency and cynicism' (*William Shakespeare: A Life* (1989), p. 95).

9.   Thomas Heywood, *An Apology for Actors* (1612), F 1^v.

10. Dick Hebdige, *Subculture: The Meaning of Style* (1979), p. 17.

11. 'Wherever Messina is found, it is defined by its codes of conduct and patterns of behaviour. Its concern with fashion is central not peripheral. Throughout the play, the text prompts us to think in fashionable terms . . . conceptually the references to fashion reinforce the importance of that which is judged and endorsed through appearances' (Pamela Mason, *Much Ado About Nothing: Text and Performance* (1992), p. 12).

12. Lisa Jardine, *Still Harping on Daughters: Women and Drama in the Age of Shakespeare*, second edn (1989), Chapter 5.

13. Phillip Stubbes, *The Anatomie of Abuses* (1583), C ii^v.

14. John Williams, *A Sermon of Apparell* (1620), pp. 28–9.

15. *The Letters and Epigrams of Sir John Harington*, ed. Egbert McClure (Philadelphia, 1930), pp. 41–2.

16. Williams, *A Sermon*, p. 18.

17. Thomas Lodge, *An Alarvm against Vsurers. Containing tryed experiences against worldly abuses* (1584), F ii^v.

18. Henry Hutton, *Follie's Anatomie or Satyres and Satyricall Epigrams* (1619), B 2^v.

19. Williams, *A Sermon*, pp. 19, 22.

20. John Earle, *Micro-cosmographie, Or A Peece of the World Discovered; in Essays and Characters* (1628), D 10^v-11^r.

21. Everard Guilpin, *Skialetheia or A shadowe of Truth, in certaine Epigrams and Satyres* (1598), A 6^v.

22. Stubbes, *Anatomy*, E 3^r; *The Second Part of The Anatomy*, E 8^v-F 2^r.

23. Benedetto Varchi, *The Blazon of Iealovsie*, trans. R[obert] T[ofte] (1615), A 3^v.

24. Heywood, *Apology*, C 1^v.

25. Martin Amis, *The Rachel Papers* (Harmondsworth, 1984), first published 1973, p. 147.

26. In *King Lear* the Duke of Burgundy is similarly put off Cordelia for political reasons (I. i. 189–246).

27. Shirley Nelson Garner, 'Male Bonding and the Myth of Women's Deception in Shakespeare's Plays', in *Shakespeare's Personality*, ed. Norman N. Holland, Sidney Holman and Bernard J. Paris (1989), 135–50, p. 146.

28. Ann Jennalie Cook notes that following the kiss of Beatrice and Benedick, she is silent for the rest of the play which 'allows Benedick to control the nuptials' (*Making a Match: Courtship in Shakespeare and his Society* (Princeton, 1991), p. 174).

29. Louis Adrian Montrose, '"The Place of a Brother" in *As You Like It*: Social Process and Comic Form', *Shakespeare Quarterly*, 32 (1981), 28–54, p. 29.

30. Cited in *The Theory of Criticism: From Plato to the Present*, ed. Raman Selden (1988), p. 533.
31. Norman N. Holland, 'Hermia's Dream', in *Representing Shakespeare: New Psychoanalytic Essays*, ed. Murray M. Schwartz and Coppélia Kahn (1980), 1–20, p. 17.
32. For an alternative reading of this moment, see Chapter 8.
33. Jonathan Goldberg, *Sodometries: Renaissance Texts, Modern Sexualities* (Stanford, California, 1992), p. 143.
34. Salman Rushdie, *The Satanic Verses* (Harmondsworth, 1988), p. 97.

3

The Flaw in the Flaw: Shakespeare's Tragic Method and a Problem of Criticism

I

At the centre of Umberto Eco's medieval thriller, *The Name of the Rose*, lies a library.[1] At the heart of this semiological maze is a book – a tract so jealously guarded that its protection and censorship cause the savage murder of anyone who gets close to it. The book is the companion volume to Aristotle's *Poetics* and contains the philosopher's account and analysis of comedy. For Jorge, the blind monk who hides, guards and eventually eats the book to stop others reading it, its existence threatens to undermine man's insecurity and his consequent religious faith. The monk explains the potential of laughter to defuse man's collective anxieties:

> Laughter frees the villein from the fear of the Devil, because in the feast of fools the Devil also appears poor and foolish, and therefore controllable. But this book could teach that freeing oneself of the fear of the Devil is wisdom. . . . Laughter, for a few moments, distracts the villein from fear. But law is imposed by fear, whose true name is fear of God. . . . And from this book there could be born the new destructive aim to destroy death through redemption from fear. . . . if laughter is the delight of the plebeians, the license [sic] of the plebeians must be restrained and humiliated, and intimidated by sternness.[2]

A humanity that laughs is a humanity that fails to take its plight seriously. A humanity that giggles at the absurdity of its own situation does not have imaginative space for a god. The blasted heath where Lear shouts and rails in a grotesquely comic way anticipates

40

the morally and theatrically naked stage where Vladimir and Estragon wait absurdly for their Godot. When, in the rhetoric of the plays, the gods do appear, they do so only as sadistic school-children or in careless recreation: 'As flies to wanton boys are we to th' gods – / They kill us for their sport' (*King Lear*, IV. i. 37–8) or as Bosola trenchantly puts it in Webster's *Duchess of Malfi*, 'We are merely the stars' tennis-balls, struck and banded / Which way please them.'[3] From the very earliest literature, right up to Ted Hughes's *Crow*, mankind is presented as little more than laughable.[4] Humanity is a walking joke but, as Jorge maintains, *we* should never be allowed to enjoy it.

The anarchy of comedy threatens to undermine authority – the authority of religious faith (as in Eco's novel) or the authority of other power structures. The feast of misrule in the classical world put slaves in authority over their masters for a single day. The slave in Cæsar's chariot whose job it was to slap his emperor in the face comically deflated the very power structures which the ruler embodied. The Renaissance moralists who wrote against the theatre singled out comedy's propensity to undercut authority: 'Comedyes make our delight exceede, for at them many times wee laugh so extreemely, that striuing to bridle our selues, wee cannot; therefore *Plato* affirmeth that great laughter breedeth a great change.'[5] Laughter subverts not just the State but individual self-control. Comedy turns the world upside down – transforms men into beasts (Bottom into an ass), and women into men (Rosalind into Ganymede, Viola into Cesario). Yet for all its radical potential to change social, political, cultural and religious structures, it is variously considered to be light, whimsical, trivial and escapist. This failure to take comedy seriously goes back a long way. Even the usually vituperative John Rainoldes underestimated the comic genre: 'I . . . perhaps thinke with *Plato*, that the seeing of *Comedies* played can doe no harme, of *tragedies* may be dangerous.'[6] The myth persists that if tragedy is serious, comedy is not. For the influential critic I. A. Richards, 'Tragedy is perhaps the most general, all-accepting, all-ordering experience known. . . . It is invulnerable.'[7] Richards goes on to separate the highest examples of the genre from the lesser kinds; unsurprisingly, he distinguishes between 'almost all Elizabethan Tragedy [and] Shakespeare's six masterpieces'.[8] Tragedy, of which Shakespearean tragedy is assumed especially by commentators earlier this century to be the most noble species, is grave, profound, forthright, *tragic*. Comedy, by contrast, offers relief – 'comic relief' – a lessening of

dramatic tension, a moment of relaxation for the wracked and terrified audience of tragedy. As recently as 1986, we find this critical
misconception being promulgated: 'comedy does not demand characters so highly developed and individuated as does tragedy'.[9]
Tragedy is, according to this analysis, the superordinate term of the
two, containing within it disjointed and trivial comic interludes.
Comedy becomes a subordinate device in the tragic scheme of things.

The problems with this oversimplified separation are legion. In
Shakespeare's drama we are not always offered the security of
knowing when comedy is comedy and tragedy is tragedy. Without
broaching the taxonomic difficulties of plays like *Measure for Measure*, *The Merchant of Venice* or *Cymbeline* (are they comedies or tragedies?) what do we do with apparent anomalies like the porter in
Macbeth, who amid the blasted nightmare of murder and savagery
(a landscape where witches brew cauldrons, old men spout blood
and horses eat each other), jokes about the difficulty of achieving an
erection when drunk? Where do we place the clown who refuses to
leave the stage in the most compellingly tragic of all Shakespearean
moments – Cleopatra's suicide – but hangs around to make lewd
jokes about women enjoying his worm? How do we account for the
exchange in *Othello* between the musician and a clown who ribs
him about the proximity of his tail and his wind instrument (an
episode to which I will return below)? And what do we do about
the Fool in *King Lear* who persistently deflates the monarch's tragic
pretensions with his stories of housewives beating eels on their
heads and simpletons who, out of kindness, spread their horses'
hay with butter? Comedy is not tragedy, nor tragedy comedy but
their disparity does not preclude the possibility of their coexistence.

As we have seen in Chapter 2, comedy has the potential to dis-
rupt, it is anarchic, it substitutes given power structures and ideologies, with an inverted scheme of things. Relations between god and
man, king and subject, men and women are turned inside out, upset
and inverted. Comedy is anarchic because it questions ideology
and may even replace it with an alternative one. The relationship of
tragedy to ideology is quite different. If comedy defies ideology,
tragedy endorses it. Graham Holderness explains: 'Tragedy for
Aristotle was really a form of cultural oppression, a means of ideological coercion by which the audience was invited to sympathise
with the tragic hero in his challenging of law, morality or fate; and
then required to cleanse that sympathy through an awed contemplation of the terrible consequences of the challenge.'[10] For example,

the audience empathises with the ambitious drive of Macbeth and the despondent deprivation of Hamlet. The sympathy that Holderness mentions is indeed forthcoming in each instance. Each hero kills a king and inevitably falls; what these tragedies offer is an object lesson in the evils of regicide. If royal murder, which is also a kind of patricide, can undo one as intellectually adroit as Hamlet or as emotionally committed as Macbeth, then what on earth, were we to commit that horror, would happen to us? Holderness concludes: 'The audience is meant to leave the theatre with all its immoral, antisocial and politically dissident impulses safely cauterised or quelled.'[11]

History plays especially were instructive in the acceptable standards of social behaviour. The subtitle of Thomas Beard's *Theatre of Gods Iudgements* (1597) clearly implies that tragedy befalls only those who deserve it: *concerning the admirable Iudgement of God vpon the transgressours of his commandments*. Tragedy is, in this analysis, a form of social control; the plays tell us how *not* to behave. For Beard, the object lessons of history, which were popular material for contemporary dramatisation, demonstrated the errors as well as the successes of the past:

> historie is accounted a very necessary and profitable thing, for that in recalling to mind the truth of things past, which otherwise would be buried in silence, it setteth before vs such effects (as warnings and admonitions touching good and euill) and laieth virtue and vice so naked before our eyes, with the punishments or rewards inflicted or bestowed vpon the followers of each of them, that it may rightly be called, an easie and profitable apprentiship or schoole for euery man to learne to get wisdome at another mans cost.[12]

Phillip Stubbes, whose *Anatomy of Abuses* published in 1583 contains a savage attack on the theatrical institutions of his day, at least concedes that some drama may contain this kind of historical object lesson and thus operate for the social good: 'when honest & chast playes, tragedies, & enterluds are used to these ends, for the Godly recreation of the mind, for the good example of life, for the avoyding of that, which is evill, and learning of that which is good, than are they very tolerable exercyses'.[13] It is no accident that *Macbeth*, written for a royal command performance and presented in front of a Scottish king, should be so uncompromising in its condemnation of regicides. Earlier in his career, when Shakespeare had dared to suggest that the usurper in *Richard II* may well have had grounds for his revolt, the play was heavily censored and the monarch, herself not at all amused, took the point: 'I am Richard II, know ye not that?'[14] In an age which brutally put to death those suspected of conspiring against the throne, the notion that Bolingbroke could depose and murder a king and not himself be publicly decapitated was indeed a dangerous one. Elizabeth's misgivings were well-founded. On the eve of the Essex rebellion in 1601 the conspirators gathered into the Globe and paid 40 shillings to watch this play of successful revolution.

II

In the classic account of Shakespearean tragedy the play focuses itself on the single eponymous hero and especially on what has become known as the 'fatal flaw'. Time after time critical accounts of what have become the four major tragedies focus on Hamlet's procrastination, Othello's jealousy, Lear's naive desire to quantify love or Macbeth's ambition. These single faults in otherwise admirable characters bring about the terrible collapse of the Shakespearean world; but tragedy has not always been like this. In Chaucer's *The Monk's Tale*, humanity grabs on to the revolving Wheel of Fortune; first rising to the apex then descending to depravity.

> I wol biwaille, in manere of tragedie,
> The harm of hem that stoode in heigh degree,
> And fillen so that ther nas no remedie
> To brynge hem out of hir adversitee.
> For certein, whan that Fortune list to flee,
> Ther may no man the cours of hire with-holde.
> Lat no man truste on blynd prosperitee;
> Be war by thise ensamples trewe and olde. [15]

Although this fall is moralised (Fortuna has no hold upon the faithful at heart) this rise and fall is part of the order of things – no little flaws or faults lurking inwardly which threaten to undermine the foundations of the universe – no less tragic perhaps but a good deal less complicated.

From the Romantic period onwards, Shakespeare's art as a

dramatist was analysed in terms of the involved theories of the 'Romantic Imagination'. Discussions of the playwright's craft became conflated with complex deliberation over ideas such as 'Imagination' or 'Nature'. Coleridge attributed Shakespeare's talents to Nature in a passage which displays the origins of the essentialism which was to become the hallmark of Shakespearean criticism thereafter:

> Nature, the prime genial artist, inexhaustible in diverse powers, is equally inexhaustible in forms. Each exterior is the physiognomy of the being within, its true image reflected and thrown out from the concave mirror. And even such is the appropriate excellence of her chosen poet, of our own Shakespeare, himself a nature humanized, a genial understanding directing self-consciously a power and an implicit wisdom deeper than consciousness.[16]

This process of dramatic composition with its 'power and . . . implicit wisdom deeper than consciousness' is typical of the internalisation of artistic creativity more generally; in an age in which the greatest literary achievement was a poem subtitled the *Growth of a Poet's Mind*, this introspection should not really surprise us.[17] The tragedies thus became related not to the externality of Fortune's Wheel, but to something inherent in the very constitution of the protagonist. The tragedy of Macbeth happens because of something rooted as firmly inside him as his bone marrow: his characteristic fatal flaw.

Following the Romantics, A. C. Bradley analysed the heroic personality's innards for clues as to their faults. For Bradley tragedy arose out of a character's flaw and they were *real* characters. Of Othello, for example, Bradley writes:

> In the first place, Othello's mind, for all its poetry, is very simple. He is not observant. His nature tends outward. . . . In the second place, for all his nature and massive calm (and he has greater dignity than any other of Shakespeare's men), he is by nature full of the most vehement passion. . . . Lastly, Othello's nature is all of one piece. His trust, where he trusts is absolute. Hesitation is almost impossible to him.[18]

Bradley's emphasis on human nature is directly descended from Coleridge's own description of Shakespeare as 'himself a nature

humanized'. This process of humanising is extended to Shakespeare's
tragic protagonists. Thus Othello is (note the present tense) a recognisable person with his own 'nature', habits and propensities. He is
not a character in a drama, he is a man with 'greater dignity than
any other of Shakespeare's men'. For Bradley, Shakespeare never
wrote characters but men; never functional figures in a drama but
people in a world as real as this one. They are people brought
down by a coincidence of unfortunate circumstances and their fatal
flaw. Implicit in this kind of approach is the assumption that Macbeth
would not have overreached himself if he had been less ambitious,
that Othello would not have killed his wife unless he had been a
'jealous type'.[19] They behaved thus because, Bradley would say, it
was in their *nature* to do so – their characters demanded it of
them. Even if one ignores its psychological naivety, this attitude is
dangerously unsound in two further ways – dramaturgically and
politically.

In the first place, it renders meaningless the dramatic relationships that Shakespeare so carefully constructs. If *Othello* is an interesting play, it is partly so because of the mystery of Iago and the
relationship between servant and master that inspires the murder
of the innocent mistress. If the fault is inherent in the hero himself,
Iago ceases to contribute to the action of the play or the morality of
its world. Othello's flaws would have precipitated the murder of
his wife anyway – likewise we can edit out the ghost of King Hamlet and the witches in *Macbeth*. Of course this makes complete non-
sense of the plays.

Politically the notion of the fatal flaw is dangerous because it
places the entire responsibility for the actions of the character
squarely and totally on his/her shoulders. In other words, Macbeth's
evil is a facet of his personality and nothing can be done about it.
Such a sociology proposes that there is no possibility of social
amelioration, that education is a waste of time, that interpersonal
relationships are futile and that everyone is self-interested and isolated. It is a sociality required by the mechanisms of capitalism. The
obsessive emphasis that Thatcherism placed on individuality and
'enterprise' is part of this divisive philosophy since reformulated in
John Major's society of equality of opportunity and underlined by
individual 'back to basics' responsibility. In 1989 Mrs Thatcher spoke
in an ITV interview with Brian Walden about what she called the
'British character': 'it's enterprising, it's responsible, it will take the
initiative it wants to look after its own family, [it] wants to make its

own decisions'. [20] If your fatal flaw is your own concern then no one should be burdened with having to help you out. If you are so weak that you cannot stand on your own two feet then you go to the wall. The literary critical device of the 'fatal flaw' plays directly into a politics which abnegates responsibility to others in the social group. In an interview that took place in 1987, Mrs Thatcher attacked the notion of social obligation:

> I think we've been through a period where too many people have been given to understand that if they have a problem, it's the government's job to cope with it. 'I have a problem, I'll get a grant.' 'I'm homeless, the government must house me.' They're casting their problem on society. And you know, there's no such thing as society. There are individual men and women and there are families. [21]

The final problem with the notion of the fatal flaw is that it internalises Shakespearean drama. It mystifies it, placing the dynamics of its ebb and flow firmly within the unlit harbour of the protagonist's character. Is this flaw behavioural, psychological, emotional? The fatal flaw remains nebulous, written in invisible ink between the lines in front of us. The assertion that the fatal flaw is there at all is extraordinary given Shakespeare's contempt for the abstract. Critics have the time to ponder at length over speeches looking with magnifying glasses for signals of the fatal flaw. An audience in the theatre just does not have time to perceive the critical problems in the same way. Shakespeare's drama was written (unlike Milton's, for example) for the stage. Shakespeare is bluntly, most of the time crudely, concrete and it is this concreteness, especially in terms of physicality, that I now wish to consider.

white in control, cleverer

III

'You promised to tell me your history, you know,' said Alice . . . 'Mine is a long and a sad tale!' said the Mouse, turning to Alice and sighing. 'It *is* a long tail, certainly,' said Alice, looking down with wonder at the Mouse's tail; 'but why do you call it sad?'[22]

Alice's confusion accidentally but not incorrectly locates the origin of narrative power in the body itself. The homophonic *tale* and *tail*

bring about the fusion of the historical with the bodily – force together, until they converge, discourse and physicality. Shakespeare's
characters are continually validating what they say with what they
organically are, habitually equating their speech with their bodies.
At the beginning of *Richard II*, for example, Bolingbroke accuses
Mowbray of lying. He threatens literally to make him eat his words:
'With a foul traitor's name stuff I thy throat' (I. i. 44) and asserts
that 'what I speak / My body shall make good' (ll. 36–7). Words are
just too slippery to be believed; we can never be sure of what has
been said. Physicality, on the other hand, is objective and determi-
nate. At the opening of *Macbeth*, Duncan seizes upon the body's
genuineness; physicality validates speech. Addressing the Bloody
Sergeant, he remarks: 'So well thy words become thee as thy
wounds; / They smack of honour both' (I. ii. 44–5). The Bloody
Sergeant himself is unable to speak further but his very body calls
out for assistance: 'I cannot tell – / But I am faint; my gashes cry for
help' (ll. 42–3). Similarly in his supremely understated incitement
to riot, Mark Antony disclaims his oratorical skills and relocates
them in the gaping cuts of the body in front of him:

> Show you sweet Cæsar's wounds, poor poor dumb mouths,
> And I bid them *speak for me*. But were I Brutus,
> And Brutus Antony, there were an Antony
> Would ruffle up your spirits, and put a tongue
> In every wound of Cæsar, that should move
> The stones of Rome to rise and mutiny.
>
> (III. ii. 225–30, my emphasis)

Previously in the same play, Casca has quite literally vocalised his
political aspirations through his destructive dexterity: 'Speak, hands,
for me!' (III. i. 76 – note the similar formulation: bodily parts speaking). Even the lowly Third Citizen in *Coriolanus* recognises the irresistible rhetorical force of wounds. He asserts that they are unable
to deny Coriolanus their voices, 'for if he show us his wounds and
tell us his deeds, we are to put our tongues into those wounds and
speak for them' (II. iii. 6). Again, this time in *I Henry IV*, wounds
speak louder than words. Hotspur tells the king that Mortimer's
bravery is evident in the physical mutilation that he has suffered in
the king's name:

> Revolted Mortimer!
> He never did fall off, my sovereign liege,

But by the chance of war; to prove that true,
Needs no more but *one tongue for all those wounds,*
Those mouthed wounds, which valiantly he took
When on the gentle Severn's sedgy bank,
In single opposition hand to hand,
He did confound the best part of an hour
In changing hardiment with great Glendower. . . .
Never did base and rotten policy
Colour her working with such deadly wounds;
Nor never could the noble Mortimer
Receive so many, and all willingly.
Then let him not be slandered with revolt.

(I. iii. 93–112, my emphases)

When Antonio pledges his purse and his person to Bassanio, he is prepared to have his body mutilated for the love of his friend. Bassanio attributes a gory physicality to the letter which tells him of the wreck of Antonio's argosy. He addresses Portia, 'Here is a letter, lady, / The paper as the body of my friend, / And every word in it a gaping wound / Issuing life-blood' (III. ii. 265–8). Bassanio, like Hotspur, judges devotion by the body.

In the drama of Shakespeare, what we experience all the time is not simply body language in the sense of gesture or movement – though this is obviously an element of performance – but much more fundamentally, *body-talk.* The texts themselves repeatedly foreground their interest in bodies and bodily parts. Shylock's nose, Antonio's heart, Gloucester's eyes, Bardolph's complexion, Barnadine's head, Lavinia's tongue and hands, Cordelia's voice, Helena's height, Richard III's deformity, Cleopatra's breast, Duncan's blood, Cloten's headless corpse, Yorick's skull, Lady Macbeth's nipple, Aguecheek's haircut, Olivia's schedule of beauty, Toby's broken pate, the colour of Othello's 'sooty bosom' and so on. Shakespeare's most common joke is physical. The sets of identical twins from *The Comedy of Errors* and *Twelfth Night* are visual puns while the recapitation of Bottom with an ass's head is a bizarre kind of malapropism. When Stephen Greenblatt writes that 'Shakespearean comedy constantly appeals to the body', he is only partly right.[23] These examples illustrate that there is no genre in which Shakespeare does not foreground bodily concerns.[24]

Shakespeare's most extended physical joke is Falstaff. Addressed by names that suit his physicality, Falstaff becomes 'Plump Jack',

'Chops' and so on. 'Falstaff sweats to death', says the Prince during the Gadshill robbery, 'And lards the lean earth as he walks along' (II. ii. 104–5). Falstaff himself uses his obesity as a comic ploy. The Lord Chief Justice challenges him at the beginning of *II Henry IV*: 'Your means are very slender, and your waste is great.' Falstaff takes up the challenge and, like Alice's confusion over the Mouse's tail, he opts for the wrong definition: 'I would it were otherwise; I would my means were greater and my waist slenderer' (I. ii. 133–5). Shakespeare was evidently fond of the pun. In *The Merry Wives of Windsor* as Falstaff tells Pistol and Nim of his plan to woo and exploit Mistresses Ford and Page, he remarks, 'I am in the waist two yards about; but I am now about no waste; I am about thrift' (I. iii. 38). The ambiguities of speech allow Falstaff creative space to play with his own bodiliness but when that physically is itself threatened, he recognises the futility of linguistic and hence socialised reward. Unlike the Bloody Sergeant, Mortimer or Cæsar, Falstaff shuns the wounds that command the respect of his fellows:

> honour pricks me on. Yea, but how if honour prick me off when I come on? How then? Can honour set to a leg? No. Or an arm? No. Or take away the grief of a wound? No. Honour hath no skill in surgery, then? No. What is honour? A word. What is in that word? Honour. What is that honour? Air. A trim reckoning! Who hath it? He that died o' Wednesday. Doth he feel it? No. Doth he hear it? No. 'Tis insensible, then? Yea, to the dead. But will it not live with the living? No. Why? Detraction will not suffer it. Therefore I'll none of it. Honour is a mere scutcheon. And so ends my catechism.
>
> (*I Henry IV*, V. i. 127–40)

Honour is interrogated according to the absolute standard of physical well-being and, in Falstaff's scheme of things, suffers a poor second.

The process of gradual demise which Falstaff undergoes throughout the course of the two parts of *Henry IV* is, not surprisingly, manifest in terms of his weakening physicality. He notes his dilapidation quite early on: 'Do I not bate [abate, grow thin]? Do I not dwindle? Why, my skin hangs about me like an old lady's loose gown; I am withered like an old apple-john' (Part I, III. iii. 2). Our first sight of him in Part II is with a urine sample that he has just received from the doctor and all is not well. The Chief Justice roundly confirms that he is past his prime, cataloguing in a kind of parodic blazon his physical decrepitude:

> Do you set down your name in the scroll of youth, that are written down old with all the characters of age? Have you not a moist eye, a dry hand, a yellow cheek, a white beard, a decreasing leg, an increasing belly? Is not your voice broken, your wind short, your chin double, your wit single, and every part about you blasted with antiquity?
>
> (I. ii. 167–72)

The development of Falstaff's physical ailments signifies the tragic momentum of *II Henry IV*. This is also the situation, but much more viciously, in the case of Pandarus. The desperate state of Troilus and Cressida's affair, which he has fostered and promoted is inseparable from the decline of his own body:

> A whoreson tisick [throat or lung disorder], a whoreson rascally tisick so troubles me, and the foolish fortune of this girl, and what one thing, what another, that I shall leave you one o' th's days; and I have a rheum in mine eyes too, and such an ache in my bones that unless a man were curs'd I cannot tell what to think on't.
>
> (V. iii. 101–6)

The play, perhaps Shakespeare's most cynical tragedy, ends with Pandarus bequeathing us his diseases. *Troilus*'s savage ending and the pathos surrounding the final rejection of Falstaff, make inseparable the tragic outcomes and the physical decline of the plays' 'chorus' figures. Pandarus's and Falstaff's bodies are only the most obvious examples of Shakespeare's corporal interest. This is not just a casual theme of Shakespearean drama, but an essential concern, for as Falstaff's speech on honour demonstrates, what the plays continually assert is that physicality, not history, the tail not the tale is the only verifiable reality. The clown of *Othello* makes this disgustingly clear:

> *Clow.*: Are these, I pray, call'd wind-instruments?
> *1 Mus.*: Ay, marry, are they, sir.
> *Clow.*: O, thereby hangs a tail.

1 Mus.:   Whereby hangs a tale, sir?
Clow.:   Marry, sir, by many a wind-instrument that I know.

                                                                (III. i. 6–10)

This moment again illustrates the centrality of the Shakespearean
body. There is no need for the abstract critical machinery of fatal
flaws – because Shakespeare sites his drama in the physicality of
his scripts and the actors speaking them. The drama is concretised
in front of us – literally, in the flesh. Linguistic accuracy is predicated on the very physicality which articulates it. It follows then
that those characters who are without bodies are the most deceptive in their use of language. Ariel, Puck, the ghost of King Hamlet,
are continually eluding the attempts to tie them down to a single
linguistic truth. Macbeth's witches are bearded sisters who vanish
into air bubbles as they wish and this physical ambiguity reflects
their linguistic sleight of hand. Ironically it is the witches who fully
understand the complexities and constraints of language. Highly-
patterned and prophetic, their speeches represent not so much a
violation of language as an adroit exploitation of it. They deceive
Macbeth not by lying but by telling him the truth, albeit they are
being 'economical' with it: they are 'imperfect speakers' but they
are not dishonest ones.

Physicality and language go quite literally hand in hand in Shakespeare's plays. At the end of *Henry V* the English king is mistrusted
by the French princess: 'Your Majestee ave fausse French enough to
deceive de most sage damoiselle dat is en France' (V. ii. 217). It is
indeed significant that previously the only English lesson we have
witnessed is her translation of bodily parts; in III. iv she has learned
'd'hand, de fingre, de nails, d'arm, d'elbow, de nick, de sin, de foot,
le count' (l. 55).[25] Bodies can puncture the deceptiveness of speech
and permeate the infinite nuances of linguistic competence. The
comfort that Katherine has despite Henry's deceptive tongue is that
a hand is a hand is a hand in whatever language it occurs.

While these scenes illustrate this idea of corporal verity, they
frequently expose the constructedness and inseparability of linguistic and political authority. Language is, according to this analysis,
a vehicle for the formulation and expression of power. Those who
can speak are those who can rule. The histories and the tragedies
in particular are concerned with the importance of linguistic/politi-
cal competence. Hal is a powerful king precisely because he has
served his apprenticeship as a student of different languages. For

example, he describes the slang associated with drinking games to Poins but not before he has noted the political consequences of knowing it:

> when I am King of England I shall command all the good lads in Eastcheap. They call drinking deep, dyeing scarlet; and when you breathe in your watering they cry 'hem!' and bid you play it off. To conclude, I am so good a proficient in one quarter of an hour that I can drink with any tinker *in his own language* during my life.
>
> (II. iv. 13–18, my emphasis)

As the three rebels bicker about the division of the kingdom in *I Henry IV*, Hotspur wants the course of the River Trent straightened by explosives in order to enlarge his share of land. Glendower opposes him:

> *Hots.*: I'll have it so; a little charge will do it.
> *Glen.*: I'll not have it alt'red.
> *Hots.*:   Will not you?
> *Glen.*: No, nor you shall not.
> *Hots.*:   Who shall say me nay?
> *Glen.*: Why, that will I.
> *Hots.*: Let me not understand you, then; speak it in Welsh.
>
> (III. i. 114–20)

Percy's hot-headed contempt elicits the following defiant insistence from Glendower that his English is as good as that spoken at court:

> I can speak English, lord, as well as you,
> For I was train'd up in the English court;
> Where, being but young, I framed to the harp
> Many an English ditty lovely well,
> And gave the tongue a helpful ornament –
> A virtue that was never seen in you.
>
> (III. i. 121–6)

That Glendower's speech is as fluent as that of the court is the proof that he is equipped linguistically and thus politically to attempt to overthrow it. With knowing irony, though, the playwright has him protest his Englishness with phrasing that is stereotypically Welsh – 'lovely well'![26] An inability to communicate, to speak the right language, is not merely a political handicap; Mortimer later moans, 'This is the deadly spite that angers me: / My wife can speak no English, I no Welsh' (ll. 192–3).

In the histories those that are powerful are those that can speak the languages of others. In *Henry V*, the king has successfully learnt to galvanise and unite Welsh, Scottish, Irish and English soldiers. Language, as the play *Richard II* insists, is power. As Richard relents and commutes Bolingbroke's banishment from ten years to six, the defendant comments on the awesome power of the King's speech: 'Four lagging winters and four wanton springs / End in a word: such is the breath of Kings' (I. iii. 214–15). Hamlet too is a prince who speaks across many different social registers. We see and hear of him chatting to the players, the gravediggers, the Norwegian captain and the pirates ('these good fellows') all in their own language. When Claudius says 'He's lov'd of the distracted multitude' (IV. iii. 4) we know why – because he speaks to them in a language that they can understand. At the other extreme are those in Shakespeare who are inarticulate and hence politically impotent. Mortimer's wife and Queen Katherine are marginalised in two ways – they are women and they are unable to speak the right language. Shakespeare's two most famous blacks are similarly deprived of the language with which to voice political power. Caliban in *The Tempest*, like thousands of the dispossessed in the golden age of exploration, is colonised and oppressed. Taught the language of the white invader, he is subjected to its grammar: 'You taught me language, and my profit on't / Is, I know how to curse. The red plague rid you / For learning me your language!' (I. ii. 363–5). Othello too is linguistically muzzled:

> Rude am I in my speech,
> And little blest with the set phrase of peace;
> For since these arms of mine had seven years' pith
> ... they have us'd
> Their dearest action in the tented field;
> And little of this great world can I speak
> More than pertains to feats of broil and battle;
> And therefore little shall I grace my cause
> In speaking for myself.
>
> (I. iii. 81–9)

Othello, with the emphasis on his 'arms', replaces linguistic with physical competence. Othello's descriptions of his war conquests which win Desdemona are not epic or poetic; they are steeped in physicality. His speech is as substantial as food – 'She'd come again, and with a greedy ear / Devour up my discourse' (I. iii. 149–50). He accounts for his reliance upon physical truth rather than oral virtuosity specifically in terms of his racial identity: 'for I am black / And have not those soft parts of conversation / That chamberers have' (III. iii. 267–9).

As well as race, sex can serve to censor the speaking of Shakespearean characters. In *The Subject of Tragedy*, Catherine Belsey relates this dramatic silence to the social position of woman in early modern England. Women, she writes, were 'enjoined to silence, discouraged from any form of speech which was not an act of submission to the authority of their fathers or husbands. Permitted to break their silence in order to acquiesce in the utterances of others, women were denied any single place from which to speak for themselves.'[27] Robert Tofte offers a contemporary poetic example of this principle: 'shee that seldome speakes and mildly then, / Is a rare Pearle amongst all other Women, / Maides must be seene, not heard, or selde or neuer, / O may I such one wed, if I, wed euer.'[28] In Shakespeare's plays, Cordelia, Desdemona and Ophelia are all put to silence. As the royal Lear turns to his youngest daughter for a reply to draw an opulent third of his kingdom she says nothing and she says 'Nothing'. As Desdemona explains to the patriarchs her love for Othello, she pleads that they will lend her voice a 'gracious ear'. The duke immediately interrupts, compelling her to speak (I. iii. 247). The whole of the final scene is a protracted study of the issues of speaking, lying and censorship. Othello remarks of the dead Desdemona that she is as 'Still as the grave' (V. ii. 97) and Emilia's attempts to revive her depend upon soliciting her speech: 'O lady, speak again! / Sweet Desdemona! O sweet mistress, speak!' (ll. 123–4). Iago attempts to shut his wife up but she is determined to speak: '*Iago*: Go to, charm your tongue. *Emil.*: I will not charm my tongue; I am bound to speak. . . . 'Twill out, 'twill out, I peace! / No I will speak as liberal as the north. / Let heaven and men and devils, let them all, / All, all cry shame against me, yet I'll speak' (ll. 186–225). Iago is silenced by his wife and, as his final words indicate, having been discovered, his is now a position untenable in the society of speaking men: 'Demand me nothing. What you know, you know. / From this time forth I never will speak word' (ll. 306–7).

Silence implies a subservience to masculine culture. Ophelia is consistently hushed; when she tells her prolix father about Hamlet's affection for her, Polonius snorts dismissively, 'Affection! Pooh! You speak like a green girl' (I. iii. 101). He goes on to forbid her 'to give words or talk with the Lord Hamlet' (l. 134) as though her silence will guarantee her temperance. Garrulousness implies lascivious immorality and Ophelia's longest public speeches are her mad songs which rail not surprisingly at the sexual inequality of her society. She sings of predatory men tumbling country girls and of violated virginity. In the 1989 Leicester Haymarket production, directed by Yuri Lyubimov, she approached the patriarchal ruler Claudius and sang accusingly 'By *Cock*, they are to blame.' Frequently in Shakespeare's plays, women are linguistically and politically impotent. It is worth reminding ourselves that the one notable exception, Lady Macbeth, has asked the gods to unsex her, to convert her into a sexless monster.

If power resides in language which is in turn ratified by the physicality of the speaker, then it follows that the amount of power that characters wield may be related to their bodily shape. Edmund's realisation of his political aspirations is intimately related to his physical attractiveness to the warring princesses. By choosing to sleep with one or other sister, he is able to fashion his own political advancement:

> To both these sisters have I sworn my love;
> Each jealous of the other, as the stung
> Are of the adder. Which one of them shall I take?
> Both? one? or neither? Neither can be enjoy'd,
> If both remain alive: to take the widow,
> Exasperates, makes mad her sister Goneril;
> And hardly shall I carry out my side,
> Her husband being alive. Now then, we'll use
> His countenance for the battle; which being done,
> Let her who would be rid of him devise
> His speedy taking off.
>
> (V. i. 55–65)

Edmund moves in this speech from a self-satisfied lust to a coldly political and manipulative calculation on the relative advantages of bedding one or other woman.

These examples ought to have made clear that Shakespeare sites his drama essentially in the web of relations between the linguistic and the bodily. The inscrutability of 'fatal flaws' and the like serves only to occlude the straightforward, though not necessarily uncomplicated, dramaturgy of the physical. As if we needed it, the plays provide us with one more crucial distraction from the red herring of fatal flaws – the technique of metadrama.

IV

When Hamlet instructs the players before the performance of *The Mousetrap* in Elsinore, he promotes what we might call a mimetic view of the drama: 'Suit the action to the word, the word to the action; with this special observance, that you o'erstep not the modesty of nature' (III. ii. 16–18). For Hamlet as a theatre director, drama should 'hold, as 'twere, the mirror up to nature; to show virtue her own feature, scorn her own image, and the very age and *body* of the time his form and pressure' (l. 22, my emphasis). Action for Hamlet should be naturalistic, as true to life as possible, an undistorting mirror. At the other extreme is the play staged by the rude mechanicals in *A Midsummer Night's Dream*. The 'tedious brief scene of young Pyramus and his love Thisby' consistently ruptures its own fictionality. The play is symbolical, a man standing for moonshine, another for a wall. It is prefaced by a speech which begs the court's indulgence and apologises for the shortcomings of the actors. Throughout, Bottom and the other players puncture the illusion of drama as they announce that the lion is not really a lion and that Pyramus has not really killed himself.

If Hamlet's is an illusionistic dramaturgy that wishes to pretend it is not there, that aspires to erase itself and simply reflect the world, Bottom's is a theatre that continually announces its own presence and goads its audience into the recognition that mimesis on stage is inseparable from the accompanying artifice of theatre. In other words, while Hamlet's theatre aspires to nature, Bottom's recognises that theatre is art. Shakespeare's own drama is closer to that of Bottom than of Hamlet. Plays like *Henry V* continually and explicitly announce their own fictionality through Chorus figures. *Pericles* is structured around the regular interpolations of a poet, Gower, who has previously written the story that Shakespeare is dramatising in the play. As well as in *Hamlet* and *A Midsummer Night's Dream*, masques and smaller 'insert plays' occur in *The*

Merchant of Venice, *Love's Labour's Lost*, *The Tempest*, *Henry VIII*, and so on. *The Taming of the Shrew* is one single artificial play performed for the benefit of Christopher Sly, which the audience happens (in the scheme of the play) to oversee.

Hamlet protests too much. While Hamlet's (the actor's) view of the drama is mimetic, *Hamlet* (the play itself) is quite the opposite. It is a play about plays; a play in which its central player becomes a director. Hamlet's view of the drama is radically inconsistent with the drama that contains it; and indeed the prince's own dramatic theory is logically defective. On the one hand, he says, drama should hold the mirror up to nature; drama becomes moral, spiritual, theological, philosophical, abstract and general. On the other hand, it should have a localised satirical purpose – to scourge 'the very age and body of the time'. By allowing us to glimpse this theatrical tension, the playwright is questioning the very notion of drama as an illusion of reality at all. *The Murder of Gonzago* or (as Hamlet prefers to call it) *The Mousetrap*, features all of the standard ingredients of the revenge drama – the genre to which *Hamlet* itself belongs – a dumb-show, a pronounced morality, virtue and vice figures, and so on: thus the inserted play is self-consciously drawing attention to the play which contains it *as a play* in a particular dramatic tradition.

Near the beginning of the play, the prince tells his mother that he is no actor. I know not 'seems', he says,

> 'Tis not alone my inky cloak, good mother,
> Nor customary suits of solemn black,
> Nor windy suspiration of forc'd breath,
> No, nor the fruitful river in the eye,
> Nor the dejected haviour of the visage,
> Together with all forms, moods, shapes of grief,
> That can denote me truly. These, indeed, seem;
> For they are actions that a man might play;
> But I have that within which passes show –
> These but the trappings and the suits of woe.
>   (I. ii. 77–86)

Hamlet casts himself as a sincere doer, not a pretentious actor. Later in the play the Prince curses himself for his own procrastination and his pale commitment next to an actor who mourns for Hecuba, or rather, performs a mourning:

What's Hecuba to him or he to Hecuba,
That he should weep for her? What would he do,
Had he the motive and the cue for passion
That I have? He would drown the stage with tears,
And cleave the general ear with horrid speech.

(II. ii. 552–6)

The Prince protests that he is no actor, but he discovers that he is worse than one – he is a ham. After the players' scene we would expect Hamlet's self-contempt to galvanise him into performing the murder that he has promised himself. Instead, of all things, he decides to direct a play.

Shakespeare is especially keen to explore this concern with acting and the dynamics of the stage. Jaques's 'All the world's a stage' is a prime example of this but it is in the tragedies that this metaphor for the world, the *theatrum mundi*, is interrogated most pessimistically. Lear equates the brevity of life with that of a play, 'When we are born, we cry that we are come / To this great stage of fools' (IV. vi. 183–4) and Shakespeare's most famous formulation of the absurdity of dramatic life occurs in what is possibly his most repellent and disturbing tragedy, *Macbeth*:

To-morrow, and to-morrow, and to-morrow,
Creeps in this petty pace from day to day
To the last syllable of recorded time,
And all our yesterdays have lighted fools
The way to dusty death. Out, out, brief candle!
Life's but a walking shadow, a poor player,
That struts and frets his hour upon the stage,
And then is heard no more; it is a tale
Told by an idiot, full of sound and fury,
Signifying nothing.

(V. v. 19–28)

I have tried to show through the examination of the issues of physicality and its relationship to speaking and metadrama, that the shady notion of the fatal flaw is an intangibility of which we, as critics of Shakespearean tragedy, should be wary. We have so much of the drama under our noses – the bodies in front of us, the lines that the actors speak and finally the self-allusion of the drama itself – that it seems perverse to start talking of psychologies and personality faults. The plays continually insist that they are plays, about fictional characters, performed on a stage by actors. If, like Bradley, we choose to ignore this insistence then the personalities that we discuss are only creations of our own imagination. The tragic flaw is itself tragically flawed, 'full of sound and fury, / Signifying nothing'. Aristotle himself is clear about the importance of subjecting the characters in a drama to its overall coherence *as a drama*: 'The first essential, the life and soul, so to speak, of Tragedy is the Plot; and . . . the Characters come second.'[29] As Hamlet puts it so concisely, 'The play's the thing.'

Notes

1. Umberto Eco, *The Name of the Rose* (1984).
2. Ibid., pp. 474–5.
3. *Plays by Webster and Ford*, selected with an introduction by G. B. Harrison (1933), pp. 179–80.
4. See especially Hughes's 'A Childish Prank', *Crow: From the Life and Songs of the Crow* (1972), first published 1970, p. 19.
5. Stephen Gosson, *Playes Confuted in fiue Actions, Prouing that they are not to be suffred in a Christian common weale* (1582), F 5ᵛ.
6. John Rainoldes, *Th'Overthrow of Stage Playes* (Oxford, 1599), p. 153.
7. I. A. Richards, 'The Balance or Reconciliation of Opposite and Discordant Qualities', in *Tragedy: Developments in Criticism*, ed. R. P. Draper (1980), pp. 145–6.
8. Ibid., p. 146.
9. James L. Hill, '"What are they children?": Shakespeare's Tragic Women and the Boy Actors', *Studies in English Literature*, 26 (1986), 235–58, p. 237.
10. Graham Holderness, '"Come in equivocator": Tragic Ambivalence in *Macbeth*', in *Critical Essays on Macbeth*, ed. Linda Cookson and Bryan Loughrey (Harlow, 1988), 61–71, p. 64.
11. Ibid., p. 64.
12. Thomas Beard, *The Theatre of Gods Iudgements* (1597), A 4ʳ.
13. Phillip Stubbes, *The Anatomy of Abuses* (1583), 6ʳ.
14. According to Stubbes, regicide was out of the question even as a method of deposing a tyrant, 'For whether the prince be wicked or godlye, hee is sent of GOD . . . if hee be a tyrant, then is he raised of GOD for a scourge to the people for their sinnes' (*The Second Part of The Anatomy of Abuses* (1583), D 1ʳ).
15. Geoffrey Chaucer, *The Works*, ed. F. N. Robinson, second edn (Oxford, 1974), p. 189.
16. *Romantic Poetry and Prose*, ed. Harold Bloom and Lionel Trilling (1973), p. 656.
17. The poem is Wordsworth's *The Prelude*.

18. A. C. Bradley, *Shakespearean Tragedy*, second edn (1974), pp. 154–5.

19. Bradley notes in addition that Othello 'is ignorant of European women.' Ibid., p. 154.

20. *The Guardian*, 30 October 1989.

21. 'Aids, Education and the Year 2000', *Woman's Own*, 31 October 1987.

22. Lewis Carroll, *Alice's Adventures in Wonderland, Through the Looking Glass and Other Writings*, introduced by Robin Denniston (1954), pp. 43–4. Shakespeare uses the same pun in *The Two Gentlemen of Verona* (II. iii. 40–2) and *The Taming of the Shrew* (II. i. 210–16). Generally for Shakespeare, and in both these instances, *tail* meant 'pudend'.

23. Stephen Greenblatt, *Shakespearean Negotiations: The Circulation of Social Energy in Renaissance England* (Oxford, 1988), p. 86. The sentence occurs in an essay entitled 'Fiction and Friction', for further discussion of which, see Chapter 8.

24. A number of valuable essays on the subject of the body in Renaissance culture, ranging from anatomy to architecture are available in *Renaissance Bodies: The Human Figure in English Culture c. 1540–1660*, ed. Lucy Gent and Nigel Llewellyn (1990).

25. In his edition Gary Taylor notes the *doubles entendres*, again linked to physicality, of the princess's speech (*Henry V* (Oxford, 1984), p. 179).

26. Another example of satire against Welsh attempts to speak English is Falstaff's reference to Hugh as a 'Welsh goat . . . one who makes fritters of English' (*The Merry Wives*, V. v. 136–42).

27. Catherine Belsey, *The Subject of Tragedy: Identity and Difference in Renaissance Drama* (1985), p. 149.

28. Benedetto Varchi, *The Blazon of Iealovsie*, trans. R[obert] T[ofte] (1615), p. 27.

29. Cited in *The Theory of Criticism: From Plato to the Present*, ed. Raman Selden (1988), p. 49.

4

Sexual Geography of the Renaissance: On the Imagery of *Antony and Cleopatra*

Though he [Antony] be painted one way like a Gorgon,
The other way's a Mars.

(II. v. 116–17)

I

Antony and Cleopatra enjoys the dubious reputation of being Shakespeare's most ambiguous drama. A sample of critical explorations yields the following remarks:

> The safest statement we can make about this play is that Shakespeare's ambivalence toward the characters, and toward their points of view, values, and modes of action, is extreme.... [There is a] marked and pervasive ambivalence which infuses the entire work.... [I]n essence *Antony and Cleopatra*, at its greatest moments, is gloriously senseless.[1]

> [A] painful ambivalence ... characterises our response to the play.... [It moves] in a dialectical process that begins with experiment and ends in failure.... This hurts.[2]

> The play seems perfectly calculated to offend the rising tide of neoclassical taste and to disappoint rational expectation.... Shakespeare insists upon ... ambivalence, for it is not simply the characteristic of his heroine but also the informing principle of the entire dramatic structure.[3]

62

For a number of critics this confusing polysemy is a symptom of the play's mixing of genres. Constance Brown Kuriyama writes, 'Falling roughly between the four great tragedies and the late romances, and clearly a transitional piece of some sort, *Antony and Cleopatra* partakes freely of both worlds.'[4] For Peter Erickson, 'the play threatens to turn into a hybrid "mongrel tragi-comedy" that falls between the two main generic categories'. He goes on (in a manner close to that of Kuriyama), 'it is convenient to call it a "transitional play," halfway between tragedy and late romance'.[5]

Another explanation of the ambiguities of the play is founded upon its double setting, 'geographically, the main theatres are two: Egypt (the Eastern world) and Rome (the Western World)'.[6] Frequently these play-worlds are associated straightforwardly with the two sexes, 'The conflict dramatized in *Antony and Cleopatra* is partly expressed through the contrast which Shakespeare establishes immediately between the flowing, feminine world of Egypt and the masculine, structured world of Rome.'[7] This uncomplicated dichotomy is only half-right, however, for just as each of the geographical settings is distinct from its own 'other', so it recognises itself as defined against that other. Thus, within the play itself there are no fewer than four competing points of view:

Rome of Rome: martial, virile, noble, ordered
Egypt of Rome: barren, frigid, pompous
Rome of Egypt: effeminate, salacious, politically and sexually unstable
Egypt of Egypt: fertile, exotic, fecund.

The audience is presented with all four of these viewpoints simultaneously and the final victory of Rome over Egypt is ambiguously open: the Romans do increase their empire and enlarge their governmental influence, but who wants a kingdom where nothing is left remarkable beneath the visiting moon? The world of Octavius is the world of love inverted: ROMA | AMOR.[8]

Antony and Cleopatra is built upon a mesh of imagery and the structural dialectic of the play (Rome versus Egypt) is the genesis of the double standard upon which so much of that imagery rests. A curiously prolific image is that of liquidity (water, clouds, melting, fading light, the sea, the Tiber and the Nile). This motif is thematically appropriate because, like the truth of the play, it remains elusive and indeterminable. A particular image does not form a consistent correlative for something, rather it is redefined upon each occasion and is thus environmentally conditioned. There is such an indeterminacy surrounding the imagery of sailing, for example. Agrippa says of Antony that 'A rarer spirit never / Did steer humanity' (V. i. 31–2). Antony is imaged as a reliable helmsman, a competent national leader. Previously, however, Antony had been likened to a ruined ship; contemplating Cleopatra's apparent denial of Antony, Enobarbus murmurs, 'Sir, sir, thou art so leaky / That we must leave thee to thy sinking, for / Thy dearest quit thee' (III. xiii. 63–5). These two antithetical metaphors do not contend, rather they coexist and their coexistence re-emphasises the abnegation of absolute standards by which we can evaluate the actions that take place in front of us.

The significance of this inconsistency in the use of imagery must be seen in the context of some thoroughly anti-sceptical traditions in Renaissance thought. In his study of the mechanisms of human apprehension, *The Order of Things*, Foucault discusses the correspondences, the parallels between different hierarchies of phenomena that were apparent to a Renaissance epistemology: 'resemblance played a constructive role in the knowledge of Western culture'.[9] This idea found expression in the well-known speculations of the Neoplatonists. From the late fifteenth century the Florentine Humanists developed the theory that classical mythology concealed the Platonic wisdom of the ancients; God could be reached through contemplation of physical beauty. The creator could be glimpsed through his creation and the landscape was thus a symbol of holy harmony. The 'Neoplatonic quest for unity' proposed that Nature and Art owe their power to God and that, while Art imitates Nature, Nature is God's Art.[10] Sir Philip Sidney explains:

> There is no art delivered to mankind that hath not the works of Nature for his principal object, without which they could not consist, and on which they so depend, as they become actors and players, as it were, of what Nature will have set forth. . . . Only the poet . . . goeth hand in hand with Nature.[11]

Well over half a century later, Sir Thomas Browne concurred: 'Now nature is not at variance with art, nor art with nature; they being both servants of his providence. . . . In briefe, all things are artificiall, for Nature is the Art of God.'[12] Instructing Perdita on the grafting of flowers the disguised Polixenes recognises this ultimate equivalence of Art and Nature:

> nature is made better by no mean
> But nature makes that mean; so over that art,
> Which you say adds to nature, is an art
> That nature makes ...
> The art itself is nature.
>   (*The Winter's Tale*, IV. iv. 89–97)

The patterns which the Renaissance projected on to its environment were easily attributable to the workings of God. In this way, as Foucault says, the universe was folded in on itself and every natural object was imbued with the presence of its creator. Turning to his comrades in exile, Duke Senior remarks upon this latent divinity, 'our life, exempt from public haunt, / Finds tongues in trees, books in the running brooks, / Sermons in stones, and good in everything' (*As You Like It*, II. i. 15–17). Under the apparent confusion of Nature, masked by the babbling brooks, the trees and stones, is a unifying harmony, a divine benevolence. The idea of *discordia concors*, 'the concealed god' (as Edgar Wind puts it), was dear to Neoplatonic theory and the ability to decode the riddle of the universe was often conceptualised as a cryptic literacy.[13] Thomas Beard's *The Theatre of Gods Iudgements* draws on this bibliographic metaphor as it discusses the miracle of creation: 'if we turne ouer euery leafe of Gods creatures from the tenth sphere to the centre of the earth, we shall find, that euery leafe and letter of this great volume, is admirable and wonderfull'.[14] In *Antony and Cleopatra*, when Charmian asks the soothsayer to produce his credentials he tells her: 'In nature's infinite book of secrecy / A little I can read' (I. ii. 8–9).

Nature is, if observed properly, an introductory manual to the ways of God, a source of information on the divine gardener. The point of reference for all of this cosmic literacy was man. Vitruvian man stands at the centre of geometry, the abstract of God's mysterious book.[15] The ever-adroit speaker of Donne's 'The Extasie' justifies his seduction by arguing that intercourse can provide an epiphany of divine love. He draws again on the idea of inscriptional physicality, 'Love's mysteries in souls do grow, / But yet the body is his book' (ll. 71–2).[16] The universe is assembled around the body and takes its meaning from it. Analogical meaning finds its fulcrum in man. Our heads are spherical because the universe is spherical, our two eyes are the sun and the moon.[17] According to Nicholas Culpeper's *Directory for Midwives*, 'There must needs be *Microcosmical Stars* in the Body of Man, because he is an exact Epitome of the Creation.'[18] Richard Hooker proposes that man is 'not only the noblest creature in all the world, but even a very world in himself'.[19] Browne is characteristically even more emphatic: 'There is no man alone, because every man is a *Microcosme*, and carries the whole world about him' while Phillip Stubbes employs the same mystical terminology: man 'is a wonderful Creature: and therefore is called in greek MICROCOSMOS, a litle world in himself, And truely he is no lesse, whether we consider his spirituall soule, or his humaine body'.[20] In order to recognise these hidden empathies, these analogical resemblances in nature, to understand the influence over us of our guiding planets, we look around us for divine signatures. In Edward Phillips's dictionary *signature* is defined in this technical sense, 'a signing, marking, or sealing; also the resemblance of any Plant or Mineral unto a mans body, or any parts thereof'.[21] The paintings of Guiseppe Arcimboldo which construct human faces out of plants and animals are precisely about this analogical relationship.[22] Their crazy fabric is exactly paralleled by John Donne's ability to find a pair of lovers in a geometrical instrument. What Dr Johnson didn't understand in his famous definition of the metaphysical conceit ('the yoking of heterogeneous images by violence together') is that Donne's images were not 'heterogeneous' to Donne.[23] The poet's ingenuity, however, also indicates the immense effort required to perceive divinity in the everyday. The strain of Donne's poetry and Arcimboldo's pictures which angles them towards the absurd is symptomatic of the epistemological uncertainties provoked by the earth-shattering work of Copernicus, Kepler, Brahe, Galileo and others. Donne's entropic 'Anatomy of the World' is gloomily ambiguous towards scientific enquiry: the 'new philosophy calls all in doubt, / The element of fire is quite put out; / The sun is lost, and th' earth, and no man's wit / Can well direct him, where to look for it' (ll. 205–8). Since Babel the perception of divine signatures has become problematic. Lorenzo understands the tragic inability of fallen man to hear the music of the spheres:

Here will we sit and let the sounds of music
Creep in our ears; soft stillness and the night

Become the touches of sweet harmony.
Sit, Jessica. Look how the floor of heaven
Is thick inlaid with patines of bright gold;
There's not the smallest orb which thou behold'st
But in his motion like an angel sings,
Still quiring to the young-ey'd cherubins;
Such harmony is in immortal souls,
But whilst this muddy vesture of decay
Doth grossly close it in, we cannot hear it.
(*The Merchant of Venice*, V. i. 55–65)

Man is the cypher of the cosmology and his ability to know his universe is dependent upon his ability to know himself (*nosce teipsum*); self-definition means universal definition. But since the fall, this is no easy thing, as Lorenzo so poignantly reminds us; whilst knowing he is at the centre of things, man cannot apprehend, except indirectly, the otherness which defines him. Thus the relativity which underlies a play like *Antony and Cleopatra* dramatises the moment of separation of mankind and the natural world. One particularly significant break with the secured analogical perspectives of the period can be seen in the land/sea images which the play associates with the two lovers.

II

Both God and (since he is fashioned in God's image) man appear in the landscape. Daniele Barbaro's *Practica della Perspettiva* places fragmented human features firmly within a natural topos:

The better to hide what he paints, in accordance with the practices indicated, the painter who is proposing to delineate the two heads or other portrayals must know how to shade and cover the image so that instead of two heads, it shows landscapes, water, hills, rocks, and other things. . . . And then one would no longer recognize that the painting represents a head, but the nose would seem one thing and the forehead another, and, for example, the painter can make the nose look like a rock and the forehead a clod of earth if he wishes.[24]

This idea of human landscapes was not only important in the visual
arts. Salomon de Caus, the writer on perspective and landscape
gardener who worked for a number of European royal patrons
including Henry, Prince of Wales (for whom he designed Richmond Gardens), frequently punctuated his gardens with anthropomorphic vegetation.

Women especially were prone to being landscaped. In *The Generation of Animals* Aristotle distinguishes between the sexes thus:
'the male as possessing the principle of movement and of generation, the female as possessing that of matter. . . . This is why in
cosmology . . . they speak of the nature of the Earth as something
female and call it "mother".'[25] Ian MacLean notes that

> the metaphorical association of woman with mother earth, nutri-
> tion, fruitfulness and the fluctuations of the moon, [was] deeply
> embedded in the substratum of ancient medieval thought, and
> sometimes explicit there. The implications of these metaphors –
> passivity, receptiveness, compassion, mutability – may account
> in part for the Renaissance view of female psychology.[26]

Milton draws upon and develops this Aristotelian idea in his
version of creation. In Book VII of *Paradise Lost*, the landscape gives
birth on a cosmic scale in response to divine insemination: 'The
earth obeyed, and straight / Opening her fertile womb teemed at a
birth / Innumerous living creatures' (ll. 453–5).[27] The commonplace
Renaissance rhyme 'womb / tomb' demonstrates that the earth is a
final resting-place as well as a source of life.[28] As Stubbes puts it,
'Dame Nature, bryngeth us all into the world, after one sorte, and
receiveth all againe, into the wombe of our mother, I meane, the
bowelles of the earth.'[29] Timon addresses the earth in accordance
with this mythical geogendering:

> Common mother, thou,
> Whose womb unmeasurable and infinite breast
> Teems and feeds all . . .
> Yield him, who all thy human sons doth hate,
> From forth thy plenteous bosom, one poor root!
> Ensear thy fertile and conceptious womb,
> Let it no more bring out ingrateful man!
>   (IV. iii. 176–87)

Infused as it is with Timon's savage misanthropy, the speech, strad-
dling the dichotomy between nature and nurture, reveals its trust
in the positive qualities of the earth-mother. The instant recognition
of this topos is testament to its ubiquity.[30] Females are landmasses
receptive (in the Renaissance scheme of things) to the insertion of
the male seed. According to Plato, the sexual organs had a life of
their own: 'in the male the privy member is mutinous and self-
willed, like a beast deaf to the voice of discourse, and fain to carry
all before it in frenzied passion'.[31] The union of animate genitals
is imaged as an agricultural process with the male 'sow[ing] the
plough-land of the womb'.[32] In Shakespeare's *Pericles*, the pimp
insists to his servant that Marina be deflowered in a similarly agricultural manner: 'if she were a thornier piece of ground than she is,
she shall be ploughed' (IV. vi. 144). Agrippa jokes with Enobarbus
about the way in which Cleopatra turns swords into ploughshares:
'She made great Cæsar lay his sword to bed. / He ploughed her,
and she cropp'd' (II. ii. 231–2) and in an exceptional departure from
his usual loutish style, Lucio, in *Measure for Measure*, describes
Claudio's sexual transgression to Isabella again in terms of sexual
ploughing:

> Your brother and his lover have embrac'd.
> As those that feed grow full, as blossoming time
> That from the seedness the bare fallow brings
> To teeming foison, even so her plenteous womb
> Expresseth his full tilth and husbandry.
>
> (I. iv. 40–4)

The final word of this speech incorporates in a single term agricultural and sexual labour. *Husbandry* appropriates for exploitation
both land and women. In a feudalistic society, the importance of
farming and the ownership of land were crucial to economic well-
being. In the words of Phillip Stubbes, 'Neither king, prince, earle,
duke, lord, knight, esquire high or low, rich nor poore, nor yet any
potentate, power or principalitie vpon the earth (how great a monarch soeuer) could liue or continue without the vse of husbandrie
and husbandmen.'[33] Power depended on the possession of land
which was frequently amassed by expedient marriage. The irony of
Claudio's situation in *Measure for Measure* is precisely that although
he has cultivated this particular land mass, he doesn't yet fully own
her. His farming is essentially illicit because he is trespassing on the

territory of another man. The bride remains the property of the father until she is 'given away'.[34] Capulet stakes his paternal claim when he tells Paris that Juliet 'is the hopeful lady of my earth' (I. ii. 15). When Ford, disguised as Master Brooke, tells Falstaff of his unrequited love for Mistress Ford, he uses a similar metaphor. His love, he says, is 'Like a fair house built on another man's ground' (*Merry Wives*, II. ii. 195). Petruchio exploits the agricultural possibilities of the metaphor when he brutally describes his wife as his farm from which he warns off potential intruders:

> She is my goods, my chattels, she is my house,
> My household stuff, my field, my barn,
> My horse, my ox, my ass, my any thing,
> And here she stands; touch her whoever dare.
> (*The Taming of the Shrew*, III. ii. 226–9)

From his earliest writing Shakespeare utilised the motif of the colonisation of the female. In *Two Gentlemen of Verona*, for example, the infatuated Valentine describes his love as a 'principality' (II. iv. 148) and in reply to Proteus's imperative to 'let her alone', he replies, 'Not for the world! Why, man, she is mine own' (l. 164). Underpinning this juvenile hyperbole is the equivalence of woman and land to be conquered and exploited; the female is reified into a commodity. The colony of the female body is often a site of invasion and struggle over possession and domain. Robert Tofte attributes one of the causes of jealousy to a perceived threat to the exclusivity of ownership: 'IEALOVSIE springeth from the Propertie or Right that we haue, when we (enioying our Lady or Mistresse) would haue her soly and wholy vnto our selues; without being able (by any meanes) to suffer or endure, that another man should haue any part or interest in her, any way, or at any time.'[35] The psychotic Ferdinand, in John Webster's *Duchess of Malfi*, offers an example of Tofte's masculine paranoia; he would rather lay waste, as a storm, to the landscape of his own sister than have her cultivated by somebody else:

> Would I could be one [a storm],
> That I might toss her palace 'bout her ears,
> Root up her goodly forests, blast her meads,
> And lay her general territory as waste,
> As she hath done her honours.
> (II. v. 17–21)

Similarly in John Ford's *'Tis Pity She's a Whore* the site of agricultural conflict is the body of the ill-fated sister who, while she provides food for Giovanni in the first place ('I digg'd for food'), is eventually destroyed by her owner-occupier:

> 'Tis Annabella's heart, 'tis; why do you startle?
> I vow 'tis hers; – this dagger's point ploughed up
> Her fruitful womb, and left to me the fame
> Of a most glorious executioner.
>
> (V. vi. 24–33)

These horrific examples of fraternal violence rely on the analogy between the sister's physicality and the possession of land: 'the female body is a supreme form of property and a locus for the contestation of authority'.[36]

The traditional exegesis of the Song of Songs as the seduction of the Church by her rightful husband, Christ, helped normalise this correlation between the female body and the landscape. Moreover the Canticles dwell, in a way uncannily appropriate to *'Tis Pity*, on the incestuous possibility of the beloved being at once wife and sister: 'Thou hast rauished my heart, my sister, *my* spouse' (4. 9).[37] In Shakespeare's erotic poem, *Venus and Adonis*, Venus offers us a secular example of this sexualised land mass. As she seduces Adonis, she transforms herself into a garden of earthly delight:

> 'Fondling,' she saith 'since I have hemm'd thee here
> Within the circuit of this ivory pale,
> I'll be a park, and thou shalt be my deer;
> Feed where thou wilt, on mountain or in dale;
> Graze on my lips; and if those hills be dry,
> Stray lower, where the pleasant fountains lie.
>
> 'Within this limit is relief enough,
> Sweet bottom-grass and high delightful plain,
> Round rising hillocks, brakes obscure and rough,
> To shelter thee from tempest and from rain;
> Then be my deer, since I am such a park;
> No dog shall rouse thee, though a thousand bark.'
>
> (ll. 229–40)

The entry of Adonis into the symbolic order requires his separation from the mother's body. The nurturance and protection that Venus

offers here is in stark contrast to the hostile briers and thorns that
tear her legs later in the poem. The movement of Adonis to the
hunt, his rejection of this eroticised maternalism, dramatises his
fear of female sexual expectation from a point of view of male
impotence. Ironically when the boar sheaths his tusk in the youth's
'soft groin' (l. 1116), out flows 'milk and blood . . . mingled both
together' (l. 902).[38] The castration of Adonis takes place amid a
bizarre instance of bestiality. His seed is spilt on to the barren ground
of the forest rather than being sown into the fecund garden which
Venus offers him.

As has been frequently noted, in its sexualised colonialism John
Donne's writing is extreme. The poet of his second elegy 'To his
Mistress Going to Bed', describes frenetic copulation in terms of
this discourse of land use: 'O my America, my new found land, /
My kingdom, safeliest when with one man manned, / My mine of
precious stones, my empery, / How blessed am I in this discover-
ing thee' (ll. 27–30). Discovery is the process of exploring and
mapping for the first time the hitherto uncharted landscape of the
female body but the word encapsulates more literally the exposure
of that body: Donne's lover is dis-covering her in the sense of pull-
ing back the bed-clothes. When Ralegh founded his new American
colony, he gave it as it were, in answer to Donne's poem, the fit-
tingly exploitative name: Virginia. Moreover his description of
Guiana in 1595 drew upon the same analogy: 'a country that hath
yet her maydenhead'.[39] While the comparison between territory and
the female body is demeaning in these examples, the topos could be
utilised in what was, for Renaissance writers, a positive and complimentary way. In 'An Anatomy of the World', Donne redeploys
the exploration motif in a serious, if not solemn manner. Of the
death of Elizabeth Drury, he writes:

> she whose rich eyes, and breast,
> Gilt the West Indies, and perfumed the East;
> Whose having breathed in this world, did bestow
> Spice on those Isles, and bade them still smell so,
> And that rich Indy which doth gold inter,
> Is but as single money, coined from her:
> She to whom this world must itself refer,
> As suburbs, or the microcosm of her,
> She, she is dead; she's dead.
>
> (ll. 229–37)

By and large though, the literature that connects the virginal woman and the unexplored landmass lacks the respect of 'The First Anniversary'. Renaissance geo-eroticism dramatises the facelessness of male desire. These landscaped women are generally supine, still, and anonymous from the neck up. In Thomas Carew's 'A Rapture' the female body is again itemised, dissected, fragmented as it melts mysteriously into a fervently eroticised landscape:

> I'll seize the rose-buds in their perfumed bed,
> The violet knots, like curious mazes spread
> O'er all the garden, taste the ripened cherry,
> The warm firm apple, tipped with coral berry;
> Then will I visit, with a wandering kiss,
> The vale of lilies and the bower of bliss;
> And, where the beauteous region doth divide
> Into two milky ways, my lips shall slide
> Down those smooth alleys, wearing as I go
> A tract for lovers on the printed snow;
> Thence climbing o'er the swelling Apennine
> Retire into thy grove of eglantine.
> (ll. 63–74)[40]

Like Donne's intrepid explorer, Carew's persona is also a cartographer leaving his trail for others to follow as they certainly will, for in this poem and in the female landscape of the Renaissance, woman is sexually available for anyone.[41] The poet of 'A Rapture' despises those 'greedy men that seek t' enclose the common / And within private arms impale free woman' (ll. 19–20) but she is not free herself, rather she is freely available to everyone else, just like Jonson's Doll Common who speaks of herself as a commonwealth, 'Have yet some care of me, o' your republic' (*The Alchemist*, I. i. 110). Land held in common and women commonly used lose their value. Tofte insists on the consequences of trespassing:

> And so puissant and potent is this our desire, which wee haue to enioy that Party (which wee loue) soly and alone, without the societie and company of any other whatsoeuer, as that (many times) when this our high-pris'd Commoditie chanceth to light into some other merchants hands, and that this our private Inclosure proueth to be a Common for others, we care no more for it, but giue it altogether ouer.[42]

Woman comes to be an object for man's libidinal pleasure rather than a presence in her own right in these pastoral landscapes. It is trenchantly significant that the Latin verb *rapere*, 'to take by force', gives us both *rapture* and *rape*. This vocabulary of geosexual assault is employed by Shakespeare. Titus addresses the raped Lavinia as 'Thou map of woe' (III. ii. 12) while the sleeping Lucrece is described, immediately prior to her rape, as a 'map of death' (l. 402). Her breasts are 'like ivory globes circled with blue, / A pair of maiden worlds unconquered' (ll. 407–8). Though tonally changed, Dromio's description of the serving woman in *The Comedy of Errors* utilises the same misogynist mapping of the female body. He tells Antipholus that she is so fat, 'she is spherical like a globe; I could find out countries in her' (III. ii. 113). In a Renaissance example of rugby-club humour her hot breath is Spain, the barren hardness of her hand is Scotland, the Indies are represented by the jewels or spots on her nose and the Netherlands provide their own rather obvious and smutty joke. Columbus himself believed 'that the newly discovered hemisphere was shaped like a woman's breast, and that the Earthly Paradise was located at a high point corresponding to the nipple.'[43]

Landscapes are female not merely physiographically but, as a number of the above examples intimate, economically and politically too. In Shakespeare's histories the concept of the motherland feeds directly into notions of nationalism. John of Gaunt's valedictory images England as 'this teeming womb of royal kings, / Fear'd by their breed, and famous by their birth' (II. i. 51–2) and Richard conceptualises rebellion as an act of maternal rape (I. iii. 125–38). In *Henry V* the French King describes the hitherto peaceful cities in terms of anthropomorphic landscapes. Their intact city walls make them politically virginal: 'you see them perspectively, the cities turned into a maid; for they are all girdled with maiden walls that war hath never ent'red' (V. ii. 315). The agrarian phenomenon of enclosure of which Carew's speaker is so contemptuous had long applied equally to women as to land. In *The Merchant's Tale*, January keeps the key to his young wife's garden, and her lover can only gain entrance to this zone of sexual indulgence after she has copied the key for him: she is his 'paradys terrestre'.[44] The faithful woman ever since the Song of Songs, and the *Romance of the Rose* had been imaged as a *hortus conclusus*: 'A garden inclosed is my sister, *my* spouse: a spring shut vp, a fountaine sealed' (4: 12). Campion employs this analogy, relying on the stock colours red and white associated with female beauty:

There is a Garden in her face,
Where Roses and white Lillies grow;
A heav'nly paradice is that place,
Wherein all pleasant fruits doe flow.
There Cherries grow which none may buy,
Till Cherry ripe themselves doe cry.
(*Fourth Booke of Ayres*, vii. 1–6)[45]

Herrick's poetry is abundant in such female gardens, excelling as he does in the *carpe florem* tradition: 'Gather ye Rose-buds while ye may, / Old Time is still a flying: / And this same flower that smiles to day, / To morrow will be dying' ('To the Virgins, To Make Much of Time', 1–4).[46] Against the blithe indulgence of this tradition, Marvell's masculine solipsism is constructed as a direct parody. The cavalier luxuriating in his misogynistic 'Garden' is prepared to satisfy his onanistic energies on anything at hand – especially soft fruit:

What wond'rous Life in this I lead!
Ripe Apples drop about my head;
The Luscious Clusters of the Vine
Upon my Mouth do crush their Wine;
The Nectaren, and curious Peach,
Into my hands themselves do reach;
Stumbling on Melons, as I pass,
Insnar'd with Flow'rs, I fall on Grass.
(ll. 33–40)[47]

In this exquisite plethora of Nature's sexualised bounty, the speaker seems to have overlooked the dark implications of the apples of that archetypal garden – Eden. This garden with its rich temptation is actually dangerous; it causes the unwary to stumble, its flowers can ensnare and the final falling echoes the fatal fall and expulsion from the most superb garden of all. The last stanza of 'The Garden', with its industrious bee and its floral sundial, bludgeoningly asserts the futility of the pastoral dream. Work and time are both results of man's first disobedience and the delights of the pastoral fantasy and sexual indulgence have cost us our immortality. As Marvell puts it in *Upon Appleton House*: 'What luckless apple did we taste, / To make us mortal and thee waste?' (ll. 327–8).

In the visual arts, the *hortus conclusus* finds its high point in the fifteenth century in the paintings of Martin Schongauer, Stefan

Lochner, and Stefano da Verona with their pictures of the Madonna in the rose garden. This Marian image is appropriated by the propaganda of the Virgin Queen herself and given a clearly nationalistic tone. _The Ditchley Portrait_ of 1592 has Elizabeth firmly established in her own territory. Her cool gaze should be enough to warn intruders off. The meniscus which falls away from the precious stone set in the silver sea indicates that Elizabeth is not simply standing on England, but on the very globe itself. England's naval domination, testified by the defeat of the Armada only four years earlier, and its burgeoning interest in geographical exploration by sea are definitively inscribed in the painting. In _The Armada Portrait_, which illustrates the triumphant English fleet routing the Armada, the Queen sits contemplating her power in front of her crown. Her hand rests significantly on a globe and the New World is quite literally under her thumb. In _The Rainbow Portrait_, the Queen is seen controlling not only the geographical areas of the earth's surface, but also the climate that they suffer. In these pictures, England most certainly does rule the waves that surround it. Ten years after the Armada, Queen Elizabeth is quite literally mapped on to the European scene. The Dutch engraving reproduced in Plate B is a superb example of the politics of female cartography. Elizabeth is imaged as Europa; Italy forms her right arm while her left is made up of England and Scotland. Maps, like those in _Tamburlaine_, _I Henry IV_ and _King Lear_, are symbols of power. They establish zones of possession and government; at first only Caliban knows the way around the island and Lear's political authority is rent along with his map. Elizabeth's mappings are profoundly ideological reworkings of the tradition of female landscape. The paradox of the monarch was her self-image as that of a man trapped inside a woman's body. Addressing her navy she divided herself between the sexes: 'I know I have the bodie but of a weak and feeble woman, but I have the heart and stomach of a King.'[48] The male part of Elizabeth governs not only her female part, but the land of which the female part is map and monarch.[49]

If woman was especially immanent in dry land, man was associated more often with water. Cellini's salt-cellar, for example (see Plate C), relies in its sexual allocation on this pattern:

> on this oval [base], with the idea of showing the embrace of the Sea and the Land, I made two figures, ... sitting with their legs intertwined, just as you can observe long arms of the sea running

up into the land. The Sea was figured by a man with a richly carved ship in his hand, which was conveniently arranged to hold a quantity of salt. Under him I had placed the four sea-horses; and in his right hand I had put his trident. The Earth I had represented as a woman, the most beautiful and graceful I could fashion or even conceive of. Near her I had placed a richly adorned temple, on which she rested her hand. This I intended for holding the pepper. In her other hand was a cornucopia decorated with every lovely ornament imaginable. Beneath this goddess, in the part which was meant to represent land, I had grouped all the fairest animals which the earth brings forth; while on the sea side I had designed every sort of beautiful fish and shell which I could get into the small space.[50]

Mother Nature or Mother Earth were assumed female; water whether sea (deified as Neptune) or rain (deified as Jove) seems more likely to be represented in male terms. Spenser offers a clear example of this imaging of male potency in terms of rain. As the Redcross Knight and Una pass through the forest, it begins to rain:

Thus as they past,
The day with cloudes was suddeine ouercast,
And angry *Ioue* an hideous storme of raine
Did poure into his Lemans lap so fast,
That euery wight to shrowd it did constrain,
And this faire couple eke to shroud themselues were fain.
(I. i. 6)[51]

In Titian's *Danae* the goddess lays supine, her legs open to receive the monetary sperm and in Botticelli's *Birth of Venus*, the goddess surfs in to the shore on a wave of divine semen. Pico writes 'Venus could not be born if the testicles of Uranus did not fall into the waters of the sea'.[52] Donne's 'Anatomy of the World' laments that, following the death of Elizabeth Drury, the sky has become impotent: 'The clouds conceive not rain, or do not pour/ In the due birth time, down the balmy shower' (ll. 381–2). The insemination of the female land by male water and seminal froth reappear in a more fecund way in *Hero and Leander*. Fresh from copulating with his love, Leander arrives at the beach to be greeted by his sister Hermione. As he shakes the water from his body, the earth responds by conceiving and giving birth to flowers:

His most kind sister all his secrets knew,
And to her singing like a shower he flew,
Sprinkling the earth, that to their tombs took in
Streams dead for love to leave his ivory skin,
Which yet a snowy foam did leave above,
As soul to the dead water that did love;
And from thence did the first white roses spring
(For love is sweet and fair in every thing)
And all the sweetened shore as he did go,
Was crowned with od'rous roses white as snow.

(III. 73–82)[53]

In *Twelfth Night* Orsino distinguishes between what he considers to
be the paucity of female love and the passion that beats in his own
male breast by invoking the elemental grandeur of the sea: 'Alas,
their [women's] love may be call'd appetite. . . . / But mine is all as
hungry as the sea, / And can digest as much' (II. iv. 96–100). His
love, in accordance with the iconographical norm, has an infinite
capacity which 'Receiveth as the sea' (I. i. 11).

In '"The Swallowing Womb": Consumed and Consuming Women
in *Titus Andronicus*', Marion Wynne-Davies demonstrates how
gendered geography is distorted and confused by the pressure of
tragedy. She cites Titus's speech from III. i:

If there were reason for these miseries,
Then into limits could I bind my woes.
When heaven doth weep, doth not the earth o'erflow?
If the winds rage, doth not the sea wax mad,
Threat'ning the welkin with his big-swol'n face?
And wilt thou have a reason for this coil?
I am the sea; hark how her sighs do blow.
She is the weeping welkin, I the earth;
Then must my sea be moved with her sighs;
Then must my earth with her continual tears
Become a deluge, overflow'd and drown'd;
For why my bowels cannot hide her woes,
But like a drunkard must I vomit them.

(ll. 220–32)

In this speech, Titus roundly acknowledges the maritime vigour of
masculinity – 'I am the sea' – but his realisation that he has just

pointlessly sacrificed his hand and the appalling condition of his daughter, persuade him that he has lost his autonomy. Consequently he images himself as the passive earth subject to the deluge of his daughter's tears. Wynne-Davies writes: 'When our pity and sympathy become overwhelming this figurehead of patriarchy ... turns to his mutilated daughter and denies difference, elemental and gender. ... [W]e are faced with the appalling consequences of tragedy, which perforce takes identity beyond its limit to a point where gender overflows itself into another.' [54] I would like to propose that a similar dissolution of 'all delineations of difference' takes place with respect to the central protagonists of *Antony and Cleopatra*.[55]

III

In her study of *Broken Nuptials in Shakespeare's Plays*, Carol Thomas Neely registers a recent propensity to wrest literary meaning from any single monolithic conceptualisation and a corresponding tendency to see it in terms of dynamic relationships between male and female. Writing of *Antony and Cleopatra* she notes, 'Recently, psychoanalytic and feminist critics have likewise found in the play the dissolution of gender boundaries.'[56] She goes on to illustrate the ways in which gender oppositions are left behind but, in doing so, relies upon the hoary notion that the love of the protagonists is transcendental and mystical. The lovers are etherialised in her account and, in their death, triumph spiritually over the world of Roman expediency. I believe that Neely is right that the gender boundaries are collapsed but my evidence is directly based on the imagery of the play. There is no need to employ quasi-divine notions of an extra-terrestrial love, because the play explicitly muddles the sexual geography and the female/male categories that it stands for.

In refuting this iconographical norm *Antony and Cleopatra* takes the anxiety implicit in the mannerist analogues of Donne and Arcimboldo a stage further. Unlike Cellini's salt-cellar, the land and sea do not merely intertwine, they actually merge; *Antony and Cleopatra* takes place against 'The varying shore o' th' world' (IV. xv. 11). In Shakespeare's play it is not the centre that cannot hold, but the boundaries. Sexual taxonomies are eroded like the beach itself, and ultimately, in places, they become peculiarly reversed. In *On*

the General Nature of Beauty, Pico discusses the old belief that attributed this kind of sexual inversion to the need for cosmic harmony:
'according to the ancient astrologers ... Venus was placed in the
centre of heaven next to Mars, because she must tame his impulse
which is by nature destructive and corrupting'.[57] In Botticelli's *Mars
and Venus*, the male is passive, supine and naked – all qualities
associated above with Titian's Danae. Venus, on the other hand, is
erect, fully dressed and voyeuristic. When Venus appears in Shakespeare's poem she picks up the unwilling and virginal Adonis and
takes him off to seduce him. The macrocosmic version of this poem,
Antony and Cleopatra, is similarly interested in the woman as a figure
of authority and potency. Along with this inversion is an appropriate reversal of the imagery of sexual geography. Cleopatra is constantly associated with water and even with Jove. Enobarbus insists
that Cleopatra's volatile emotions are sincere: 'We cannot call her
winds and waters sighs and tears; they are greater storms and tem-
pests than almanacs can report. This cannot be cunning in her; if it
be, she makes a show'r of rain as well as Jove' (I. ii. 145). Cleopatra
later promises a messenger that she will 'set thee in a shower of
gold' (II. v. 45) if he brings her good news and the raining kisses of
Act III reiterate this motif (xiii. 85).

Complementing this association of the female with virile symbol-
ism is the emasculation of the play's male characters. Octavius is
scathing of the blurring of sexual categories which takes place in
Egypt: Antony 'is not more manlike / Than Cleopatra, nor the queen
of Ptolemy / More womanly than he' (I. iv. 5–7). Antony's fellow
Romans are similarly anxious about the compromise of their general's machismo. Philo describes Antony as 'the bellows and the
fan / To cool a gipsy's lust' (I. i. 9–10) and the play immediately
realises this image with the stage direction: '*Enter* ANTONY, CLEO-
PATRA, *her Ladies*, ... *with* Eunuchs *fanning her*': in Egypt, only eunuchs wield fans.

In his youth Antony was conventionally identified with the man-
nishness of the sea; his old school master introduces himself to
Cæsar 'As is the morn-dew on the myrtle leaf / To his grand sea'
(III. xii. 8–9). However, the play continually represents him as
effeminised and accordingly he is associated with land ('On the
Alps / It is reported ...', I. iv. 66). The sea is no longer Antony's
element. This transsexual movement is sometimes concurrent with
post-orgasmic exhaustion (as in Botticelli's picture); reminiscing,
Cleopatra reminds us of this particular instance of sexual reversal:

O times!
I laugh'd him out of patience; and that night
I laugh'd him into patience, and next morn,
Ere the ninth hour, I drunk him to his bed,
Then put my tires and mantles on him, whilst
I wore his sword Philippan.

(II. v. 18–23)

Cleopatra, like her archetype *Venus armata*, adopts the weapons
for her own and usurps Mars / Antony's belligerence.[58] Her appropriation of his sword signifies the transference of phallic power
from male to female. Antony's later 'O, thy vile lady! / She has
robb'd me of my sword' (IV. xiv. 22–3) bewails his recognition of
impotence. Romeo too recognises the sexual compromise that results from female intimacy: 'O sweet Juliet, / Thy beauty hath made
me effeminate, / And in my temper soft'ned valour's steel!' (III. i.
110–12): burnished masculinity is rendered flaccid in a woman's
hand. Antony is no longer, phallically or militarily 'the firm Roman' (I. v. 43). Antony's address to Cleopatra as 'Thetis' (III. vii. 60)
is, in this sense, doubly ironic. First Thetis is a sea nymph and so
rhetorically Antony has allocated the queen to the male element,
but moreover, Thetis is the mother of Achilles for whom she carries
armour. In IV. iv Cleopatra insists on arming her lover and symbolically this scene indicates that Antony's manhood can be confis-
cated and conferred by woman: 'my queen's a squire' (l. 14). Mars
represents the fusion of masculinity and martial virtuosity and the
suggestion is that the collapse of either will result in the decay of
the other. Antony's transvestism (like that of Hercules, Achilles and
Samson) anticipates his defeat. But this desiccation of virility is by
no means confined to the leading male; this castration and the
military demise it initiates, are pervasive and percolate down from
Antony to Enobarbus, thence to Antony's forces. Resigning as his
leader, Antony prompts the following bitter response from
Enobarbus, 'Look, they weep; / And I, an ass, am onion-ey'd. For
shame! / Transform us not to women' (IV. ii. 34–6). These tears
stand for the evaporation of the troops' virility and their consequent military prostration. This idea of emasculation is coupled
with the traditional iconography of land and sea and the issue of
the site of the imminent battle is thus imbued with a mythological
significance:

Sold.: O noble Emperor, do not fight by sea;
          Trust not to rotten planks. Do you misdoubt
          This sword and these my wounds? Let th' Egyptians
          And the Phœnicians go a-ducking; we
          Have us'd to conquer standing on the earth
          And fighting foot to foot.
Anto.:   Well, well – away.
                    [Exeunt Antony, Cleopatra, and Enobarbus.
Sold.: By Hercules, I think I am i' th' right.
Cani.: Soldier, thou art; but his whole action grows
          Not in the power on't. So our leader's led,
          And we are women's men.
                                        (III. vii. 61–70)

Soldierly pragmatism is overruled by Cleopatra's maritime determination – clearly Antony and his army are governed by her.
Moreover, she says that she wants to 'Appear there for a man' (III.
vii. 18) – we are reminded of Elizabeth galvanising her navy with
the suggestion that she has the heart and the stomach of a king. In
attempting to win a victory at sea, Antony is redefining his masculinity in terms of it; that is, Cæsar's challenge at sea demands a
marine response:

Anto.: . . . we
          Will fight with him by sea.
Cleo.:   By sea! What else?
Cani.: Why will my lord do so?
Anto.:   For that he dares us to 't.
                                        (III. vii. 27–9)

In Shakespeare's source, Plutarch has Antony fight at sea in deference to Cleopatra's wishes. Shakespeare, by drawing attention to
the dare, makes Actium a battle-zone not merely of politics but of
masculinity.

   Marlowe's *Dido, Queen of Carthage* offers an interesting contrast
here. Aeneas receives advice from his general, Achates, who alerts
him to the imminence of his own uxorious decline:

Acha.: Banish that ticing dame from forth your mouth,
          And follow your foreseeing stars in all;

This is no life for men-at-arms to live,
Where dalliance doth consume a soldier's strength,
And wanton motions of alluring eyes
Effeminate our minds inur'd to war.

(IV. iii. 31–6)

Unlike Antony, Aeneas takes the advice and eight lines later he resolves to act upon it. In accordance with the 'proper' sexual geography, his break from this 'ticing dame' is marked by a return to the virile sea in quest of his motherland: 'Trojans aboard, and I will follow you. / . . . To sea, Aeneas! Find out Italy' (ll. 45–56). In *Antony and Cleopatra*, however, the sea challenges rather than embodies virile sexuality and questions Antony's masculine potency.

The association that the play forges between Cleopatra and moisture underlies much of the Egyptian 'magic', forming a curiously inevitable dramatic sub-structure. Enobarbus mentions that 'When she first met Mark Antony she purs'd up his heart, upon the river of Cydnus' (II. ii. 190) and Cleopatra reiterates this just before her suicide: 'I am again for Cydnus, / To meet Mark Antony' (V. ii. 227–8). The affair seems to be sanctioned by an aquatic puissance. It is entirely apt that Cleopatra 'purs'd up his heart' while on her golden barge. Enobarbus's description ascribes her to the male element yet portrays her as a kind of siren: irresistible but inaccessible, surrounded by water. Moreover, the vacillations of her mood have about them the cyclical rhythms of ebb and flow. Given Cleopatra's supernatural kinship with water and especially the Nile, her hysterical alternative to Roman denigration is vehemently ironic: 'Rather a ditch in Egypt / Be gentle grave unto me! Rather on Nilus' mud / Lay me stark-nak'd, and let the water-flies / Blow me into abhorring!' (V. ii. 57–60). Despite the horror and violence of such a death there is about it a peculiar aptness as well as an uncomfortable eroticism.

Elsewhere the Nile functions as a kind of sexual totem.[59] The swelling Nile of Antony's speech emphasises its phallic significance as well as its importance as a fertility symbol: 'The higher Nilus swells / The more it promises; as it ebbs, the seedsman / Upon the slime and ooze scatters his grain, / And shortly comes to harvest' (II. vii. 20–3).[60] In Egyptian mythology, according to Plutarch, the flooding of the Nile symbolised the fertilisation of the female earth (Isis) by male moisture (Osiris).[61] This impregnation of the female land by a male water exactly matches the usual geosexual categories.

It is in Shakespeare's play, wherein the female ruler of Egypt is associated with its major river, that the pattern is reversed.

In addition to its erotic role the Nile has a more mysterious consequence; its magnitude is indicative of Egypt's agricultural yield. The sinister destructive force of the Nile associated with Cleopatra's uncomfortable deathwish is here subsumed by a more bountiful attitude. The river's and hence Cleopatra's phallicism is reinforced by its (and her) association with snakes and serpents. She imagines Antony murmuring to himself, somewhat unflatteringly, 'Where's my serpent of old Nile?' (I. v. 25) and in an attempt to placate the messenger she has just threatened, she assures her servants that she will keep her fangs in: 'Melt Egypt into Nile! and kindly creatures / Turn all to serpents! Call the slave again, / Though I am mad, I will not bite him' (II. v. 78–80). As Cleopatra kisses farewell to her waiting woman before her suicide, Iras falls and dies. Cleopatra wonders if she has actually turned into a snake: 'Have I the aspic in my lips?' (V. ii. 291). Earlier she alludes to the head of the Medusa – the female gorgon with snakey hair that Antony is said to resemble when looked at from an alternative angle.[62] If your news is bad, she tells the messenger, 'Thou shouldst come like a Fury crown'd with snakes, / Not like a formal man' (II. v. 40–1). In his essay *Medusa's Head*, Freud suggests that the head functions as a focus for both anxiety and security about phallic potency. On the one hand, the fact that the head is severed implies castration but, on the other, the paralysis induced by the sight of the head suggests erection, thus the head 'offers consolation to the spectator: he is still in possession of a penis, and the stiffening reassures him of the fact'.[63] Like that of Milton's Sin, Cleopatra's sex is problematised by the snake imagery that penetrates her realisation. This phallic confusion is intimately related to the blurring of sexual geography for, as the play consistently re-emphasises, the origin of the snake (like its fellow reptile the crocodile) is the pre-genital slime of the Nile itself. Cleopatra asks the clown for 'the pretty worm of Nilus' (V. ii. 241) and the first soldier recognises the slime on the fig leaves as that which 'th' aspic leaves / Upon the caves of Nile' (ll. 349–50). With characteristic ambivalence, the sources of life and death are rooted in the same images. The asp is a child of the Nile, sucking its life from the breast of the Egyptian Queen and, as she is drained, the moisture which is her life force ebbs from her.

Just before his remorseful death Enobarbus invokes the moon: 'O sovereign mistress of true melancholy, / The poisonous damp of night dispange upon me, / That life, a very rebel to my will, / May hang no longer on me' (IV. ix. 12–15). Moisture here is associated with a kind of cosmic virulence as Enobarbus's conscious faculties are submerged beneath a sea of 'poisonous damp'. In stark opposition to the fecundity associated with the swelling Nile, death and fluidity are linked here. The synthesis of destruction and liquefaction is, usually in a moment of wrathful outburst, directed towards a whole nation: thus we have Cleopatra's curse 'Melt Egypt into Nile!' (II. v. 78) recalling Antony's former execration 'Let Rome in Tiber melt' (I. i. 33). The firm imperatives imply a destructive determination but their terseness hints at an underlying unsophistication, a childlike damnation of whatever conflicts with their own aspirations. Elsewhere this civic destruction is even more violently articulated and even more selfish: 'Sink Rome, and let their tongues rot / That speak against us!' (III. vii. 14–15).

The sea's immutability and infinite capacity make it a common image of destructive potential in Shakespeare: 'I have seen the hungry ocean gain / Advantage on the kingdom of the shore' (Sonnet 64. 5–6). Antony's love for Cleopatra has something of this 'never-surfeited' appetite (*The Tempest*, III. iii. 55). Pompey refers to him as 'The ne'er-lust-wearied Antony' (II. i. 38) and the very opening lines of the play regard Antony's love as fulsome: 'Nay, but this dotage of our general's / O'erflows the measure' (I. i. 1–2). Antony is clearly unable to confine his passions within the modest limits of order and we wait with Philo for the terrible moment when the dam will break.

Just as the collation of these instances of liquefaction signifying death and violent destruction with those in which it is an image of fecundity, indicates its ambivalence, the absence of moisture, as in the case of Cleopatra's death, does not necessarily imply vitality. Despite these evocations of maritime disaster, the annihilation of civilisation by water and Antony's own passionate saturation, wetness is nonetheless a life-force. Enobarbus's heart 'being dried with grief, will break to powder' (IV. ix. 17) while with pastoral simplicity, Cleopatra notes the equivalence between desiccation and death: 'Now no more / The juice of Egypt's grape shall moist this lip' (V. ii. 279–80).

IV

Antony and Cleopatra is a play haunted by the relativity of truth, a play that is characterised by its ability to hold 'contradictory modes of living and understanding in its wide embrace'.[64] Its very opening words are a fragment of a larger argument: 'Nay, but ... ' (I. i. 1). Repeatedly within the drama, characters have their most confident expectations and assessments of situations rebuffed. So Cleopatra is surprised by Antony's marriage to Octavia, Antony suspects Cleopatra of collusion with Cæsar and later believes that she is dead. Cleopatra, after the battle of Actium, protests 'I little thought / You would have followed' (III. xi. 55–6). Despite Antony's expectation that the Romans will fight at sea (IV. x. 1) Cæsar decides to deploy his soldiers (IV. xi. 1). *Antony and Cleopatra* probably contains more messengers than any other Shakespearean play and this is symptomatic of the indeterminacy of the 'truths' that they speak. Their messages are nearly always formulated to manipulate or direct subsequent action rather than to convey information neutrally. The go-between that denigrates Octavia also flatters Cleopatra, the messenger that brings the news of Fulvia's rebellion hints that Antony should really have taken her in hand and prevented it, and Mardian's bluff that the Queen has killed herself has been designed to wreak revenge in the form of remorse on Antony for his rejection of Cleopatra. The plethora of messengers seems designed to foreground the relativity of their messages. Rumour, when he appears in Shakespeare, is maliciously delighted in the erroneous possibilities of communication:

> The posts come tiring on,
> And not a man of them brings other news
> Than they have learnt of me. From Rumour's tongues
> They bring smooth comforts false, worse than true wrongs.
> (*II Henry IV*, Induction. 37–40)

Truth is shown to be untamed in both action and word and fact is substituted with elusiveness. Indeed throughout *Antony and Cleopatra*, 'There is scarce truth enough alive to make societies secure' (*Measure for Measure*, III. ii. 215). This disparity between different kinds of actuality precipitates much of the action of the plot.

Just as this sort of lacuna constitutes the play's own narrative principle, so a similar breach drives the play in dramatic terms. This second discrepancy lies between the traditional grandeur and range of the ancient world and the theatrical production in front of us, and is not simply repeated throughout the play but is enacted by the whole of it. Prognosticating the dramatisation of her story, Cleopatra muses,

> the quick comedians
> Extemporally will stage us, and present
> Our Alexandrian revels; Antony
> Shall be brought drunken forth, and I shall see
> Some squeaking Cleopatra boy my greatness
> I' th' posture of a whore.
>
> (V. ii. 215–20)

The speech has a metatheatricality about it, bridging the gap between the legendary magnanimity of 'A pair so famous' (V. ii. 357) and their Elizabethan representation in which boys took the role of women. Nowhere does the audience *see* the goddess on her barge, nowhere the mighty Mars-like Antony: instead all we have direct access to are the actions and rhetoric of a selfish woman and an impotent man who cannot even fall properly on his own sword as they are played out by two actors on a restricted stage, against a flat backdrop. All we really see is an actor boying Cleopatra's greatness and a man playing a drunk in place of a demi-god. If a queen of fire and air or an emperor Antony do become accessible, they do so only contingently as an effort of the poetry's self-assertion or the actors' gifts.

Antony and Cleopatra is built upon infinitely regressive ironies: the stage, the cast, the characters, the characters' ideas and lastly the ideas themselves and we are shown that in the smallest of these Chinese boxes, where we would expect an absolute standard, we in fact find only a relativity which undermines our most fundamental conceptions about the interplay between female and male. The multivalency of *Antony and Cleopatra* is partly related to its status as a dramatic illusion, which is something that the play continually insists on, but it is also the result of the play's appropriation and subversion of the sexual geography of the Renaissance.

Notes

1.   Constance Brown Kuriyama, 'The Mother of the World: A Psycho-analytic Interpretation of Shakespeare's *Antony and Cleopatra*', *ELR*, 7 (1977), 324–51, pp. 327, 328, 349.
2.   Peter Erickson, *Patriarchal Structures in Shakespeare's Drama* (1985), pp. 133, 144.
3.   Phyllis Rackin, 'Shakespeare's Boy Cleopatra, the Decorum of Nature, and the Golden World of Poetry', *PMLA*, 87 (1972), 201–12, pp. 201, 206.
4.   Kuriyama, 'Mother of the World', p. 324.
5.   Erickson, *Patriarchal Structures*, pp. 123, 143.
6.   A. A. Ansari, '*Antony and Cleopatra*: An Image of Liquifaction', *The Aligarn Journal of English Studies*, 8 (1983), 79–93, p. 79.
7.   Kuriyama, 'Mother of the World', p. 338.
8.   I am grateful to Richard Wilson for this suggestion.
9.   Michel Foucault, *The Order of Things*, (1970), p. 17.
10.   A. Bartlett Giamatti, *Exile and Change in Renaissance Literature* (1984), p. 118.
11.   Sir Philip Sidney, *An Apology for Poetry*, ed. Geoffrey Shepherd (Manchester, 1973), pp. 99–100.
12.   Sir Thomas Browne, *Religio Medici*, in *Works*, ed. Sir Geoffrey Keynes, 4 vols (1964), I, 26.
13.   Edgar Wind, *Pagan Mysteries in the Renaissance* (Oxford, 1980), first published 1958, Chapter 14.
14.   Thomas Beard, *The Theatre of Gods Iudgements* (1597), A 2^r.
15.   Dympna Callaghan points out that in the engraving of Robert Fludd's *Utriusque Cosmi Historia* (1617) the male 'genitals are at the very centre of this series of circles rather than the navel, which provides the centre of Leonardo's figure following Vitruvius's specifications' (*Woman and Gender in Renaissance Tragedy* (Hemel Hempstead, 1989), p. 1). You can't get more phallocentric than that.
16.   References to Donne are from John Carey's edition (Oxford, 1990).
17.   Foucault, *Order of Things*, p. 19.
18.   Nicholas Culpeper, *A Directory for Midwives: or A Guide for Women, In their Conception, Bearing; And Suckling their Children. Newly Corrected from many gross errors* (1675), p. 58.
19.   Richard Hooker, *The Works*, arranged by J. Keeble, revised by R. W. Church and F. Paget (Oxford, 1888), I, 237.
20.   Browne, *Works*, I, 86; Phillip Stubbes, *The Anatomy of Abuses* (1583), ¶2^r.
21.   Edward Phillips, *The New World of English Words* (1658).
22.   See the generously illustrated *The Arcimboldo Effect*, introduced by Feliciano Benvenuti (1987).
23.   John Carey senses the mannerist satisfaction in Donne's forcing us to concede likeness in unlikeness: Donne 'liked joining things [but] he also liked the joint to show' (*John Donne: Life, Mind and Art* (1981), p. 261). But at the same time, Carey's atomisation is in danger of missing the continuity of Donne's anthropocentric world.

24. Published in Venice, 1559. Cited by Jurgis Baltrušaitis, *Anamorphic Art*, trans. W. J. Strachan (Cambridge, 1977), p. 32.
25. Aristotle, *The Generation of Animals*, trans. A. L. Peck (1953), p. 11.
26. Ian MacLean, *The Renaissance Notion of Woman* (Cambridge, 1980), p. 44.
27. References to Milton are from the edition by Stephen Orgel and Jonathan Goldberg (Oxford, 1991).
28. See, for example, Richard Barnfield's *Cassandra*: 'Happy are they that die in infancie: / Whose sins are cancell'd in their mothers wombe: / Whose cradle is their graue, whose lap their tomb' (*Poems 1594–1598*, ed. Edward Arber (Birmingham, 1883), p. 79). Also Milton's 'Epitaph on the Marchioness of Winchester', ll. 31–4. Though he does not employ the rhyme, Romeo apostrophises Juliet's tomb as 'Thou detestable maw, thou womb of death' (V. iii. 45). See also G. A. E. Parfitt, 'Renaissance Wombs, Renaissance Tombs', *Renaissance and Modern Studies*, 15 (1971), 23–33.
29. Stubbes, *Anatomie*, B vii^r.
30. The Celtic Danu, the Scandinavian Nerthus, the Aztec Chicomecoatl, the Egyptian Renenet and Isis (with whom Cleopatra is explicitly identified in the play), the Roman Maia, Vesta and Ceres, the Greek Gaea, Rhea, Demeter, and Cybele, the Amerindian Coatlicue are all versions of Earth goddesses. In each case their femaleness functions as a point of convergence for ideas of fertility, plenitude and growth. See *The New Larousse Encyclopedia of Mythology*, introduced by R. Graves (1968).
31. Plato, *Timaeus and Critias*, trans. A. E. Taylor (1929), *Timaeus* 91b, p. 98. Montaigne notes the wilfulness of the penis: 'Men have reason to checke the indocile libertie of this member [since it refuses] with such fiercenes and obsinacie our solicitations both mentall and manuall' (*Essayes*, trans. John Florio, 3 vols (1904), I, 102). For a lively illustration of this phallic disobedience see the cockney's exhortation to the eels, 'Down, wantons, down!' (*King Lear*, II. iv. 121).
32. Ibid., p. 99.
33. Stubbes, *Second part of the Anatomie of Abuses* (1583), G 6^v.
34. See Ann Jennalie Cook, *Making a Match: Courtship in Shakespeare and His Society* (Princeton, 1991).
35. Benedetto Varchi, *The Blazon of Iealovsie*, trans. R[obert] T[ofte] (1615), E 2^r.
36. Louis Adrian Montrose, ' "Shaping Fantasies" Figurations of Gender and Power in Elizabethan Culture', *Representations*, 1 (1983), 61–94, p. 68.
37. See Jean-Marie Maguin, 'The Anagogy of *Measure for Measure*', *Cahiers Elisabéthains*, 16 (1979), 19–26, p. 25. Also Stanley Stewart, *The Enclosed Garden: The Tradition and the Image in Seventeenth Century Poetry* (1966) and Patricia Parker, *Literary Fat Ladies* (1987) especially Chapters 6 and 7. For the motif of woman's chastity imaged as a private place, see Georgianna Ziegler, 'My lady's chamber: female space, female chastity in Shakespeare', *Textual Practice*, 4 (1990), 73–90.

38. This bizarre cocktail may allude to the confluent mixture of blood and water that flowed from the side of the punctured Christ.
39. Cited by Montrose, 'Shaping Fantasies', p. 77 and Parker, *Literary Fat Ladies*, p. 140.
40. *Cavalier Poets*, ed. Thomas Clayton (Oxford, 1978).
41. On the voyeuristic male conspiracy of the blazon, see Parker, *Literary Fat Ladies*, pp. 128, 129, 153. Nancy J. Vickers makes the following telling remark, 'bodies fetishized by a poetic voice logically do not have a voice of their own' ('Diana Described: Scattered Woman and Scattered Rhyme', *Critical Inquiry*, 8 (1981–82), 265–79, p. 277).
42. Varchi, *Iealovsie*, trans. T[ofte], E 2ᵛ.
43. Harry Levin, *The Myth of the Golden Age in the Renaissance* (New York, 1972), p. 183.
44. Geoffrey Chaucer, *The Works*, ed. F. N. Robinson, second edn (Oxford, 1974), p. 116.
45. References to Campion are from the edition by Joan Hart (Manchester, 1989).
46. References to Herrick are from the edition by F. W. Moorman (Oxford, 1921).
47. References to Marvell are from *The Metaphysical Poets*, ed. Helen Gardner (Harmondsworth, 1972), first published 1957.
48. Cited by Helen Morris, 'Queen Elizabeth I "shadowed" in Cleopatra', *Huntingdon Library Quarterly*, 32 (1968–9), 271–8, p. 276.
49. Given the tendency of this topos to legitimate a patriarchal agrarian economy and to exculpate the sexual exploitation of woman, it is peculiar to find its adoption by feminists. Rachel Blau DuPlessis writes that 'Woman as mother translates into . . . woman/nature' ('Washing Blood', *Feminist Studies*, 4 (1978), 1–12, p. 9), while Hélène Cixous believes that the writing woman enjoys a security and intimacy with a mythical Good Mother. In a moment of mystical topography she employs the imagery of the female landscape: 'I am myself the earth, everything that happens on it, all the lives that live me in my different forms' (cited by Toril Moi, *Sexual/Textual Politics* (1985), p. 116).
50. *The Life of Benvenuto Cellini*, trans. Anne MacDonell (1926), p. 203.
51. Edmund Spenser, *The Faerie Queene*, ed. A. C. Hamilton (1987).
52. Cited by Wind, *Pagan Mysteries*, p. 133.
53. Christopher Marlowe, *The Complete Poems and Translations*, ed. Stephen Orgel (Harmondsworth, 1971). The passage quoted is Chapman's.
54. In *The Matter of Difference* ed. Valerie Wayne (Hemel Hempstead, 1991), pp. 129–51, 143–4.
55. Ibid., p. 143.
56. Carol Thomas Neely, *Broken Nuptials in Shakespeare's Plays* (1985), p. 136.
57. Cited by Wind, *Pagan Mysteries*, p. 89.
58. For a picture of *Venus armata*, see *Pagan Mysteries*, plate 73. Peter Stallybrass describes *Venus Victrix* as a 'fantasy of female rule, of rebellion at the heart of family and state alike' ('The World Turned

Upside Down: Inversion, Gender and the State', in *The Matter of Difference*, 201–20, p. 216).

59. The fertility of Egypt was proverbial. Culpeper notes that 'In Ægypt many times women have five or six children at one birth; the reason is supposed to be the fruitfulness of the place, and if so (as is probable) then let women that would be fruitful, live in fruitful places' (*Directory for Midwives*, p. 104, misnumbered as p. 140).

60. Spenser alludes to its fertility specifically in masculine terms: 'As when old father *Nilus* gins to swell / With timely pride aboue the *Aegyptian* vale, / His fattie waues do fertile slime outwell, / And ouerflow each plaine and lowly dale ...' (*The Faerie Queene*, I. i. 21).

61. 'Of Isis and Osiris', trans. William Baxter in *The Writings of Plutarch*, ed. William W. Goodwin (New York, 1905), IV, 98. In Thomas Nashe's 'The choise of valentines', the emission of sexual fluids finds its objective correlative in the swelling Nile: 'As Aprill-drops not half so pleasant be, / Nor Nilus overflowe, to Ægipt-plaines, / As this sweete-streames, that all hir joints imbaynes' (*The Penguin Book of Renaissance Verse 1509–1659*, ed. H. R. Woudhuysen (Harmondsworth, 1992), p. 259).

62. See headnote to this chapter.

63. *The Standard Edition of the Complete Psychological Works of Sigmund Freud*, trans. James Strachey *et al.*, 24 vols (1966–74), XVIII, 273.

64. Richard P. Wheeler, ' "Since first we were dissevered": Trust and Autonomy in Shakespearean Tragedy and Romance', in *Representing Shakespeare: New Psychoanalytic Essays*, ed. Murray M. Schwartz and Coppélia Kahn (1980), 150–69, p. 159.

A *Much Ado about Nothing*, dir. Alexandru Darie, Oxford Stage Co., 1992. Diane Parish as Hero.

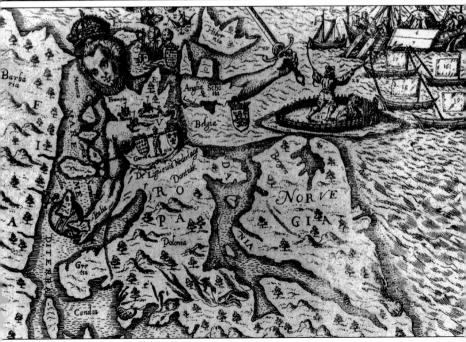

B Dutch engraving of Elizabeth I as Europa.

C   Salt-cellar by Cellir

D   *The Winter's Tale*, dir.
     Simon Usher, Leicester
     Haymarket, 1991. Kevin
     Costello as Leontes with
     the statue of Hermione.

E *Cymbeline*, dir. Bill Alexander, RSC, 1987. Harriet Walter as Innogen and Donald Sumpter as Iachimo.

F *Romeo and Juliet*, dir. David Leveaux, RSC, 1991. Michael Maloney as Romeo (foreground) and Kevin Doyle as Benvolio.

G *Romeo and Juliet*, dir. Terry Hands, RSC, 1989. L to R: Patrick Brennan as Benvolio, Mark Rylance as Romeo and David O'Hara as Mercutio.

H *The Merchant of Venice*, dir. Tim Luscombe, ESC, 1990. Gary Raymond as Antoni and Hugh Sullivan as the Duke.

I   *The Merchant of Venice*, dir. David Thacker, RSC, 1993. Designed by Shelagh Keegan. David Calder as Shylock (centre).

J   *The Jew of Malta*, dir. Barry Kyle, RSC, 1987. John Carlisle as Machevill.

K *The Merchant of Venice*,
   dir. Bill Alexander, RSC,
   1987. Antony Sher as
   Shylock.

L *As You Like It*, dir. Declan
   Donnellan, Cheek by Jowl,
   1991. Adrian Lester as
   Rosalind and Patrick Toomey
   as Orlando.

M   *Troilus and Cressida*, dir.
    Sam Mendes, RSC, 1990.
    Norman Rodway as Pan-
    darus and Sally Dexter as
    Helen.

N   *Troilus and Cressida*, dir.
    Sam Mendes, RSC, 1990.
    Ciaran Hinds as Achilles.

O *Coriolanus*, dir. Tim Supple, Renaissance Theatre Co., 1992. Kenneth Branagh as Coriolanus and James Simmons as Lartius.

P *Coriolanus*, dir. Michael Bogdanov, ESC, 1990. L to R: Vivian Munn as Roman Senator, Michael Pennington as Coriolanus and Bernard Lloyd as Menenius Agrippa.

Part II
Dramaturgy and Language

5

Dreaming Drama and Dramatising Dreams: Towards a Reading of Sexuality in *Cymbeline*

I

Dreams, then, are often most profound when they seem most crazy.... The Prince in the play ... was behaving just as dreams do in reality; so that we can say of dreams what Hamlet said of himself ... 'I am but mad north-north-west; when the wind is southerly, I know a hawk from a hand-saw!'[1]

Shakespeare's is a drama of dreams. The plays deal with fantasies like those of *Twelfth Night*. Having been proposed to by a beautiful widow whom he has just met, Sebastian expresses his ecstasy in terms of illusion: 'What relish is in this? How runs the stream? / Or I am mad, or else this is a dream. / Let fancy still my sense in Lethe steep; / If it be thus to dream, still let me sleep!' (IV. i. 59–62). Elsewhere in the same play, Viola (who is dressed as a boy) hopes that Olivia has not fallen for her: 'Poor lady, she were better love a dream' (II. ii. 24) and even the profoundly prosaic Malvolio has fantasies, as Toby tells Maria, 'thou hast put him in such a dream that when the image of it leaves him he must run mad' (II. v. 173).

Long before Freud interpreted dreams as the bubbling to the surface of instants of wish-fulfilment, Shakespeare understood their relationship to the unarticulated desires of individuals. Peculiarly, it is from the mouth of one of his severest cynics that Shakespeare expresses the fragile magic of the dream world. In I. iv of *Romeo and Juliet*, Mercutio points out that the dream and the dreamer share an obvious affinity. The monarch of dreams, Queen Mab, 'gallops night by night / Through lovers' brains, and then they dream of love; / O'er courtiers' knees, that dream on curtsies straight; / O'er lawyers'

fingers who straight dream on fees; / O'er ladies' lips, who straight
on kisses dream . . . / Sometime she driveth o'er a soldier's neck, /
And then dreams he of cutting foreign throats' (I. iv. 70–83). Romeo's
self-centred impatience punctures Mercutio's mysticism:

> Rome.:　Peace, peace, Mercutio, peace!
> 　　　　　Thou talk'st of nothing.
> Merc.:　　　　　　　　　　　　　True, I talk of dreams,
> 　　　　　Which are the children of an idle brain,
> 　　　　　Begot of nothing but vain fantasy;
> 　　　　　Which is as thin of substance as the air,
> 　　　　　And more inconstant than the wind.
> 　　　　　　　　　　　　　　　　　　(I. iv. 95–100)

For all his ironic self-deprecation, there is about Mercutio's dream-
speak an eerie grandiloquence and psychological magnificence. This
is not merely the result of the other-worldliness of Mab, or even of
the horror she inspires but is, in part, caused by our recognition of
the potency of dreaming and fantasy.[2] Nothing is more authentic to
each of us than our own imaginations and like our own dreams,
drama offers 'an experience at once unreal and yet more real than
real'.[3]

In a moment of indulgent reverie, Cleopatra relishes the libera-
tion of imagination (or 'fancy' as Shakespeare called it) that sleep
permits: 'I dreamt there was an Emperor Antony— / O, such another sleep' (V. ii. 76–7). Shylock's anxieties are suitably materialistic: 'I did dream of money-bags to-night' (II. v. 18). For Romeo,
Juliet is just too good to be true: 'O blessed, blessed night! I am
afeard, / Being in night, all this is but a dream, / Too flattering-
sweet to be substantial' (II. ii. 139–41). These kinds of dreams offer
the sleeper an idealised territory for the examination and fulfilment
of secret desire. Such inspirations are not always so welcome, though.
Antigonus in *The Winter's Tale*, delivers the baby Perdita to the
hostile elements and recounts the vision of its mother which, inspired by his guilt at his part in this infanticide, haunts him:

> Come, poor babe.
> I have heard, but not believ'd, the spirits o' th' dead
> May walk again. If such thing be, thy mother
> Appear'd to me last night; for ne'er was dream
> So like a waking.
> 　　　　　　　　　　　　　(III. iii. 15–19)

The hallucination of Hermione goes on to tell him that his punishment is never to see his wife again. The dream comes true – twenty lines later there follows the absurd and tragic stage direction: *Exit, pursued by a bear*.

Macbeth, that sustained nightmare of history, dwells hauntingly on the iniquitous nature of dreams: 'Now o'er the one half-world / Nature seems dead, and wicked dreams abuse / The curtain'd sleep' (II. i. 49–51). Nightmares dog the couple. Macbeth hath murdered sleep and can neither eat nor sleep in peace because of 'the affliction of these terrible dreams / That shake us nightly' (III. ii. 18–19). 'I dreamt last night of the three Weird Sisters', Banquo tells him. 'I think not of them' (II. i. 20–2), the Thane evasively replies. It is a nightmare, we remember, about washing blood that drives Lady Macbeth to suicide. Hamlet too is in desperate need of sedatives: 'I could be bounded in a nutshell and count myself a king of infinite space, were it not that I have bad dreams' (II. ii. 253). Even his resolve to follow Lady Macbeth in suicide is thwarted by the possibility of imaginative anarchy: 'To die, to sleep; / To sleep, perchance to dream. Ay, there's the rub; / For in that sleep of death what dreams may come, / When we have shuffled off this mortal coil, / Must give us pause' (III. i. 64–8).

Dreams as omens or prophecies also fascinate the playwright. Richard of Gloucester's fantasies are, appropriately, political: 'I do but dream on sovereignty . . . I'll make my heaven to dream upon the crown' (*III Henry VI*, III. ii. 134, 168), yet he is alert to the gullibility of dreamers inciting Edward to imprison their brother George, Duke of Clarence, by encouraging the King to believe that the name of his heirs' assassin begins with the letter G. Clarence laments, 'He hearkens after prophecies and dreams, / And from the cross-row plucks the letter G . . . / And, for my name of George begins with G, / It follows in his thought that I am he' (*Richard III*, I. i. 54–9). Richard's contempt for prediction – he refers dismissively to 'drunken prophecies, libels, and dreams' (l. 33) – rebounds upon him as the audience realises that the King's misgivings about the letter G are not unfounded but need only be transferred to Gloucester to make the omen truthful. The play seems to bear out the portentous authenticity of dreaming. On the eve of Bosworth, Richmond speaks of the 'sweetest sleep and fairest-boding dreams' (V. iii. 227) that forecast his victory: Richard has been wrong to write them off so easily. Like Macbeth and Hamlet, Richard's unquiet soul is wracked by insomnia that results from Margaret's earlier curse: 'No sleep close up that deadly eye of thine, / Unless it be while some tormenting dream / Affrights thee with a hell of ugly devils!' (I. iii. 225–7).

Calphurnia's dream of her husband's statue spouting blood which prognosticates his slaughter is adroitly reinterpreted by the scheming Decius, who has been sent to ensure that the Emperor will attend the Senate to be killed:

> This dream is all amiss interpreted;
> It was a vision fair and fortunate.
> Your statue spouting blood in many pipes,
> In which so many smiling Romans bath'd,
> Signifies that from you great Rome shall suck
> Reviving blood, and that great men shall press
> For tinctures, stains, relics, and cognizance.
> This by Calphurnia's dream is signified.
>   (*Julius Cæsar*, II. ii. 83–90)

Decius refutes the literalness of the vision, interpreting the spouting statue allegorically. Later in the play, however, when the conspirators stoop to wash their hands in Cæsar's blood, Calphurnia's prescience is horribly reified. In a play full of auguries, omens and dreams, Cæsar's tragedy is that, like Richard III, he refuses to be literal-minded about them. With unconscious irony he dismisses the soothsayer who warns him of the ides of March: 'He is a dreamer; let us leave him. Pass' (I. ii. 24). Cæsar's stubborn persona forces him to overlook the possibilities of clairvoyance which the play seems to ratify. The most pointless death in Shakespeare, that of Cinna the poet, is anticipated by his uneasy forebodings: 'I dreamt to-night that I did feast with Cæsar, / And things unluckily charge my fantasy' (III. iii. 1–2). The brutal murders of Cæsar and Cinna demonstrate the plays' faith in visionary authority. Likewise, in *Troilus and Cressida* the dreams of the woeful Andromache are discounted even though their forecast of Hector's death accords with the visions of Cassandra: 'My dreams will, sure, prove ominous to the day' (V. iii. 6). Even King Priam's patriarchal authority is not enough to validate these prophecies:

> Come, Hector, come, go back.
> Thy wife hath dreamt; thy mother hath had visions;
> Cassandra doth foresee; and I myself

Am like a prophet suddenly enrapt
To tell thee that this day is ominous.
Therefore, come back.

(V. iii. 62–7)

Like Cæsar though, Hector's sense of the importance of public display blinds him to the authenticity of these talismanic visions and, like Cæsar, Hector is slaughtered.

Leontes, on the other hand, is prepared to overrule all external evidence which gives the lie to his own privileged grasp of 'reality' as it is inscribed in his ominous dreaming. Early in *The Winter's Tale*, he debates with himself as to whether he should believe the evidence under his nose – that he has a loving wife – or whether he should follow the absurd misgivings of his own fancy which suggest to him that she is sleeping with his best friend. During the trial scene, Hermione pathetically tries to reassure her husband that she is the woman of his dreams. He accepts that she is but, tragically, it is in his dreams that she is unfaithful:

Herm.: My life stands in the level of your dreams,
    Which I'll lay down.
Leon.:   Your actions are my dreams.
    You had a bastard by Polixenes,
    And I but dream'd it.

(III. ii. 79–82)

Brabantio is similarly precipitate in believing the truth of his fancy before the confirmation of hard fact. Iago and Roderigo inform him that his precious daughter is making the 'beast with two backs'. 'This accident', he replies, 'is not unlike my dream' (I. i. 143). Later in the play, it is the story of Cassio's wet-dream which convinces Othello of his wife's infidelity. Despite the fact that Iago has scripted the dream, it is given a dangerous credence because it tallies with Othello's existing suspicions:

Othe.: O monstrous! monstrous!
Iago: Nay, this was but his dream.
Othe.: But this denoted a foregone conclusion.
Iago: 'Tis a shrewd doubt, though it be but a dream,
    And this may help to thicken other proofs
    That do demonstrate thinly.

(III. iii. 431–5)

In *The Winter's Tale* and *Othello*, the characters prioritise their own dreams in the teeth of factual opposition, and this is what makes these plays studies in psychosis. The audience knows that it should rely on the instinctive virtues of Hermione and Desdemona while the fantasies of jealous husbands, albeit ratified by their own paranoid dreams, are likely to be increasingly unsound as they become more intensively expressed.

At the end of his 'Ode to a Nightingale', the speaker of Keats's poem challenges himself to determine whether or not he is in the land of consciousness: 'Was it a vision, or a waking dream? / Fled is that music: – Do I wake or sleep?'[4] Shakespearean characters have frequently to ask themselves the same question. Master Ford in *The Merry Wives of Windsor* cannot believe his ears having been informed (while in disguise) that Falstaff intends to act as his wife's pimp: 'Hum! ha! Is this a vision? Is this a dream? Do I sleep? Master Ford, awake; awake Master Ford' (III. v. 123). Propositioned by his twin brother's wife (whom he has never met), Antipholus of Syracuse interrogates himself thus: 'What, was I married to her in my dream? / Or sleep I now, and think I hear all this? / What error drives our eyes and ears amiss?' (*The Comedy of Errors*, II. ii. 181–3). In a rather more savage example, Leonato in *Much Ado About Nothing* finds it impossible to accept that the slanders of sexual misconduct levelled at his daughter on her wedding day come from anywhere except his darkest nightmares: 'Are these things spoken, or do I but dream?' (IV. i. 65). By way of answer, the cruelly adamant Claudio cynically dispels any doubt by asking a series of absurd rhetorical questions: 'Leonato, stand I here? / Is this the Prince? Is this the Prince's brother? / Is this face Hero's? Are our eyes our own?' (IV. i. 68–70). Romeo too has to ask himself whether his fears are founded in the real world or are merely the misgivings of his own worst conceits:

> What said my man, when my betossed soul
> Did not attend him as we rode? I think
> He told me Paris should have married Juliet.
> Said he not so, or did I dream it so?
> Or am I mad, hearing him talk of Juliet,
> To think it was so?
>
> (V. iii. 76–81)

Romeo's dread about the potential deception of dreaming is a fear shared with the audience as *Romeo and Juliet* begins its final act.

Juliet has died at the end of Act IV and this is immediately followed by the blithe entrance of Romeo celebrating a vision of reverie with his beloved, 'If I may trust the flattering truth of sleep, / My dreams presage some joyful news at hand' (V. i. 1–2). In David Leveaux's 1991 production for the RSC the contrast between Romeo's fantasy and the reality of Juliet's death was heightened by having her suspended in her bedchamber (which later doubled as her tomb) above the ecstatic lover. Not all visions are to be believed; tragically in *Romeo and Juliet*, dreams only come true when linked to images of death. Balthasar, Romeo's servant, tells Lawrence how he has dreamt of the violence of Romeo, a vision which transpires to coincide with the death of Paris: 'As I did sleep under this yew tree here, / I dreamt my master and another fought, / And that my master slew him' (V. iii. 137–9). The uncertainty of the dream facilitates the parallel of Paris's murder with the earlier stabbing of Tybalt.

With characteristic profundity, *King Lear* takes the idea of dreaming ever closer to the borders of nihilism. When he awakes in front of his youngest daughter after his madness on the heath, the king has not merely returned from the land of sleep but, it seems, from the land of the dead. Significantly the self-questioning that we have witnessed above is here substituted by a moving certainty that Lear's vision of hell is terrifyingly true. To begin with, others ask him the questions:

> Cord.: How does my royal lord? How fares your Majesty?
> Lear: You do me wrong to take me out o' th' grave.
> Thou art a soul in bliss; but I am bound
> Upon a wheel of fire, that mine own tears
> Do scald like molten lead.
> Cord.: Sir, do you know me?
> Lear: You are a spirit, I know. Where did you die?
> (IV. vii. 44–9)

Gradually, as Lear comes round from the horror of his imaginative hell, he begins to ask himself questions which signify his attempt to separate himself from the landscape of his mind: 'Where have I been? Where am I? Fair daylight?' (l. 52). Finally, with the aid of external evidence, Lear establishes that he is alive but questions continue to rupture his certitude: 'I will not swear these are my hands. Let's see. / I feel this pin prick. Would I were assur'd / Of my condition! .... Be your tears wet? .... Am I in France?' (ll. 55–76).

In each of the above cases the bewilderment is caused by the erosion of the boundaries between the conscious and the subconscious mind. Shakespeare's dreamers are consistently attempting to limit the compass of their creative imaginations, effectively to separate their internal private fantasies from their socialised personae. This dichotomy feeds directly into the notion of drama itself, for what we are asked to perform, as an audience, is an imaginative act of faith – a collective dream. At the end of *The Winter's Tale*, Paulina tells Leontes that the statue of his wife will come to life for him but 'It is requir'd / You do awake your faith' (V. iii. 94–5). The art of Hermione's statue will become life only if Leontes believes that it can. *The Winter's Tale* is unusual in Shakespeare's canon in that the audience is not allowed to know of the concealed life of Hermione. Typically, as I have shown in Chapter 2, the audience is privy to Shakespeare's secrets but here the statue awakes not merely for Leontes but for the audience too. This doubt in the audience's mind is vital to balance the seemingly unsubstantiated jealousy earlier on. What this means is that, in the final scene, Hermione is life pretending to be art while Leontes and the audience see her as art pretending to be life. If our dreams come true, if the statue does come to life, it is because we have learned along with Polixenes that 'art itself is nature' (IV. iv. 97) and that the theatre is able to dodge rationalistic desires for consistency and truth. In the Leicester Haymarket production of 1991, Simon Usher punctured the dream world of the play. For the first and only time in my experience, the statue was actually a statue – usually it is Hermione standing very still (see Plate D). As the real Hermione entered, on crutches and physically scarred, Leontes had a very real choice between idealised art and imperfect nature. The production challenged the play's faith in the efficacy of dreaming; dreams don't always come true.

Shakespeare's is a drama of dreams not merely in the sense that characters in it have nightmares, fantasies and prophetic imaginings but also in the sense that Shakespeare's theatre itself is a place in which we are willing to suspend our disbelief; Shakespeare continually promotes the idea of drama as a shared fantasy. Towards the end of *The Tempest* Prospero remarks upon the fusion of dramatic and rhapsodic illusion:

Our revels now are ended. These our actors,
As I foretold you, were all spirits, and
Are melted into air, into thin air;

And, like the baseless fabric of this vision,
The cloud-capp'd towers, the gorgeous palaces,
The solemn temples, the great globe itself,
Yea, all which it inherit, shall dissolve,
And, like this insubstantial pageant faded,
Leave not a rack behind. We are such stuff
As dreams are made on; and our little life
Is rounded with a sleep.

(IV. i. 148–58)

The speech is studded with references to Shakespeare's stagecraft. 'The cloud-capp'd towers, the gorgeous palaces', the temples and racks are references to the increasingly elaborate stage machinery of the court masques with which the late plays have so much in common.[5] The descent of Jupiter in *Cymbeline* and the masque of the goddesses and the disappearing feast in *The Tempest* are masque-like features of the late plays. But Shakespeare has fond memories of his old stamping grounds – it is difficult to overlook 'the great globe itself' as a reference to the Globe theatre which opened in 1599 with a production of *Julius Cæsar* and was burned down in 1613 after a cannon set fire to the thatched roof during a performance of *Henry VIII*.

Shakespeare's is an urgently self-conscious art. The dream that the audience is required to indulge is constantly foregrounded by the playwright. In *Henry V* Shakespeare apologises to the audience for the confined space of the theatre:

But pardon, gentles all,
The flat unraised spirits that hath dar'd
On this unworthy scaffold to bring forth
So great an object. Can this cockpit hold
The vasty fields of France? Or may we cram
Within this wooden O the very casques
That did affright the air at Agincourt?
O, pardon! since a crooked figure may
Attest in little place a million;
And let us, ciphers to this great accompt,
On your imaginary forces work.

(Prologue. 8–18)

The Renaissance open-air theatre appears again as 'this wooden O' and the audience are asked at the beginning of each act to place

themselves in the illusion of the drama: 'Still be kind, / And eke
out our performance with your mind' (Prologue. III. 34–5).[6]

Perhaps Shakespeare's most extended meditation on the dream
of drama and the drama of dream is *A Midsummer Night's Dream*.
The dreamscape of the Athenian forest is punctuated with phantas-
magoric fantasies inscribing the hinterlands of adolescent sexual
desire within the acceptable boundaries of socialised behaviour. It
is only in the forest that Hermia could dream of a snake that eats
her heart away while her lover looks on voyeuristically, only in the
forest where a fairy queen could desire to couple with an ass. These
fanciful misconstructions are aberrations caused by a negation of
the 'correct' / normalised / socialised frames of reference. The solipsism of dreaming corresponds to the imaginative autonomy of
the audience itself. It is no accident that the romantic delicacy of the
forest is continually broken by the assembly of rude mechanicals
who are rehearsing a play. The insistent references to eyes and
seeing enforce the potentiality of misinterpretation, both of dreams
and of drama. Puck's love-juice rubbed on the eyes causes love at
first sight and yet we have already heard that this is the most
unreliable kind of involvement: 'Love looks not with the eyes, but
with the mind; / And therefore is wing'd Cupid painted blind. /
Nor hath Love's mind of any judgement taste; / Wings and no
eyes figure unheedy haste' (I. i. 234–7). *A Midsummer Night's Dream*
is a sustained exploration into the nature, value and function of the
art of illusion: drama – where actors pretend to be characters they
are not, where they pretend to speak spontaneously lines which
have been deliberately committed to memory. The illusions generated by the characters themselves, and the illusions that they foist
on each other form the superordinate illusion, the one which governs and dictates the structure of all others – the play itself: *A
Midsummer Night's Dream*. Puck, a malevolent version of Cupid,
plays the parts of Lysander to Demetrius and Demetrius to Lysander
as he leads each through the forest. He also plays director to Oberon's
producer, as the lovers are made to fall in love with each other.
When the lovers awake, they are quick to attribute the story of the
night to their own overactive dreams:

> Deme.:   Are you sure
>   That we are awake? It seems to me
>   That yet we sleep, we dream. Do not you think
>   The Duke was here, and bid us follow him?

Herm.:	Yea, and my father.
Hele.:	And Hippolyta.
Lysa.:	And he did bid us follow to the temple.
Deme.:	Why, then, we are awake; let's follow him;
	And by the way let us recount our dreams.

(IV. i. 189–96)

The suggestion that the characters have been sleeping conflicts directly with the audience's experience of the play. Had these four really been lying on the ground for twelve hours, the play would be quite different from the one we have just watched. We know, even if they do not, that their dreams are our drama; and the waking of Bottom, which immediately follows their exit, reinforces this equation:

> [*Awaking*] When my cue comes, call me, and I will answer. My next is 'Most fair Pyramus'. Heigh-ho! Peter Quince! Flute, the bellows-mender! Snout, the tinker! Starveling! God's my life, stol'n hence, and left me asleep! I have had a most rare vision. I have had a dream, past the wit of man to say what dream it was. Man is but an ass if he go about to expound this dream. . . . I will get Peter Quince to write a ballad of this dream. It shall be call'd 'Bottom's Dream' because it hath no bottom; and I will sing it in the latter end of a play, before the Duke.

(l. 197–215)

Bottom, the gross actor-manager who would if he could, take all the available parts in the rustics' play, is the focus for these twinned issues of drama and dream. He is, of all the play's mortals, the only one to see the fairies, and yet his literal-mindedness demands that the peculiarities of his vision be adapted for the stage. Paradoxically the most obvious clown in the whole play recognises the synonymous nature of dreams and drama. It would be foolish to interpret the dream, he says, because it has taken place in his own head; all he can do is re-enact it through a play. It is called 'Bottom's Dream', firstly because it belongs to him and secondly because it has no imaginative or dramatic life unless he is its author. *Bottom's Dream* is literally Bottom's dream; the play *is* the dream, the art itself *is* nature. Bottom's propensity to interrupt the court entertainment points up his inability to separate drama and dream and indicates his belief in their power. To assuage the ladies' fears, they must be informed that the actor is not really a lion, that the stage deaths are not real and so on. Framed as it is within the larger comic benevolence of the *Dream*, the tragical story of Pyramus and Thisby is completely defused. It is comical precisely because the dream of its illusion is continually ruptured. The court audience and the theatre audience are consistently woken from the illusion of the drama by the actors' intrusions. If such intrusions had not occurred, such a play could indeed require us to respond to it as a tragedy. Shakespeare at about the same time as he wrote the *Dream*, was composing a version of 'A tedious brief scene of young Pyramus / And his love Thisby' (V. i. 56–7) without its ingressive interruptions; this play he called *The Most Excellent and Lamentable Tragedy of Romeo and Juliet*.

A *Midsummer Night's Dream* leaves us by emphasising the necessity of our tolerance while making us aware of the importance of fantasy and dreaming:

> If we shadows have offended,
> Think but this, and all is mended,
> That you have but slumb'red here
> While these visions did appear.
> And this weak and idle theme,
> No more yielding but a dream,
> Gentles, do not reprehend.
> If you pardon, we will mend.
>   (V. i. 412–19)

Puck attempts to persuade those of us who are upset by the *Dream* that it is nothing more than the product of our own fantasies: that the drama is dream. As Norman N. Holland succinctly puts it, 'what has happened [in *A Midsummer Night's Dream*] is *our* dream.'[7] In Shakespeare's English the word *shadow* meant 'spirit' or 'ghost' but it also meant 'actor'. Macbeth uses the word thus: 'Life's but a walking shadow, a poor player, / That struts and frets his hour on the stage, / And then is heard no more' (V. v. 24–6) and Hamlet plays with the pun as he asserts lugubriously that 'A dream itself is but a shadow' (II. ii. 259).[8] In *A Midsummer Night's Dream*, Theseus plays on the word when he notes of the players that 'The best in this kind are but shadows' (V. i. 210) and the opening line of Puck's epilogue draws attention through this pun to the acting of the *Dream* itself. Dreaming and drama blur in the audience imagination.

Shakespeare's most sustained consideration of the fusion of dreaming and acting takes place in the induction to *The Taming of the Shrew*. The drunk Christopher Sly, having been ejected from a pub, falls down and asleep in the street. A hunt passes by and a lord suggests that Sly be picked up and taken back to his chamber. The lord instructs his servants to pretend that the drunk has been in a coma for fifteen years and that he is really a noble aristocrat:

> Some one be ready with a costly suit,
> And ask him what apparel he will wear;
> Another tell him of his hounds and horse,
> And that his lady mourns at his disease;
> Persuade him that he hath been lunatic,
> And, when he says he is, say that he dreams,
> For he is nothing but a mighty lord.
> (Induction. I. 57–63)

Sly's response to all this trickery is predictably gullible:

> Am I a lord and have I such a lady?
> Or do I dream? Or have I dream'd till now?
> I do not sleep: I see, I hear, I speak;
> I smell sweet savours, and I feel soft things.
> Upon my life, I am a lord indeed,
> And not a tinker, nor Christopher Sly.
> (Induction. II. 66–71)

Like Master Ford, the lovers in *A Midsummer Night's Dream* and Lear, Sly cannot tell the difference between consciousness and unconsciousness. This time the evidence seems to imply that he really is a lord and that the life of Christopher Sly that he believes is real has been nothing but a sustained dream. The life he is sure he remembers has formed the basis of his dormant mutterings: 'though you lay here in this goodly chamber, / Yet would you say ye were beaten out of door; / And rail upon the hostess of the house' (Induction. II. 82–4). The irony of this servant's report is that this is exactly how the play opens. In other words, the beginning of *The Shrew*, that we have just witnessed, has now become the substance of a dream; the dream has subsumed the drama. But the twist is that the dream is a confidence trick and therefore the drama is more real than the dream. This confusion is something that the play anticipates as the lord of the hunt remarks that Sly will find the whole situation as strange 'Even as a flatt'ring dream or worthless fancy' (Induction. I. 42). The fusion between drama and dream does not merely confuse Sly, but the audience of the *Shrew*. As Richard Dutton puts it, 'Sly's "dream" and the experience of watching a play become one and the same thing.'[9] In Bill Alexander's 1992 RSC version, Sly and the aristocrats of the induction sat on a raised dais facing down stage and watched the entire play as it took place in front of them. The actors in the main play had their backs to the on-stage audience and the theatre audience accepted this as a convention which allowed them to see the play. This was an interesting though not entirely successful way of sustaining our awareness of the illusory nature of dramatic representation.[10] In *The Shrew* and elsewhere, Shakespeare's drama is continually urging us to recognise that without our own inspiration, our own imaginative contribution, the drama will never be as real as our wildest dreams.

II

Critical opinions of *Cymbeline* have often been negative. In his *General Observations on the Plays of Shakespeare* (1756), Dr Johnson wrote with impenitent gusto: 'To remark the folly of the fiction, the absurdity of the conduct, the confusion of the names and manners of different times, and the impossibility of the events in any system of life, were to waste criticism upon unresisting imbecillity, upon faults too evident for detection, and too gross for aggravation.'[11] Johnson's impatience is symptomatic of the peculiar difficulties of *Cymbeline* which arise out of the play's propensity to take the dream/drama conflation one stage further. Indeed, D. E. Landry begins her essay on the play with the sentence, '*Cymbeline* is most remarkably a play about dreams, about the various and often inexplicable functions of the unconscious mind.'[12] For Landry, it is the very confusion of the play which makes it so dreamlike, 'a world of doublings, disguises, misnamings, and mistaken identities, the conventions both of romantic or tragicomic drama and of dreams.'[13] That these kinds of qualities and confusions belong to drama has been demonstrated above in Chapter 2; that they belong to dream, Freud testifies:

> There is often a passage in even the most thoroughly interpreted dream which has to be left obscure . . . because . . . there is a tangle

of dream thoughts which cannot be unravelled. This is the dream's navel, the spot where it reaches down into the unknown. The dream thoughts . . . cannot, from the nature of things, have any definite endings; they are bound to branch out in every direction into the intricate network of our world of thought.[14]

Complications in the play are legion. It is frequently noted that although the play takes place historically around AD10, Iachimo in his compelling adroitness, his capacity to reverse his arguments and to manipulate the English naivety of Posthumus and Innogen, represents an incarnation of the Elizabethan Italianate bogeyman, Machiavelli. *Cymbeline* then straddles about fourteen centuries and shifts from the one to the other without apparent difficulty. Much else in Johnson's objection points up the dream-like aspects of the play. He mentions its improbability and in relation to this accusation the play does not have a leg to stand on. Innogen is mistaken for Fidele by her own husband and father while she herself mistakes the corpse of Cloten for that of her husband. Fleeing from the court, she happens to stumble into the hovel of her long-lost brothers. The battle-scenes hinge on the belligerent magnificence of these brothers, an exiled courtier and a despairing husband. Between the four of them they successfully demolish the entire Roman army. Again, Johnson is worried about the plethora of pseudonyms in the play. Belarius, Guiderius and Arviragus all have alternative names, while at different points in the play, in addition to these three, Innogen, Posthumus, Cloten and Iachimo all disguise themselves. The final scene with its mysterious, prophetic resolution and its almost comical series of dénouements would seem to be all the evidence that Johnson would require. But perhaps the most pointed instance of far-fetchedness would be the dream of Posthumus and the descent of Jupiter. In all of these ways, *Cymbeline* is the stuff that dreams are made on.

The virtues of a play with improbable action and a want of coherence comprise precisely the kinds of dramaturgy that I have been considering above. As the critic Meredith Skura writes: 'I think . . . what happens as we look at *Cymbeline* . . . is that we can see the terms conscious and unconscious as a misleading polarity. What we really experience instead of either of these extremes is a range of different ways of being aware.'[15] *Cymbeline* then forces us to problematise the taxonomic distinction between reality and dreaming while at the same time it problematises the distinction between reality and drama. In the words of Roger Warren, the play is marked by 'its capacity to astonish and to move an audience at the same time.'[16] He calls this quality 'theatrical virtuosity' and his further description of the idiosyncrasy is germane here: 'in the moments of extremest theatrical virtuosity, the action on stage can emerge as the externalisation of ... dreams'.[17] In this sense, *Cymbeline* can be thought of as a series of dream sequences and in production this is an aspect of the play with which directors have recently engaged.[18]

The paradox of dreaming is that it is real and unreal at the same time. Just like a dream, the drama is real for the course of its duration, and after its close it is just a drama. The director of the BBC Shakespeare *Cymbeline*, Elijah Moshinsky (whose previous production was significantly *A Midsummer Night's Dream*), remarks on the play's dreamlike quality: 'for me the centre of it is that there are two levels of action. There's an objective level of action and there's a subjective level of action and the subjective level of action is like a series of nightmares. ... I think the play centres round ... therapeutic dreams.'[19] Moshinsky's recognition of Shakespeare's fantastic dramatic technique helps us to deal with the objections of Johnson. In requiring the play to make literal sense, Johnson's pragmatism is in danger of occluding the imaginative flexibility that *Cymbeline* offers us, the plasticity of dream. I wish to focus on one particular aspect of this plasticity – that of sexual fantasy.

In a nutshell Freud argued that desires undergo a process of repression as the child matures and takes its place in the social formation. Thus, as we have seen in Chapter 2, having undergone their sexual initiation, the lovers in *A Midsummer Night's Dream*, *As You Like It* and *The Winter's Tale* can return to the court where their sexual activity is ratified by the socialised structure of marriage. The situation in *Cymbeline* is somewhat different. Posthumus and Innogen are married and have already slept together – this is how Posthumus knows about the mole on Innogen's breast. What we have here then is not a movement towards sexual union but a rupturing of it where it has already occurred. Innogen is exposed in the absence of her husband to two suitors: Iachimo and Cloten. The first, as he tells Posthumus, makes his 'wager rather against your confidence than her reputation' (I. iv. 106); in other words, there is no initial sexual motivation. It is not until he meets Innogen that his poetry becomes sexually charged.

In the trunk scene, Shakespeare has gone to a good deal of trouble to reinforce the dramaturgy of dreaming. Iachimo's first words imply both the silence of the bedchamber and the vulnerability of the sleeping beauty: 'The crickets sing, and man's o'er-labour'd sense / Repairs itself by rest' (II. ii. 11–12). Innogen has apparently just been reading the story of the rape of Philomel from Ovid's *Metamorphoses*. In *Titus Andronicus*, the raped and mutilated Lavinia (whose tongue has been cut out) informs her family of her suffering by opening the book at the same page. Symbolically the trunk scene is an act of rape: 'Our Tarquin thus / Did softly press the rushes ere he waken'd / The chastity he wounded' (ll. 12–14). Yet to begin with, the chamber itself is jotted down in a fairly neutral tone: 'I will write all down: / Such and such pictures; there the window; such / Th' adornment of her bed; the arras, figures— / Why, such and such; and the contents o' th' story' (ll. 24–7). But by the time the description is recounted to Posthumus, it is imbued with a dramatic eroticism. The exotic tapestry depicting Cleopatra's meeting with Antony is thematically appropriate, and the detail of the swelling Cydnus is more important for its connotations than its accuracy.[20] The 'two winking Cupids' and the 'golden cherubins' (II. iv. 88–9) seem coyly to assent to the sexual activity which Iachimo claims to have enjoyed. Perhaps the most energised feature of his later description is the carving on the chimney:

> The chimney
> Is south the chamber, and the chimney-piece
> Chaste Dian bathing. Never saw I figures
> So likely to report themselves. The cutter
> Was as another nature, dumb; outwent her,
> Motion and breath left out.
>
> (ll. 80–5)

To look at this sculpture is to cast oneself in the voyeuristic position of Acteon (again from Ovid) who, while hunting, peered through the rushes to see the naked goddess. He was spotted, transformed into a stag and torn to pieces by his own hounds.[21] The relevance of this work of art is that Diana is the goddess of chastity and our watching her represents a violation. Before resorting to hiding in the trunk Iachimo had attempted to incite Innogen to infidelity by contrasting her faithfulness with what he pretends is Posthumus's licentiousness: 'Should he make me / Live like Diana's priest betwixt cold sheets, / Whiles he is vaulting variable ramps, / In your despite, upon your purse? Revenge it' (I. vi. 131–4). At the end of the play, this motif of Diana is reiterated. During the course of his explanation as to how he came to possess Posthumus's ring, Iachimo tells Cymbeline that Posthumus had spoken of his wife 'as Dian had hot dreams / And she alone were cold' (V. v. 180–1). The trunk scene itself becomes a 'hot dream' as Iachimo changes focus from the room to the body of Innogen:

> Cytherea,
> How bravely thou becom'st thy bed! fresh lily,
> And whiter than the sheets! That I might touch!
> But kiss; one kiss! Rubies unparagon'd,
> How dearly they do't!
>
> (II. ii. 14–18)

Robert Lindsay, who played Iachimo in Moshinsky's production, regards the scene as 'pornographic' and Tim Pigott-Smith who took the role in Peter Hall's 1988 National Theatre production speaks even more strongly of the intrusion: Iachimo 'has let loose the potential of something diabolic. He has seen, for the first time, the ideal woman – and then he goes ahead and blasphemes the temple.'[22] Iachimo compares her to the lily and indeed we know she is fair because Pisanio tells her that in her affectation of a boy's disguise, she will have to cast off the mask she wears to protect her complexion: 'you must / Forget that rarest treasure of your cheek, / Exposing it . . . to the greedy touch / Of common-kissing Titan' (III. iv. 158–62). Again at her mock funeral, Guiderius addresses his dead sister as 'O sweetest, fairest lily' (IV. ii. 202). As we have seen in Chapter 4, Renaissance sexual geography associated women with horticultural fecundity. Here, like Perdita and Ophelia, Innogen is imaged in terms of the natural world and especially flowers. 'On her left breast / A mole cinque-spotted, like the crimson drops / I' th' bottom of a cowslip' (II. ii. 37–9); the moment is again a blend of dark voyeurism and vulnerable nescience. The 1987 RSC production of *Cymbeline* was staged in the round of The (old) Other Place: a tiny space which seated less than two hundred. Jim Hiley identified the sense of involvement: 'It's hard to scoff at Iachimo filching the bracelet from a sleeping Imogen . . . when it happens inches away, causing us to hold our breath.'[23] As Donald Sumpter's Iachimo pulled back the sheets, and unlaced Innogen's night-shirt, the first three or four rows of necks craned forwards to have a peep at the naked Harriet Walter (see Plate E). Stephen Wall noted

pertinently that 'the audience can hardly help becoming the voyeur's accomplices'.[24]

In the sources of the story, the mole is likened to a rose or a
violet. The change to the cowslip is significant. In *A Midsummer
Night's Dream* one of the fairies tells Puck that 'I must go and seek
some dewdrops here, / And hang a pearl in every cowslip's ear' (II.
i. 14–15) and in *The Tempest* Ariel sings: 'Where the bee sucks, there
suck I; / In a cowslip's bell I lie' (V. i. 88–9). In both these instances
the cowslip appears in a context that is gentle, undefiled, playful
and, most important, innocent. This is critical in the trunk scene
and contributes to the delicate sensuousness of Innogen; indeed it
is her very innocence that incenses Iachimo even further. In his
misogynist ranting Posthumus confirms that Innogen was sexually
modest even with her husband:

> Me of my lawful pleasure she restrain'd,
> And pray'd me oft forbearance; did it with
> A pudency so rosy, the sweet view on't
> Might well have warm'd old Saturn; that I thought her
> As chaste as unsunn'd snow.
>
> (II. v. 9–13)

The sweet view of the 'pudency so rosy' refers to Innogen's flushed
embarrassment but in addition, if we remember that the words
pudency and *pudendum* are cognate, 'the sweet view on't' is also
the ultimate act of scopophilia. This reading is substantiated when
we remember that the love tokens that signify Innogen's virginity
are also virginal symbols. At the end of *The Merchant of Venice* the
thuggish loudmouth Gratiano makes explicit the connection between the possession of his wife's ring and her fidelity: 'Well, while
I live, I'll fear no other thing / So sore as keeping safe Nerissa's
ring' (V. i. 306–7). Here, the obscene punning makes the double
meaning of the ring perfectly clear. In the wager scene of the BBC
Cymbeline, Robert Lindsay's Iachimo balanced Posthumus's diamond
ring (which he has received from his wife as a token of her fidelity)
lewdly on his finger tip, while in the 1987 RSC version of the play,
Iachimo thrust the amulet on his arm in a sexual gesture in the
despairing face of Posthumus. The cover of the 1989 RSC programme
emphasised the importance of the bracelet as a sexual totem. Naomi
Wirthner's naked Innogen lay contorted in sleep and we saw her
just as Iachimo would. On her arm, highlighted by a slightly golden

tint, was the amulet, Posthumus's 'manacle of love' (I. i. 122). In the words of Posthumus, the bracelet has become a 'corporal sign' (II. iv. 119) as much as the mole: 'symbolically, it presents the sight of the female genitals to Posthumus'.[25] In fact, it is its possession that convinces him of Innogen's betrayal even before the mole is mentioned.

This subtle mediation of sexual fantasy through symbols, through literary reference (to Ovid) and through the teasing evocation of the erotic (Iachimo's description of the bedchamber), is grossly parodied by the sexuality that Cloten represents. Iachimo's sexuality is sublimated into the eroticisation of sight and touch. Cloten, by contrast, represents a strutting, swaggering sexuality which is related to his sense of self-importance: 'I must go up and down like a cock that nobody can match' (II. i. 21). Cloten's sexuality is pregenital; he is repeatedly associated with anality through a cluster of excretory vocabulary: 'reek', 'rot', 'vent', 'backside', 'smell', 'offence', 'south-fog' and so on. He talks about sex through a series of smutty jokes. Before the aubade outside Innogen's chamber Cloten remarks, 'I am advised to give her music a mornings; they say it will penetrate. Come on, tune. If you can penetrate her with your fingering, so. We'll try with tongue too' (II. iii. 11–14). Both Iachimo and Cloten see fidelity as something to be violated but the latter's infantile sexual pursuit, while it threatens rape, is altogether less alarming than Iachimo's manipulative prowess. Iachimo never has time to formulate plans ahead but consistently moulds them according to the situation – his witty reversal in front of Innogen when he protests that he is testing her is an example of this. Cloten on the other hand is, as it were, 'all mouth and no trousers'. He decides to follow Innogen to Milford-Haven in the clothes of her husband:

> She said upon a time ... that she held the very garment of Posthumus in more respect than my noble and natural person, together with the adornment of my qualities. With that suit upon my back will I ravish her; first kill him ... when my lust hath dined – which, as I say, to vex her I will execute in the clothes that she so prais'd – to the court I'll knock her back, foot her home again. She hath despis'd me rejoicingly, and I'll be merry in my revenge.
>
> (III. v. 134–46)

At the beginning of Act IV, Cloten enters in the garments of Posthumus and enjoys another dirty joke: "'tis said a woman's fitness comes by fits' (IV. i. 6). He then almost completely reiterates his earlier intentions: 'Posthumus, thy head, which now is growing upon thy shoulders, shall within this hour be off; thy mistress enforced; thy garments cut to pieces before her face; and all this done, spurn her home to her father' (ll. 17–19). This repetition implies his own insecurity; his plan needs constant restating because fundamentally, Cloten is impotent. In *Medusa's Head*, Freud writes: 'decapitation = castration'.[26] Cloten's desire to sever Posthumus's head represents his wish to emasculate the husband so that Innogen will be available as his own sexual partner. Of course, it is Cloten that loses his head. Guiderius remarks: 'This Cloten was a fool, an empty purse; / There was no money in't. Not Hercules / Could have knock'd out his brains, for he had none' (IV. ii. 114–16). Not only does Cloten have no brains, but he is 'an empty purse'. Cloten's impotence is again reinforced; since the mid-fifteenth century, the word *purse* was a slang expression for 'scrotum'.[27]

Perhaps the most notable scene which brings together the issues of dream and sexuality is that in which Innogen awakes next to the headless corpse of Cloten which she assumes to be that of her husband. Granville-Barker called this scene 'dramatically inexcusable' and noted its injustice, 'Imogen herself is put, quite needlessly, quite heartlessly, on exhibition.'[28] It is a disturbing episode in a play that ends, for the most part, happily. Like those countless examples we have considered, Innogen requires confirmation that she is not simply having a nightmare: 'I hope I dream . . . / The dream's here still. Even when I wake it is / Without me, as within me; not imagin'd, felt' (IV. ii. 298–308) – not imagined, but as real as a dream, as real as a drama. Paradoxically, as she surveys the body, she recognises not its clothes but its features. After all the fuss that Cloten has made about ravishing Innogen in her husband's clothes and after the playwright has contrived to arrange Innogen's awakening next to a headless corpse dressed as Posthumus, we would expect her to focus on the costume to the exclusion of all else but it is very quickly dismissed:

A headless man? The garments of Posthumus?
I know the shape of's leg; this is his hand,
His foot Mercurial, his Martial thigh,
The brawns of Hercules; but his Jovial face –
Murder in heaven! How! 'Tis gone.

(ll. 309–13)

Just as Iachimo surveys her body for 'corporal signs' with which to
verify his story, Innogen surveys the corpse for evidence with which
to prove its identity. Michael Taylor notes the dark sexuality of the
scene, writing of Innogen's 'necrophiliac embrace'.[29] At the joint
burial of the corpse and Fidele, the brothers sing her to 'Quiet consummation' (IV. ii. 281) and this consummation is symbolised by
the disturbing close to the scene where she daubs her face hys-
terically with the blood from the severed neck. This is plainly a rite
of passage – just like the smearing of blood on the face of the
freshman at the fox-hunt. Innogen makes the same error as Pyramus
in the production staged at the end of *A Midsummer Night's Dream*,
connecting blood and bereavement all too rapidly. The smudging
of her face with blood is an initiation into the mystery of death as
in the parallel passage from *Venus and Adonis*: 'she falleth in the
place she stood, / And stains her face with his congealed blood' (ll.
1121–2). Of course the corpse next to Innogen is that of her potential rapist, Cloten (whose name may itself suggest *blood clot*), and so
while this ritual symbolises an affinity with the dead, a kind of
bizarre communion for Innogen herself, for the audience it stands
for her victory over Cloten just as the gore that drenches Posthumus
is a signifier of his martial virtuosity.[30] A similar initiation occurs in
As You Like It when Rosalind receives the bloody handkerchief and
assumes it signifies the death of Orlando. Blood, in both these instances, is a positive emblem yet it is accompanied by illness; both
Rosalind and Innogen swoon. The presence of blood, their fainting,
growing pale and Innogen's insistent desire to be left alone imply
that the women are menstruating.

> Guid.: Go you to hunting; I'll abide with him.
> Inno.: So sick I am not, yet I am not well;. . . .
>   I am ill, but your being by me
>   Cannot amend me; *society is no comfort*
>   *To one not sociable*. I am not very sick,
>   Since I can reason of it.
>   (IV. ii. 6–14, my emphasis)

In effect, Innogen is 'languish[ing] / A drop of blood a day' (I. i.
156–7) though the last thing she needs dressed as a boy and surrounded by three men is the onset of menstrual bleeding.[31] In *As
You Like It*, Oliver attributes Rosalind's fainting to general squeam-
ishness but Celia insists mysteriously that 'There is more in it' (IV.

iii. 158). Both Fidele and Ganymede have their assumed maleness subverted by a biological process and the consequent resumption of their female identities is rapidly followed by marital re/union. Perhaps this biological determinism is responsible for the nineteenth-century impression of Innogen's 'total femininity which she cannot effectively conceal under her male disguise'.[32] The patterns of sexuality that emerge in the course of *Cymbeline* do so through the mechanisms of dream. Innogen's femaleness, like that of Rosalind, is biologically fixed, however, and even the dynamics of Shakespearean sexuality must submit to the exigencies of gender and human reproduction.

In V. iv, *Cymbeline* offers us the most extended corollary of drama and dream. The descent of Jupiter is, in Warren's terms, one of the play's most obvious moments of 'theatrical virtuosity'. It is not a dream recollected in tranquillity like Hermia's, which is described for us after the event. Posthumus's dream, like Lady Macbeth's, is played out in front of us, *dramatised* for us as it happens.[33] Moreover, although the vision of Jupiter involves the on-stage audience of the dreamer's family, we are never allowed to forget that the whole episode is the product of Posthumus's own mentality. The device of the wooden-sounding fourteeners that prefix the descent of the god 'emphasise that Posthumus is dreaming'.[34] Peter Hall echoes this interpretation of the obsolete style of verse, urging his actors (in the 1988 National Theatre version) to speak the lines quickly and rhythmically to suggest 'the pace and cross-cutting of dreams'.[35] Posthumus's dream, which sets up the dramatic riddle for the final scene to solve, finally fuses the biology of generation with drama and dream. Posthumus, born without a family (as his name indicates), finds that the child is father of the man: 'Sleep, thou hast been a grandsire and begot / A father to me' (V. iv. 123–4). Shakespearean dramaturgy illustrates that dream and drama are similarly related and that while dream is the father of drama, it is drama that is always the progenitor of dream.

Notes

1. Freud, *The Interpretation of Dreams*, ed. James Strachey (New York, 1965), pp. 480–1.

2. Julia Kristeva calls Mab, a 'gnomelike ghost, fascinating and hideous, ruler of amorous bodies, the dark, drunken, and murderous other side of loving radiance' (*'Romeo and Juliet*: Love-hatred in the couple', in *Shakespearean Tragedy*, ed. John Drakakis (1992), 296–315, p. 305).

3. Richard Dutton, *William Shakespeare: A Life* (1989), p. 90.

4. Keats, *Selected Poems and Letters*, ed. Roger Sharrock (Oxford, 1964), p. 101.

5. Jonson's *Hymenaei* had been recently staged (1606). Its scenery, which had aroused much comment, included a great globe. (I am indebted to Richard Dutton for this.)

6. The 'wooden O' is commonly mistaken for the Globe. The references to Essex in the chorus to Act V date the play to summer 1599. *Julius Cæsar* was staged in September that year and is the earliest known play to have been performed at the Globe.

7. Norman N. Holland, 'Hermia's Dream', in *Representing Shakespeare: New Psychoanalytic Essays*, ed. Murray M. Schwartz and Coppélia Kahn (1980), 1–20, p. 11.

8. Interestingly the verb *to cast* is used in several relevant senses here. To cast a shadow is noted by the OED from 1300. To cast actors in the sense of allotting parts is recorded as 1711 though it is unlikely that the word was not in use earlier than this. Another pertinent meaning of cast is to 'to interpret a dream', first recorded as 1382.

9. Dutton, *William Shakespeare*, p. 91.

10. Part of the trouble was that this convention was not used consistently. Actors in the play often had to turn upstage to address 'their' audience and the playing direction was thus unfortunately Janusfaced. For a fuller account of this production, see my review, *Cahiers Elisabéthains*, 42 (1992), 89–91.

11. Samuel Johnson, *The Yale Edition of the Works of Samuel Johnson*, ed. Allen T. Hazen *et al.*, 14 vols (1958–78), VIII, 908.

12. D. E. Landry, 'Dreams as History: The Strange Unity of *Cymbeline*', *Shakespeare Quarterly*, 33 (1982), 68–79, p. 68.

13. Ibid., p. 70.

14. Freud, *Interpretation of Dreams*, p. 564.

15. Meredith Skura, 'Interpreting Posthumus' Dream from Above and Below: Families, Psychoanalysts, and Literary Critics', in *Representing Shakespeare*, 203–16, p. 204.

16. Roger Warren, *Cymbeline: Shakespeare in Performance* (Manchester and New York, 1989), p. 1. Warren's book is a valuable analysis of recent productions up to that of Peter Hall for the National Theatre in 1988. Though he includes Bill Alexander's 1987 RSC version, he has nothing to say about Alexander's 1989 RSC revival. It is most likely that his MS went to print before this production opened. Perhaps this is just as well as the production closed early. For an account of it, see my review in *Cahiers Elisabéthains*, 36 (1989), 106–9.

17. Warren, *Cymbeline: Shakespeare in Performance*, p. 21.
18. These include Hall and Moshinsky (see below) and William Gaskill (see Roger Warren, *Staging Shakespeare's Late Plays* (Oxford, 1990), p. 81).
19. Introduction to the BBC *Cymbeline*, ed. John Wilders (1983), p. 17.
20. On the rivers Cydnus and Nile as sexual totems, see Chapter 4.
21. See *Twelfth Night*, I. i. 21–3.
22. Lindsay in BBC *Cymbeline*, p. 24; Pigott-Smith in Warren, *Staging Shakespeare's Late Plays*, p. 44.
23. Jim Hiley, *The Listener*, 19 November 1987.
24. Stephen Wall, *The Times Literary Supplement*, 4 December 1987.
25. Murray M. Schwartz, 'Between Fantasy and Imagination: A Psychological Exploration of *Cymbeline*', in *Psychoanalysis and Literary Process*, ed. Frederick Crews (Cambridge, Mass., 1970), 219–83, p. 242.
26. *The Standard Edition of the Complete Psychological Works of Sigmund Freud*, trans. James Strachey *et al.*, 24 vols (1966–74), XVIII, 273.
27. Compare Antonio's offer to Bassanio of 'My purse, my person' (*The Merchant of Venice*, I. i. 138). See also the discussion of jewels and stones in Chapter 7 below.
28. Harley Granville-Barker, *Prefaces to Shakespeare*, 2 vols (1958), first published 1930, I, 539.
29. Michael Taylor, 'The Pastoral Reckoning in *Cymbeline*', *Shakespeare Survey*, 36 (1983), 97–106, p. 98.
30. This was a strong feature of Hall's National production. A picture of the blood-drenched Peter Woodward playing the part is conveniently available in Warren, *Staging Shakespeare's Late Plays*, Plate 3.
31. For the theatricalisation of this idea in Hall's production, see Warren, *Staging Shakespeare's Late Plays*, p. 92.
32. Ann Thompson, '*Cymbeline's* Other Endings', in *The Appropriation of Shakespeare*, ed. Jean I. Marsden (1991), 203–20, pp. 211–12.
33. Julia Bardsley's 1993 *Macbeth* for the Leicester Haymarket had Lady Macbeth traverse the stage on a line of pillows placed, like stepping-stones, in front of her.
34. Warren, *Cymbeline: Shakespeare in Performance*, p. 20.
35. Cited by Warren, *Staging Shakespeare's Late Plays*, p. 78.

6

Re(-)fusing the Sign: Linguistic Ambiguity and the Subversion of Patriarchy in *Romeo and Juliet* and *The Two Gentlemen of Verona*

I

I am eating fish and chips in Stratford-upon-Avon. To be precise, I am doing so while leaning on a lock-gate at the point where the Stratford canal flows into the river Avon. Slightly to my left is the Royal Shakespeare Theatre where I have just attended a performance of *The Tempest*. Slightly to my right is a fish-and-chip shop.[1]

Thus begins Terence Hawkes's irreverent and incisive book, one of the first examinations of the cultural construction of the Shakespearean canon, *That Shakespeherian Rag* – a title adroitly culled from the name of a twenties jazz song that appears in Eliot's *The Waste Land*.[2] Towards the end of his book, Hawkes draws a parallel between the activities of the poststructuralist critic and the jazz musician:

what I propose [is] the sense of a text as a site, or an area of conflicting and often contradictory potential interpretations, no one or group of which can claim 'intrinsic' primacy or 'inherent' authority. . . .

The abstract model I reach for is of course that of jazz music . . . interpretation *constitutes* the art of the jazz musician. The same unservile principle seems to me to be appropriate to the critic's

120

activity. . . . . Responding to, improvising on, 'playing' with, re-
creating, synthesizing and interpreting 'given' structures of all
kinds.[3]

In the course of this chapter, I will keep Hawkes's methodology in
mind and offer readings of *Romeo and Juliet* and *The Two Gentlemen
of Verona* which may in themselves be not only 'conflicting and
often contradictory' but which will aim to expose the way in which
the texts in performance have been and continue to be predicated
on such contrarieties.

Just along the road from Hawkes's fish-and-chip shop, between
The Other Place and The Swan Theatres, is a pub. If you approach
the pub from the direction of The Other Place, the sign will read
'The Black Swan'. If you approach it from the direction of The Swan
Theatre, the sign reads 'The Dirty Duck'.[4] Two signifiers, two
signifieds – but only one sign. Perhaps we should agree with Claudio
that 'there is no believing old signs' (*Much Ado*, III. ii. 37) or hold
them in the kind of contempt with which Aaron refers to his enemies,
'ye alehouse painted signs!' (*Titus Andronicus*, IV. ii. 98). Queen
Margaret dismisses them too in the fury of her self-denigration:
'make my image but an alehouse sign' (*II Henry VI*, III. ii. 81). But
not so fast – later in the same play, Richard of York kills Somerset
under the sign of the Castle pub: 'So, lie thou there; / For under-
neath an alehouse' paltry sign, / The Castle in Saint Albans, Somerset / Hath made the wizard famous in his death' (V. ii. 67–9). The
prophecy, that the duke should 'shun castles; / Safer shall he be
upon the sandy plains / Than where castles mounted stand' (I. iv.
67–9), has come ironically true and the truth is valorised by the
sign. Shakespeare's attitude to signs then seems, even in this single
play, to be ambiguous. The pub sign may be the extreme of
Margaret's wrath, an absurd token or, as is the case for dreaming
which we examined in Chapter 5, it may display the secret truth of
prophecy (albeit that Somerset expected to die outside a very different sort of castle than a public house).[5] The pub sign is the origin
and object of an interpretative crux: one sign, two meanings like so
many of the pairs of Shakespearean twins – 'One face, one voice,
one habit, and two persons! / A natural perspective, that is and is
not' (*Twelfth Night*, V. i. 208–9). Of course, we can explain the transformation of the one into the other. The Stratford pub sign rehearses
the fairy tale of the ugly duckling who is transformed in the course
of its growth into a beautiful swan. Shakespeare himself achieved

just such an avian transformation. Near the beginning of his career in 1592 he was notoriously described by his bilious contemporary, Robert Greene as: 'an vpstart Crow, beautified with our feathers, that with his *Tygers hart wrapt in a Players hyde*, supposes he is as well able to bombast out a blanke verse as the best of you: and beeing an absolute *Iohannes fac totum*, is in his owne conceit the onely Shake-scene in a countrey'.[6] The pun on Shake-scene and the deliberate misquotation from *III Henry VI* (in which Margaret is derided by the Duke of York, 'O tiger's heart wrapp'd in a woman's hide!' I. iv. 137) make clear that the target is Shakespeare. Our poet is then 'an upstart crow' – an actor, got up as a playwright and by the sound of it he is not too bothered about lining his nest with the literary feathers of other playwrights. Yet the force of Greene's anxiety seems excessive on such a fledgling talent notwithstanding the norms of satiric language and the pressures of commercial rivalry. The implication of Greene's extreme paranoia is that even this early, Shakespeare was preparing to stretch his wings.

Seven years after Shakespeare's death, when the actors Heminge and Condell published the first folio of the plays, Ben Jonson wrote a commendatory poem in which he referred to the playwright as 'Sweet Swan of *Auon*!' The image recalls that of the Shakespearean coat of arms on top of which a bird shakes a spear (thus onomastically performing the family name).[7] Jonson's poem embeds the same pun when he notes that in each line of his plays, Shakespeare 'seemes to shake a Lance, / As brandish't at the eyes of Ignorance' (69–70). No longer an earthly sign, Shakespeare is apotheosised into a celestial constellation, a guiding star of dramatic creativity:

> But stay, I see thee in the Hemisphere
> Aduanc'd, and made a Constellation there!
> Shine forth, thou Starre of Poets, and with rage,
> Or influence, chide, or cheere the drooping Stage;
> Which, since *thy flight from hence*, hath mourn'd like night,
> And despaires day, but for thy Volumes light.
>
> (75–81, my emphasis)

Shakespeare's fairy-tale transformation certainly helps to contextualise the pub sign. (It also incidentally enlightens the name of Stratford's Swan Theatre.) But the transformation of the cygnet into the swan is unsatisfactory as a way of explaining the double presence of the (two-in-one) sign. It is after all, to pose a diachronic solution to a synchronic problem. Moreover, this diachronic explanation reinforces rather than challenges the mutual exclusivity of the two signifiers. Shakespeare becomes the swan at the expense of the duckling; in becoming the former, he sheds the ugly plumage of the latter. Our sign though is both duck and swan, swan and duck and neither takes precedence. Both are equally available, both are instantly present. In addition, our pub sign figures the simultaneous presence not merely of two different signifiers, but of two different signifieds, and its meaning is contingent upon the position of the viewer. If you have come from The Swan Theatre, you'll be drinking in The Dirty Duck; from The Other Place, The Black Swan. Like Hawkes's critical model, then, the sign holds contraries in equilibrium, balancing alternative possibilities in dynamic reciprocity.

The actor is a site as well as a product of at least two major signifying practices – physical and verbal. Shakespeare is fully aware of the multivalency of dramatic signification, pointing up, in the case of Lavinia, the visual by silencing the verbal. With her hands lopped off and her tongue cut out, Lavinia becomes a walking sign – 'Thou map of woe, that thus dost talk in signs!' (*Titus*, III. ii. 12). Unable to speak, her physical movement becomes heightened as a signifying practice – a code which Titus claims to be able to read: 'Mark, Marcus, mark! I understand her signs' (III. i. 143). The linguistic competence of the handless renders his own hand superfluous and, while his brother and son argue about which of them will sacrifice his hand to save that of Titus, Lavinia's father requests help for the amputation of his own: 'Come hither, Aaron, I'll deceive them both; / Lend me thy hand, and I will give thee mine' (ll. 187–8). In exchange for his hand, Titus has been promised the return of his two sons; instead he receives their severed heads. His response is revealing. While Marcus and Lucius lament hyperbolically, Titus merely laughs; Lavinia, unable to speak, simply kisses her father. The language of the mutilated is the language of action not words. To read Lavinia's aphonic signs is to speak them with her, not physically to speak but to speak physically. Titus speaks a little of both languages but not enough to understand fully the machinations of Aaron nor the kiss of his daughter. As Titus implores his daughter to die, his brother Marcus tactlessly employs a figure of speech from the language of the dextrous, 'Teach her not thus to lay / Such violent hands upon her tender life' (III. ii. 21–2). Titus is quick to reprimand him, 'O, handle not the theme, to talk of hands, / Lest we remember still that we have none' (ll. 29–30).

Uncle and niece no longer speak the same language. Titus speaks both and neither.

In its simultaneous presence of two different signs, our pub sign occupies the same middle ground as Titus between two discourses. Usually in Shakespeare's work to speak across a discursive barrier is to come semantically unstuck. As Henry woos Kate at the end of *Henry V*, she remarks upon her double separation from him, 'O bon Dieu! les langues des hommes sont pleines de tromperies' (V. ii. 116). Alice translates for us 'dat de tongues of de mans is be full of deceits' (l. 120). Kate is isolated from the English King by her Frenchness and her femaleness.[8] In Chapter 3 we saw the way in which political power was dependent upon linguistic competence. *Richard II* offers an extended instance of the political dangers of semantic indeterminacy. Towards the end of the play, the Duchess of York pleads for the life of her son, Aumerle, whose plot to betray the new king has just come to light. She implores Bolingbroke to say 'Pardon' to her son, 'The word is short, but not so short as sweet; / No word like "pardon" for kings' mouths so meet' (V. iii. 117–18). Aumerle's father, York, places a higher value on loyalty to his sovereign than the life of his son and instructs Bolingbroke to render his pardon meaningless by proffering it in another language, 'Speak it in French, King, say "pardonne moy"' (l. 119). The duchess responds ferociously:

> Dost thou teach pardon pardon to destroy?
> Ah, my sour husband, my hard-hearted lord,
> That *sets the word itself against the word!*
> Speak 'pardon' as 'tis current in our land;
> The chopping French we do not understand.
> (ll. 120–4, my emphasis)

The linguistic anarchy, pardon destroying pardon, the word against the word, is the result of weak government. The corruption of Richard's court finds its voice in the slipperiness of language. Two scenes later, the imprisoned king enters lamenting his inability to order his thoughts: 'The better sort, / As thoughts of things divine, are intermix'd / With scruples, and do *set the word itself / Against the word* (V. v. 11–14, my emphasis). This linguistic conflict results in a state of political aphasia. Words or signs struggle against each other and their internecine dissension makes all of them ultimately meaningless. Words 'have words' with other words. The correlation between linguistic ambiguity and political subversion is important for the following discussion of the plays specified in the title of this chapter. It is a correlation noted by Terry Eagleton: 'a stability of signs – each word securely in place, each signifier (mark or sound) corresponding to its signified (or meaning) – is an integral part of any social order: settled meanings, shared definitions and regularities of grammar both reflect, and help to constitute, a well-ordered political state. Yet it is all this which Shakespeare's flamboyant punning, troping and riddling threaten to put into question.'[9]

Our duck and swan are set against one another – if not face to face then certainly back to back – positioning themselves for a duel. Yet they are also united – there is only one pub. Paradoxically what separates them joins them and, as Hawkes tells us, we cannot expect to solve this *discordia concors*: we can only accept and acknowledge it; this is why the critic's position must eschew '"intrinsic" primacy [and] "inherent" authority'. On their way to Capulet's party Benvolio assures the love-sick Romeo that he will see women the like of whom will put Rosaline's beauty to shame: 'Compare her face with some that I shall show, / And I will make thee think thy swan a crow' (I. ii. 86–7).[10] Romeo is adamant in his adoration of Rosaline: 'I'll go along, no such sight to be shown, / But to rejoice in splendour of mine own' (ll. 100–1). When he sees the true swan, Juliet, Rosaline, the ugly duckling, is discarded. In choosing one sign over the other Romeo re-fuses Hawkes's critical equivocality and thus refuses the hovering stasis that is the vantage point of the bird of prey.

II

This kind of debate about signs and signification runs throughout *Romeo and Juliet* and *The Two Gentlemen of Verona*. Both plays are about the reading and the writing of signs – about the question of interpretation – interpretation which is always a problem. The illiterate servant in *Romeo and Juliet* assumes that the initiated can read everything. Of Romeo he enquires, 'I pray, can you read anything you see?' (I. ii. 60) Romeo responds with mischievous literalism, 'Ay, if I know the letters and the language' (l. 61). Similarly in *The Two Gentlemen of Verona*, Launce 'proves' that Speed cannot read by arbitrarily misinterpreting him:

Laun.: Fie on thee, jolt-head; thou canst not read.
Spee.: Thou liest; I can.
Laun.: I will try thee. Tell me this: Who begot thee?
Spee.: Marry, the son of my grandfather.
Laun.: O illiterate loiterer. It was the son of thy grandmother.
This proves that thou canst not read.

(III. i. 285–90)

Interpretation depends, as with the pub sign, on which direction you are facing, on which language you are speaking, on which grandparent you are choosing and the relativity of reading and interpretation is something that these two plays continually insist upon. Even Gregory and Sampson's violent jesting in the first scene of *Romeo and Juliet* is open to interpretation – 'take it in what sense thou wilt' (I. i. 26).

Despite this relativity, throughout *Romeo and Juliet*, the patriarchs attempt to impose a single interpretation on their world. Capulet is contemptuous of his daughter's 'chopt logic' (III. v. 149) while Lawrence admonishes Romeo for his crazed speechifying, threatening him with a bogus absolution unless the offence is spelt out: 'Be plain, good son, and homely in thy drift; / Riddling confession finds but riddling shrift' (II. iii. 55–6). But of all the patriarchal figures, it is the prince who is most obviously guilty of transgressing Hawkes's indeterminacy. To him an inquest is vital to apportion blame, 'Some shall be pardon'd and some punished (V. iii. 307). Uncertainty spells trouble: 'Seal up the mouth of outrage for a while, / Till we can *clear these ambiguities*, / And know their spring, their head, their true descent; / And then will I be general of your woes, / And lead you even to death' (ll. 215–19, my emphasis). The prince will once again stamp his version of the truth on to the truth to restore his rule.

In David Leveaux's 1991 RSC production this emphasis on patriarchy was brought out through the performance of Julian Glover as the prince. Never has a production made so clear that the root of all problems is the aggressively pacific politic of Escalus. A towering presence, Glover was more martial and threatening than either the quietist Capulet (who would allow the Montagues to stay at his party and prevents Tybalt breaking the peace), or the meek and marginal Montague. Glover's Escalus swept around the stage with the unguarded authority of an absolute ruler and it was clear that the vehemence of the families' feud originated from his intransigence.

The first sword fight was slowed right down and, as blows were struck amid darkness and smoke, the images of civil strife were closer to the brutality of a history play than the usual sparring set in the hot and volatile dog-days. In this *Romeo* there was little violence erupting spontaneously to counter insults and jibes. Instead there was a pervasive atmosphere of blunt and brutish danger in which the actual fighting was a welcome relief.

This was an unusual interpretation of a play which has a tendency to find its own level of heat, sweat and passion. Jean Kalman's lighting was extremely bleak, shadowy, monochrome and costumes were generally dark. The contrast between this sombre production and the play's more usual warmth can be seen in the contrast with Terry Hands's 1989 RSC production in The Swan (compare Plates F and G). Leveaux's production emphasised cold intelligence and manipulative strategies. His *Romeo* was less the tragedy of 'A pair of star-cross'd lovers' (Prologue. 6) than an emphatic indictment of a ruler who divides his people with threats and savagery. Escalus never attempts to make the peace; instead, he continually laments that he has not been cruel enough in putting down the discord; the state is divided against itself. This was a political rather than a passionate production. Alison Chitty foregrounded the political by setting the play in front of a series of screens on which were enlarged sections of various paintings by Renaissance masters. The action seemed to be taking place in a Medici villa and the sliding of the shutters into different configurations with characters coming between and ducking behind them made the atmosphere all the more Machiavellian. In particular, she had chosen to enlarge those fragments of paintings that contained fingers and hands. Characters on-stage were continually being pointed at, implicated and singled out. We were not so far from the treacherous intrigue of *Hamlet*.

The various fights of the tomb-scene passed off in shadow, smoke and silhouette. Escalus stepped in to claim the credit for the final cessation of the violence. The ease with which Capulet took Montague's hand implied that there was little of the fighting spirit left – if indeed there had ever really been any at all. The production ended with the stark re-emergence of the power of Escalus insisting that while 'Some shall be pardon'd' others will be punished. If the apothecary, the nurse or Lawrence are to be dealt the retribution of the state, they will have the satisfaction of knowing that it is their suffering that keeps Escalus in office. In eschewing the romanticised ending with a pair of mythologised lovers, Leveaux took us back pessimistically, irredeemably and irrevocably to the absolute power of the state. In his final stage-centre, rigid stance and unwavering pronouncements, Julian Glover's Escalus demonstrated that he was fit to occupy this position of power. Someone has to write history and, as *Nineteen Eighty Four* makes plain, they that control the past control the future. There was only room in Leveaux's Verona for one Big Brother. Simon Trussler invokes the parallel futurist fantasy in his description of the difficulties of communication in the play when he describes *Romeo and Juliet* as 'this brave new world of words'.[11]

Shakespearean comedies are, as Ernst Cassirer puts it, built upon the 'game of the pure self-activity of the word'.[12] In this sense, the patriarchs of *Romeo and Juliet* are at odds with the comic spirit that underlies these early plays and that underpins the rejection (in line with Hawkes's plurality) of a dogmatic critical stance. *Romeo and Juliet*, albeit a tragedy, is itself keen to expose the fault of adopting a definite position in relation to the signifying practices that inhere in its world, for *Romeo and Juliet* is profoundly opposed to authority both in the political sense and the literary sense (auctoritee).[13] Moreover, parts of the play (notably those surrounding Mercutio) seem resistant to and subversive of the heterosexist authority upon which the patriarchy of Verona is predicated. In particular, Mercutio's opposition to the Verona he sees around him is marked in his almost plethorically sexualised word-play. In this role, Mercutio performs what Jonathan Dollimore has termed 'transgressive reinscription'. Dollimore defines this as 'a mode of transgression which seeks not an escape from existing structures but rather a subversive reinscription within them, and in the process their dislocation or displacement'.[14] Furthermore, Dollimore mentions exactly those features which characterise Mercutio when he points out that 'irony and ambiguity [tend] to be intrinsic to transgressive reinscription'.[15] The analogy between linguistic and political order noted by Eagleton above is here overlaid by issues of gender and sexuality. In one respect, ambiguous language is always sexually suspect; as Viola puts it, 'they that dally nicely with words may quickly make them wanton' (*Twelfth Night*, III. i. 13).[16] Subversive rhetorical strategies are inseparable from sexual transgression.

Romeo and Juliet has long been identified as one of Shakespeare's most quibbling plays.[17] The sexual nature of this punning is obvious from the very first scene in which Gregory and Sampson swap jokes about sexual assault. There is a marked contrast between the mythology of the play as a story of romantic love and the extremity of its sadistic wordplay. These quibbles involve the association of violence and sexuality. The substitution of swords and daggers for the phallus occurs throughout. This association was particularly pronounced at the opening of the 1989 RSC production directed by Terry Hands. Lolling on the ground, Sampson and Gregory's puerile phallicism was accompanied by gesticulating with and fondling the tips of their swords – 'Draw thy tool' (I. i. 31). The production was full of the fantasies of adolescent boys, self-appointed studs, over-eager to assert manhood both in terms of maturity and potency. Vincent Regan's Tybalt entered with swords strapped round his waist and across his torso – a swaggering Rambo. The other young bucks brandished and consistently polished daggers and swords. These opening scenes dwelt on the phallicism of weaponry and visually reinforced the destructiveness of patriarchal power.

In his fascinating history of swearing, Geoffrey Hughes notes that the vocabulary of phallicism and intercourse is often of a violent nature. He cites 'the slang terms for sexual intercourse, *bang*, *knock*, and the recently fashionable *bonk*. The metaphors for "penis" are no less suggestive: *tool*, *prick*, *chopper* and *weapon*, the last of which . . . goes right back to Anglo-Saxon.'[18] Of these words, *Romeo and Juliet* uses 'tool' (I. i. 31), 'prick' (I. iv. 26, 28, and II. iv. 109) and 'weapon' (I. i. 34, 85, II. iv. 153, and III. i. 83). The violence implicit in the armament of phallicism is symptomatic of the subjugation of the female throughout. Julia Kristeva writes: 'Under the guise of sex, it is hatred that prevails, and that comes out most obviously in the very first pages of the text. In the first scene, the two servants' remarks, peppered with puns and obscenities, cause the darkness of sex and inversions of all sorts to hang over this presumably pure romance.'[19]

As Mercutio, Benvolio and Romeo make their way to Capulet's feast, the love-sick Romeo staggers through a series of self-indulgent puns. He will bear the light since his mood is heavy, he has a soul of lead while the others are suited to dancing because they have light soles. He is too sorely wounded with Love's arrow to soar with Cupid's wing, too bound to the earth to bound upwards. Mercutio's reaction is to puncture this over-earnest love lamentation with puns about masturbation, 'If love be rough with you, be rough with love; / Prick love for pricking, and you beat love down' (I. iv. 27–8). Gibbons notes squeamishly in his Arden edition, 'The sense of *beat love down* includes "causing sexual detumescence".'[20] The humour then becomes scatological:

Rome.: The game was ne'er so fair, and I am done.
Merc.: Tut, dun's the mouse, the constable's own word;
        If thou art Dun, we'll draw thee from the mire
        Of this sir-reverence love, wherein thou stickest
        Up to the ears.

                                              (ll. 39–43)

Gibbons explains, 'The gist of Mercutio's reply is that Romeo is dull and heavy as if he were a bogged cart-horse, that being in love is like being up to the ears in ordure ... and he must be freed from the misery by dancing.'[21] Mercutio's humour is extreme in its anality; the *OED* defines *sir-reverence* as 'human excrement [or] a piece or lump of this'.[22] In the light of this, it may be appropriate to suggest that there is an aural association between *ears* and *arse*. Mercutio's phallicism is noted by Joseph A. Porter who calls him 'easily, in terms of what he talks about, Shakespeare's most phallic character'.[23] Mercutio's bawdy represents the high point of libidinous repartee. As he and Benvolio seek the missing Romeo, who is at that moment under the balcony of Juliet, Mercutio allows his sexual innuendoes to run riot:

Merc.: I conjure thee by Rosaline's bright eyes,
        By her high forehead and her scarlet lip,
        By her fine foot, straight leg, and quivering thigh,
        And the demesnes that there adjacent lie,
        That in thy likeness thou appear to us.
Benv.: An if he hear thee, thou wilt anger him.
Merc.: This cannot anger him: 'twould anger him
        To raise a spirit in his mistress' circle
        Of some strange nature, letting it there stand
        Till she had laid it and conjur'd it down;
        That were some spite. My invocation
        Is fair and honest: in his mistress' name,
        I conjure only but to raise up him.

                                              (II. i. 17–29)

In the 1991 RSC production, Tim McInnerny's Mercutio was sitting on the ground next to Benvolio. As he got to the line about

Rosaline's demesnes, he thrust his forearm between the legs of the seated Benvolio and fist-fucked the air. Mercutio's phallocentricity continues in his description of an intercourse that vacillates between a fruit, suggestive of female pudenda, and sodomy:

> Now will he sit under a medlar tree
> And wish his mistress were that kind of fruit
> As maids call medlars when they laugh alone.
> O Romeo, that she were, O that she were
> An open-arse and thou a poperin pear!
> (Arden edition, ll. 34–8)

The *OED*, in its botanical description of the medlar fruit, suggests the lewd sense in which Mercutio is using the word: 'The fruit of the medlar tree, resembling a small brown-skinned apple with a large cup-shaped "eye" between the persistent calyx-lobes.' As well as its association with female pudenda, the word *medlar* connotes its homonym *meddler* ('one who interferes with' but also 'one who has sexual intercourse with').[24] Q1, which prints 'open *Et cetera*' instead of 'open-ars' is glossed by Eric Partridge as follows:

> the pun on *medlar*, slangily known as 'an *open-arse*', and *poperin pear*, shape-resembling penis and scrotum, is so forcibly obvious that 'an open *et-caetera*' must here mean 'an open arse'. Yet my interpretation of Shakespeare's 'open *et-caetera*' as 'pudend' is correct, for the opening clearly refers to the female cleft, not to the human anus. With the human bottom regarded as involving and connoting the primary sexual area, compare the slangy use of *tail* for the human bottom in general and for the female pudend in particular. 'Open *et-caetera*' therefore suggests 'open cunt' – admissive organ – desirous girl.[25]

I cite this entry at length in order to demonstrate that within the joke is the possibility of both hetero- and homosexual intercourse. Mercutio's priapic sexuality defies the easily categorical. He is the sexual analogue of our indeterminate sign refusing to be read one way or the other.[26]

Romeo's conversion from a narcissistic lover to a witty comrade for Mercutio is marked by a shift in his word play. Mercutio weans Romeo off the cloying and stale formulae of the languishing lover to a repartee that is deft and mercurial. Mercutio notes the change of mood and rhetoric of his friend: 'Why, is not this better now than groaning for love? Now art thou sociable, now art thou Romeo; now art thou what thou art by art as well as by nature; for this drivelling love is like a great natural that runs lolling up and down to hide his bauble in a hole' (II. iv. 85–9). Romeo has now returned to Mercutio's ideal of him in a way that suggests that his previous melancholy was mere affectation – 'now art thou *Romeo*'. Mercutio attacks the heterosexual relationship by remarking that, at its best, it is unsatisfying and banal: intercourse is the mere hiding of a 'bauble in a hole'! This opinion of sex offers the play's audience an unresolved ambiguity. For if we share Mercutio's cynical attitude towards physical love, we are nonetheless hard-pressed to dismiss the passionate rhetoric of the lovers as they celebrate it later in the play. On the other hand, Mercutio's charm and wit and his ability to evoke such qualities in those around him (notably, as here, Romeo) make him a popular figure with audiences. Dryden suggested as early as 1672 that Mercutio's attractiveness threatens to take over the play so much so that Shakespeare 'was forc'd to kill him in the third Act to prevent being kill'd by him'.[27] Mercutio's appeal results not from a misanthropic rejection of romantic love so much as a healthy suspicion of its linguistic intensity. Dramatically, his acute commentary on Romeo's clichéd formulations insulates the audience from the lover's indulgence and provides it with a sympathetic focus. That is why the early death of Mercutio comes as such a shock. His punning exit-line – 'Ask for me to-morrow, and you shall find me a grave man' (III. i. 94) – is not merely another joke, but the final desperate and ironic demonstration of the inability of verbal adroitness to deal with the brutal world of Verona. With Mercutio gone, the play darkens considerably in tone. Verbal quibbles and the subversive strategies that they voice, completely dry up.

The situation in *The Two Gentlemen of Verona* is similar in respect of the play's interest in the difficulties of interpretation and the manner in which this is articulated through verbal juggling. Despite the marked difference in tone, the play has about it the seriousness of *Romeo and Juliet* in relation to the relativity of meaning and signification. The jokes in *The Two Gentlemen of Verona* range from the simple, based on aural similarities, to the complex, involving shifting connotation. The following is a typical example of both:

> *Spee.:*   How now, Signior Launce! What news with your mastership?

Laun.: With my master's ship? Why, it is at sea.
Spee.: Well, your old vice still: mistake the word. What news,
         then, in your paper?
Laun.: The black'st news that ever thou heard'st.
Spee.: Why, man? how black?
Laun.: Why, as black as ink.

(III. i. 276–83)

The quibble on *ship* has occurred near the outset of the play when
Proteus and Speed slide the word across another, *sheep*.[28] The joke
on 'black'st news' depends upon the literalisation of the colour's
connotative properties. Speed assumes that a black letter is a letter
that contains dark or foreboding news; Launce simply means that
it is written in black ink. Throughout, characters 'mistake the word'
and this calculated misapprehension, though lacking the sexual
obsessiveness of the word-play of *Romeo and Juliet*, points up the
difficulties of interpersonal communication. Moreover there is, in
The Two Gentlemen of Verona, a laboured insistence about the jesting
which is closer to that of the self-consciousness of Romeo than the
verbal improvisation of Mercutio. Next to the relaxed jocosity of
Mercutio, their stagey bluster betrays a certain inexperience and
immaturity.

The Two Gentlemen of Verona is similar to *Romeo and Juliet* in its
growing movement away from the harmless comedy of words to
the increasing awareness of the potential dangers of language. In
the notorious attempted-rape scene, Proteus makes it clear that there
is another, more malevolent aspect to the sparkle of verbal wooing:
'Nay, if the gentle spirit of moving words / Can no way change
you to a milder form, / I'll woo you like a soldier, at arms' end, /
And love you 'gainst the nature of love – force ye' (V. iv. 54–7).
Force is the final weapon of a wooer who is linguistically exhausted,
yet it arises paradoxically as the successor to 'the force of heaven-
bred poesy' (III. ii. 72). In accordance with the text's Renaissance
misogyny, the rape is seen to be an extreme but entirely contiguous
outcome of the earlier linguistic violence. The intensity of this attack echoes Julia's earlier insistence which itself articulates the
popular misogynist myth that girls who say 'no' really mean 'yes':
'What fool is she, that knows I am a maid / And would not force
the letter to my view! / Since maids, in modesty, say "No" to that /
Which they would have the profferer construe "Ay"' (I. ii. 53–6).[29]
Moreover, Julia is not the only one to espouse such a belief in the

cussedness of women. As Valentine instructs the duke in his wooing of the fictional lady, he remarks upon what he takes to be this
female perversity:

> A woman sometime scorns what best contents her.
> Send her another [present]; never give her o'er,
> For scorn at first makes after-love the more.
> If she do frown, 'tis not in hate of you,
> But rather to beget more love in you;
> If she do chide, 'tis not to have you gone,
> For why the fools are mad if left alone.
> Take no repulse, whatever she doth say;
> For, 'Get you gone' she doth not mean 'Away!'
>   (III. i. 93–101)

In the light of this kind of reversal, the text, in the most disturbing
manner, attempts to exculpate Proteus from blame for the attempted
rape of Silvia. Her refusal is thus contextualised as a part of the
coquettish armoury of every woman who, according to the play's
oppressive ideology articulated by Valentine, Proteus and even Julia,
deny that which they really want. (When David Thacker directed
the play for the RSC in 1991, Richard Bonneville played Valentine.
His charming performance rendered Valentine as gauche and naive
and this speech worked therefore as a satire on male prejudice.)

The inverse scenario which makes just as plain the equivocation
of speakers is that in which characters ask for something they would
rather be denied. As Julia woos Silvia in the guise of Sebastian, she
voices her bewilderment at the self-contradictory mission in which
she is engaged:

> And now am I, unhappy messenger,
> To plead for that which I would not obtain,
> To carry that which I would have refus'd,
> To praise his faith, which I would have disprais'd.
> I am my master's true confirmed love,
> But cannot be true servant to my master
> Unless I prove false traitor to myself.
> Yet will I woo for him, but yet so coldly,
> As, heaven it knows, I would not have him speed.
>   (IV. iv. 95–103)

The frequency of the repetition of the first person pronoun (eight times in nine lines) makes explicit the personal nature of the frustration and this contrasts pointedly with the generality of the previous aphorisms, the most proverbial of which must be Valentine's woefully dangerous formulation, 'That man that hath a tongue, I say, is no man, / If with his tongue he cannot win a woman' (III. i. 104–5).

Repeatedly, then, these plays examine and emphasise the slippage between sign and referent. Language seems to be out of step with the world. In places, this is the cause of humour; in others, it is the source of danger and death. As *Romeo and Juliet* moves towards its double suicide and as *The Two Gentlemen of Verona* moves towards rape, so linguistic play fast evaporates. In *Romeo and Juliet* the 'flowery' language is literally cut down by death: 'O son, the night before thy wedding day / Hath Death lain with thy wife. There she lies, / Flower as she was, deflowered by him' (IV. v. 35–7). In raping Juliet, Death performs the same act as that attempted by Proteus on Silvia. Language surrenders its polysemic multivalence to the transcendental signified of death. As with Lavinia, physicality replaces speech.

III

While speaking attempts to evade the fixity of a single positionality (and in this it is successful in the earlier parts of the plays at least), it is not the only form of communicative act. Both *Romeo and Juliet* and *The Two Gentlemen of Verona* are concerned to demonstrate the relative freedom of speaking by contrasting it particularly with written communication. Books figure largely in *Romeo and Juliet* and they are usually the object of the play's moral scorn. They symbolise the impoverishment of a single viewpoint (what Hawkes called '"intrinsic" primacy or "inherent" authority'). When Mercutio denigrates Tybalt, he notes that he is 'A braggart, a rogue, a villain, that fights by the book of arithmetic!' (III. i. 98). Juliet remarks upon Romeo's endearing inexperience in matters sexual which renders his kissing technically perfect though lacking improvisation, 'You kiss by th' book' (I. v. 108). Having slain him, Romeo fatalistically addresses the corpse of Paris on their sealed doom, 'O, give me thy hand, / One writ with me in sour misfortune's book!' (V. iii. 81–2). The book represents the kind of certitude against which are set the

protean qualities of speaking. The whole point about Romeo's love
for Juliet is that it is beyond prediction or pronouncement; it is
richer than its prescription (in the literal sense of being 'pre-
written') could ever allow. In the light of the special contempt reserved for the book, it is appropriate that the callow immaturity of
Paris be described as one, despite the fact that Lady Capulet is here
attempting to convince her daughter of the suitor's worth:

> Read o'er the volume of young Paris' face,
> And find delight writ there with beauty's pen;
> Examine every married lineament,
> And see how one another lends content;
> And what obscur'd in this fair volume lies
> Find written in the margent of his eyes.
> This precious book of love, this unbound lover,
> To beautify him, only lacks a cover. . . .
> That book in many's eyes doth share the glory
> That in gold clasps locks in the golden story.
>   (I. iii. 82–93)

Juliet speaks of Romeo as a book only once, at the moment of her
most vehement anger towards him, when the nurse tells her that
her husband has killed her cousin: 'Was ever book containing such
vile matter / So fairly bound?' (III. ii. 83–4). In its suspicion of the
delimitation of the written word over the play of speech, *The Two
Gentlemen of Verona* is at one with *Romeo and Juliet*. However, letters
rather than books function in *The Two Gentlemen of Verona* as symbols of an over-prescriptive authority/auctoritee. Letters are every-
where in this play. Speed carries Proteus's letter to Julia with which
we see her toying in the second scene. Proteus holds back Julia's
letter from his father claiming that it is from Valentine. Valentine
writes Silvia a letter which she then gives to him. The arrival of
Proteus is anticipated by a letter to the duke (II. iv. 47) who later
discovers Valentine's letter to Silvia detailing the arrangements for
their imminent elopement. Proteus assures Valentine that though
the latter is banished, 'Thy letters may be here, though thou art
hence' (III. i. 248). Launce's 'cate-log' (III. i. 273) of his mistress's
qualities is a parody of these letters while being another example of
one. Sebastian delivers the letters of Proteus to Silvia and at the
crucial moment produces the wrong paper which, with tragic irony,
is likely to be the one from Proteus that we saw her (as Julia) tear

and reconstruct in the second scene of the play. No other play has so many lines on the delivery and reception of love-letters and no other play (with the possible exception of *Love's Labour's Lost*) is so roundly distrustful of the language of love. As Julia leaves Proteus, for the last time before he betrays her, she goes without a word and Proteus comes nearer to speaking the truth here than anywhere else:

Julia, farewell!   [*Exit Julia*]
        What, gone without a word?
Ay, so true love should do: it cannot speak;
For truth hath better deeds than words to grace it. . . .
Alas! this parting strikes poor lovers dumb.
                                        (II. ii. 16–21)

Julia's emotional commitment is signalled here by her speechlessness. Like Cordelia, she prefers to 'Love, and be silent' (*King Lear*, I. i. 61). In this world of linguistic duplicity, her silence is what informs the audience (though significantly not Proteus) of Julia's strength of feeling. *The Two Gentlemen of Verona* juxtaposes a silent sincerity against the fulsome love-talk of conventional Petrarchan compliment (II. i. 87–91).

Romeo's self-dramatising hyperbole, the target of Mercutio's merciless *double entendres*, is diagnosed as an overdose of Petrarchanism:

Benv.: Here comes Romeo, here comes Romeo.
Merc.: Without his roe, like a dried herring. O flesh, flesh, how art thou fishified! Now is he for the numbers that Petrarch flow'd in.
                                        (II. iv. 36–9)

Romeo's roe has been wrung out of him by his assignation with Juliet and he is now good for nothing but to write Petrarchan poetry which takes as its central tenet the unlikelihood of sexual contact.[30] Petrarchanism, Mercutio suggests, is essentially impotent. In their shared plight as hopeless Petrarchan lovers, Romeo and Proteus are strikingly similar – first Romeo:

O brawling love! O loving hate!
O anything, of nothing first create!
O heavy lightness! serious vanity!

Mis-shapen chaos of well-seeming forms!
Feather of lead, bright smoke, cold fire, sick health!
Still-waking sleep, that is not what it is!
This love feel I, that feel no love in this.

(I. i. 174–80)

Now Proteus (occurring similarly in the first scene):

To be in love – where scorn is bought with groans,
Coy looks with heart-sore sighs, one fading moment's mirth
With twenty watchful, weary, tedious nights;
If haply won, perhaps a hapless gain;
If lost, why then a grievous labour won;
However, but a folly bought with wit,
Or else a wit by folly vanquished.

(I. i. 29–35)

The 1590s saw a burgeoning in the cycles of Petrarchan poetry
and sonnet sequences. The effect of the sonnet on *Romeo and Juliet*
has itself often been remarked (note the presence of two sonnets to
introduce the first two acts) but we should also note its presence
in *The Two Gentlemen of Verona*.[31] For example, the only letter to be
read out in its entirety is that of Valentine to Silvia (III. i. 140–9)
which approximates formally to the English sonnet with its characteristic closing couplet (though it is missing one quatrain).

Saturated by these conventions of love-talk, the plays illustrate
the fierce paradox of Petrarchanism itself – that the chaos of emotional rapture is distinctly at odds with the highly sophisticated
and disciplined poetic strategies demanded by the genre. Such an
artificial poetry is deeply suspicious. Proteus's advice to the dull
Thurio to acquire some of these poems is sinister in its association
of wooing with entrapment: 'You must lay lime to tangle her desires / By wailful sonnets, whose composed rhymes / Should be
full-fraught with serviceable vows' (III. ii. 68–70). Even Thurio knows
the force of the sonnet and arms himself in accordance with Proteus's
advice with 'a sonnet that will serve the turn' (l. 93). The very
sonnet form protests its own permanence and immortality. It is,
though, as scholars of Shakespeare's own sonnets know to their
bitter cost, one of the most enigmatic and elusive of poetic media,
obscuring behind types and conventionalities the individuals and
specificities of particular relationships.

In the face of this male preoccupation with the 'correct' formulae of love, Julia, Silvia, and Juliet, with the mental and emotional agility that will characterise Shakespeare's later romantic women, reject the empty conventions of expression.[32] We have already seen Julia take her leave of Proteus in a silence that says more than his protesting could ever do. Silvia is the only one of the four lovers not to write or receive a letter; instead, in a gesture which itself questions the uniqueness of such letters, she gets Valentine to write his own. His lines she finds stilted and artificial, noting that they are 'very clerkly done' (II. i. 97). She maintains that she 'would have had them writ more movingly' (l. 117); these men write 'by th' book'. For Proteus, Valentine and Romeo love is first and foremost the correct emulation of a model of behaviour and expression, and this model is a literary one; they are besotted by a linguistic code. In the sense that Shakespeare exposes their naivety, both plays are implied criticisms of the Petrarchan conventions.

The reason for rejecting the convention is made graphically clear by Proteus's 'hateful siege / Of contraries'.[33] At the opening of II. vi, he weighs in the balance his betrayal of Julia and Valentine against the prospect of winning Silvia:

> To leave my Julia, shall I be forsworn;
> To love fair Silvia, shall I be forsworn;
> To wrong my friend, I shall be much forsworn.
> And ev'n that pow'r which gave me first my oath
> Provokes me to this threefold perjury:
> Love bade me swear, and Love bids me forswear.
> O sweet-suggesting Love, if thou hast sinn'd,
> Teach me, thy tempted subject, to excuse it!
> At first I did adore a twinkling star,
> But now I worship a celestial sun.
> Unheedful vows may heedfully be broken;
> And he wants wit, that wants resolved will
> To learn his wit, t' exchange the bad for better.
>
> (ll. 1–13)

In the very next scene, Julia makes tragically clear the mistake of taking Proteus at his word: 'truer stars did govern Proteus' birth; / His words are bonds, his oaths are oracles, / His love sincere, his thoughts immaculate, / His tears pure messengers sent from his heart, / His heart as far from fraud as heaven from earth' (II. vii.

74–8). Faced with this duplicity, we might concede to Juliet's nurse that 'There's no trust, / No faith, no honesty in men; all perjur'd, / All forsworn, all naught, all dissemblers' (III. ii. 85–7). In her conversion of Romeo from a Protean youth to a steadfast lover, however, Juliet proves the nurse wrong. The moment at which this occurs is in Romeo's voluntary abnegation of the hackneyed and threadbare discourse of poetic love. Standing under her balcony, Romeo makes to inscribe his new love within what he takes to be the fealty of linguistic oath:

> Rome.: Lady, by yonder blessed moon I vow,
>   That tips with silver all these fruit-tree tops—
> Juli.: O, swear not by the moon, th' inconstant moon,
>   That monthly changes in her circled orb,
>   Lest that thy love prove likewise variable.
> Rome.: What shall I swear by?
> Juli.:   Do not swear at all.
>   (II. ii. 107–12)

Romeo protests too much and Juliet has a healthy mistrust of Petrarchanism. In her refusal to allow Romeo the comfort of masculine protestation, Juliet, like Mercutio, re-fuses the sexual dichotomies of gendered relationships.

The most important single thing about Petrarchanism, implicit in Mercutio's association of the convention with impotence, is that it celebrates a relationship which is inherently impossible. 'My Love is of a birth as rare / As 'tis for object strange and high: / It was begotten by despair / Upon Impossibility.'[34] The irony of this opening stanza from Marvell's 'The Definition of Love' is the presence of the verb 'begotten', for the whole point of Petrarchan love is that it is never consummated. In the case of *Romeo and Juliet* the love that was unattainable, Rosaline, fulfilled Romeo's requirement for a Petrarchan mistress. The fatal thing about the affair with Juliet and the way in which their relationship transgresses the Petrarchan boundaries, is in its consummation. The second balcony scene (III. v) takes place on the morning after the couple have slept together. Juliet is now the quibbling double-speaker of love, the deliberate misreader of signs. Once again the confusion is over types of bird; Juliet assures Romeo that 'It was the nightingale, and not the lark, / That pierc'd the fearful hollow of thine ear' (ll. 2–3). No longer subscribing to the self-conscious display of quibbling love talk,

Romeo recognises the dangers that await in the outside world and the patriarchal determinism of the political realities of Verona comes crashing through the linguistic play of the lovers, 'It was the lark, the herald of the morn, / No nightingale. . . . I must be gone and live, or stay and die' (ll. 6–11). With this, Juliet has no option but to agree, 'It is the lark that sings so out of tune, / Straining harsh discords and unpleasing sharps' (ll. 27–8). In this postlapsarian world the indulgence of love-speak is misplaced. As the nurse reprimands Romeo in Lawrence's cell for his despair, she encourages him to get up: 'Stand up, stand up; stand, an you be a man; / For Juliet's sake, for her sake, rise and stand; / Why should you fall into so deep an O?' (III. iii. 88–90). The *double entendres* of standing (to achieve an erection) and 'so deep an O' are just the kind of joke that Mercutio and the others would have relished in the earlier part of the play but contained within the word 'fall' is the despair of Edenic loss. Like Adam and Eve, Romeo and Juliet are no longer nescient and the innocence of play – linguistic and sexual – is now lost to them. This is why the nurse's jokes seem so out of place, clumsy, tactless, even unintentional.

IV

By the end of both plays there is no pleasure left in the ambiguities of language. The double sign has brought us only as far as the forest in which Silvia is assaulted (and whose designation/destination is implicit in her name) and the Capulet tomb. The endings of both plays refuse the kinds of linguistic ambiguity that each had relished earlier on, ending in a declaratory obviousness. In *The Two Gentlemen of Verona* Valentine will rehearse the events that have brought the characters to this point:

> I'll tell you, as we pass along,
> That you will wonder what hath fortuned.
> Come, Proteus, 'tis your penance but to hear,
> The story of your loves discovered.
> That done, our day of marriage shall be yours;
> One feast, one house, one mutual happiness!
> (V. iv. 168–73)

There is something poetically just about Proteus undergoing the humiliation of hearing his offences publicly recounted. But whatever its effect, the retelling will surely be without the verbal adroitness that has characterised its occurrence: the law has no space for quibbles. The ending of *Romeo and Juliet* is even more peremptory. Again the re-establishment of state power rests upon the elimination of all unsolved evidence. Escalus demands a clear synopsis, intercepting Romeo's letter to his father:

> Give me the letter, I will look on it. . . .
> This letter doth make good the friar's words. . . .
> Go hence, to have more talk of these sad things;
> Some shall be pardon'd and some punished;
> For never was a story of more woe
> Than this of Juliet and her Romeo.
>
> (V. iii. 277–309)

The conclusiveness of the repetition of the play's title (albeit in inverted form) is emphatic and Ruth Nevo has commented also on the appropriateness of our other play's title to its ending: '*The Two Gentlemen of Verona* is properly named . . . [for] this is still a play in which the masculine view and the masculine initiative dominates.' [35] The mystery of the sign is not permitted since, as we have seen, it has the potential to subvert social relationships between ruler and ruled, master and servant, and man and woman. Ambiguities are refused, signs at variance are forcibly re-fused into a system of signification that, above all else, makes complete sense. As Lucentio leaves Biondello, so Shakespeare leaves each of us 'here behind to expound the meaning or moral of his signs' (*Shrew*, IV. iv. 78). Given the extraordinary richness of the Shakespearean sign and its subversive possibilities, Hawkes's attitude towards the text as 'an area of conflicting and often contradictory potential interpretations' could be considered as something of a comfort.

Notes

1. Terence Hawkes, *That Shakespeherian Rag: Essays on a Critical Process* (1986), p. 1.
2. More recent constructivist studies include: *The Shakespeare Myth* (Manchester, 1988), ed. Graham Holderness; Gary Taylor, *Shakespeare Reinvented* (1990); and Hugh Grady, *The Modernist Shakespeare* (Oxford, 1991).

3. Hawkes, *Shakespeherian Rag*, pp. 117–18.
4. Bill Alexander's *The Taming of the Shrew* (RSC, 1992) wittily alluded to the theatre's local. At the beginning of the production, Christopher Sly was thrown out of a pub called 'The Ugly Duckling' while we first saw Petruchio outside the sign of 'The Swan'. The pub signs were flown in stage right and left respectively. They clearly symbolised the superiority of the play's hero to the play's drunk.
5. For similar ironic prophecies see the Jerusalem chamber in *II Henry IV* (IV. v. 235) and Richard III's anxiety over Rugemount and Richmond (IV. ii. 107–9).
6. Robert Greene, *A Groats-worth of Witte bought with a Million of Repentance* (Westport, Conn., 1970), pp. 45–6.
7. A sketch of the Shakespeare coat of arms is conveniently available in *The Complete Works*, Compact Edition, ed. Stanley Wells *et al.* (Oxford, 1988), p. xvii.
8. Another example illustrating female ignorance of foreign languages occurs in William's Latin lesson in *The Merry Wives of Windsor*: '*Evans*: I pray you have your remembrance, child. *Accusativo*: "*hung, hang, hog*". *Mistress Quickly*: "Hang-hog" is Latin for bacon, I warrant you' (IV. i. 41–4).
9. Terry Eagleton, *William Shakespeare* (Oxford, 1986), p. 1.
10. Allan Shickman notes a similar avian metamorphosis in George Chapman's *All Fools* wherein Rynaldo describes beauty as 'like a cousoning picture which one way / Shewes like a Crowe, another like a Swanne'. He suggests that both poets may have seen the same anamorphic picture. 'Turning Pictures in Shakespeare's England', *Art Bulletin*, 59 (1977), 67–70, p. 67. See also Jurgis Baltrušaitis, *Anamorphic Art*, trans. W. J. Strachan (Cambridge, 1977).
11. Programme note for 1989 RSC production, p. XIV. The title of Huxley's novel is of course dialogically engaged with *The Tempest*.
12. Cited by Keir Elam, *Shakespeare's Universe of Discourse: Language Games in the Comedies* (Cambridge, 1984), p. 1.
13. For a comparison of *Romeo and Juliet* with the early comedies rather than with the later tragedies, see *Shakespeare: A Bibliographical Guide*, ed. Stanley Wells, new edn (Oxford, 1990), p. 190.
14. Jonathan Dollimore, *Sexual Dissidence* (Oxford, 1991), p. 285.
15. Ibid., p. 292.
16. *Dally* has a specifically sexual charge in the plays of Shakespeare. Compare 'dallying with a brace of courtezans', *Richard III* (III. vii. 74) and the 'primrose path of dalliance', *Hamlet* (I. iii. 50).
17. See, for example, M. M. Mahood, *Shakespeare's Wordplay* (1957), p. 56.
18. Geoffrey Hughes, *Swearing: A Social History of Foul Language, Oaths and Profanity in English* (Oxford, 1991), p. 27.
19. Julia Kristeva, '*Romeo and Juliet*: Love-hatred in the couple', in *Shakespearean Tragedy*, ed. John Drakakis (1992), 296–315, p. 305.
20. *Romeo and Juliet*, ed. Brian Gibbons (1980), p. 107.
21. Ibid., p. 108.
22. The *OED* cites an example from Greene of 1592, about three years before the composition of *Romeo and Juliet*.

23. Joseph A. Porter, *Shakespeare's Mercutio: His History and Drama* (1988), p. 155.

24. This reading of the *medlar* is reinforced by stage practice. In Trevor Nunn's *Measure for Measure* (RSC, 1991), Lucio (played by Roger Hyams) grasped his genitals and shook his head disapprovingly when he noted that, having got 'a wench with child', he had nearly been forced to marry 'the rotten medlar' (IV. iii. 165–9). The gesture implied that the woman was diseased (the whole production emphasised a prevailing venerial unhealth) and so *medlar* translates quite literally here as 'cunt'. Later in the same production, when Lucio told the Duke, 'I know him; 'tis a meddling friar' (V. i. 127), the word *meddling* was accompanied with a salacious gesture.

25. Eric Partridge, *Shakespeare's Bawdy*, third edn (1968), pp. 101–2. There is another example of this arboreal indecency at the opening of IV. i of Tourneur's *The Atheist's Tragedy*. For a more modern usage of the euphemism see e e cummings, 'my sweet old etcetera'. The poem ends with a soldier in the trenches dreaming of 'Your smile / eyes knees and of your Etcetera'. *The Penguin Book of First World War Poetry*, ed. Jon Silkin, second edn (Harmondsworth, 1981), p. 140.

26. Gregory W. Bredbeck writes 'the invocation of sodomy is truly punning, for it stresses the fact that the one signifier, *sodomy*, carried with it several senses that were all equally valid if slippery referents' (*Sodomy and Interpretation: Marlowe to Milton* (1991), pp. 12–13).

27. Cited in *Shakespeare: A Bibliographical Guide*, ed. Wells, p. 194.

28. For another instance of the *ship / sheep* quibble, see *Love's Labour's Lost*, II. i. 218f.

29. For a terrifying restatement of this myth, note Judge David Wild's summing-up at a rape trial in 1986: 'Women who say no do not always mean no. It is not just a question of saying no. It is a question of how she says it, how she shows it and makes it clear. If she doesn't want it, she only has to keep her legs shut and there would be marks of force being used' (cited by Marion Wynne-Davies, '"The Swallowing Womb": Consumed and Consuming Women in *Titus Andronicus*', in *The Matter of Difference: Materialist Feminist Criticism of Shakespeare*, ed. Valerie Wayne (1991), 129–51, p. 129). See also Buckingham's advice to Richard to 'Play the maid's part: still answer nay, and take it' (*Richard III*, III. vii. 51).

30. For another example of male impotence and its association with desiccation, see *Macbeth*, I. iii. 18.

31. See Jill L. Levenson, 'The Definition of Love: Shakespeare's Phrasing in *Romeo and Juliet*', *Shakespeare Studies*, 15 (1982), 21–36; Gayle Whittier, 'The Sonnet's Body and the Body Sonnetized in *Romeo and Juliet*', *Shakespeare Quarterly*, 40 (1989), 27–41. The latter suggests that the Petrarchan influence must have been irresistible since Shakespeare 'wrote at or near Petrarch's English zenith' (p. 27).

32. Compare with Rosalind's pragmatic words to Orlando cited in Chapter 2 above, 'men have died from time to time, and worms have eaten them, but not for love' (*As You Like It*, IV. i. 95). Orlando is another Petrarchan sonneteer.

33. *Paradise Lost*, IX. 121.
34. *The Poems of Andrew Marvell*, ed. Hugh MacDonald (1956), first published 1952, p. 34.
35. Ruth Nevo, *Comic Transformations in Shakespeare* (1980), p. 56.

Part III
Society and Culture

7

The Eternal Mushroom of Humanity: Racism and Jewishness in *The Jew of Malta* and *The Merchant of Venice*

I

> I was repelled by the conglomeration of races which the capital showed me, repelled by this whole mixture of Czechs, Poles, Hungarians, Ruthenians, Serbs, and Croats, and everywhere, the eternal mushroom of humanity – Jews and more Jews. To me the giant city seemed the embodiment of racial desecration.[1]

Thus the author of *Mein Kampf* remembers the Vienna of his youth. That the wholesale slaughter of European 'inferiors' resulted solely from the psychotic ravings of this single maniac of ferocious genius, is a myth that has long been superseded by an awareness of the economic and political problems of prewar Germany. The marginalisation and destruction of the Jews provided an outlet for racial aggression and, at the same time, fertilised the soil in which the roots of an iniquitous nationalism could flourish. The mission of National Socialism was to weed its green and pleasant land free of those alien races who, it alleged, were absorbing more than their fair share of sustenance. The confident magnificence of the Berlin Olympic stadium or Milan central station is accompanied by the long and mournful shadow of Auschwitz and Belsen. In the words of Walter Benjamin, one of the most significant cultural critics of Hitler's Germany, who took his own life while fleeing from the Nazis: 'There is no document of civilisation which is not at the same time a document of barbarism.'[2]

It is with the paradoxical duality of Benjamin's notion of a cultural document that I want to explore *The Jew of Malta* and *The Merchant of Venice* and reread both plays in the light of the suggestion that what we are actually doing when we watch, teach and act these plays is nothing less than rejuvenating and re-experiencing racist texts. In a society where the promotion of racial hatred is illegal and generally felt to be morally obscene, we do need to consider the implications of those texts inscribed at the centre of our literature and our national identity. When these texts contain sentiments like those of Hitler it is time to ensure that we are aware of the responsibilities we must shoulder in their continued promulgation. The German critic Ernst Schumacher recently drew attention to the way in which *The Merchant of Venice* was appropriated and deployed in the cause of Nazism:

> Hitler used it, Goebbels used it, and it contributed directly to the extermination of the Jews, the 'final solution' of 1943. The Minister for Propaganda is quoted in the six files for the extermination of the Jewish people as ordering a performance of *The Merchant of Venice....* It is impossible in my view to play *The Merchant of Venice* in Germany after this example.[3]

This is an attitude to the work shared by some of its most distinguished commentators. In a letter to Ellen Terry (whose Portia was playing opposite Henry Irving's Shylock at the time), Lewis Carroll suggested that the court's sentence upon Shylock – that he convert to Christianity – be cut: 'It is a sentiment that is entirely horrible and revolting to the feelings of all who believe in the Gospel of Love. Why should our ears be shocked by such words merely because they are Shakespeare's?'[4] More recently, D. M. Cohen opens his sensitive article on the play with the sentence, 'Current criticism notwithstanding, *The Merchant of Venice* seems to me a profoundly and crudely anti-Semitic play.'[5] Of the introduction to the Arden edition, Cohen writes,

> It is all very well for John Russell Brown to say *The Merchant of Venice* is not anti-Jewish, and that 'there are only two slurs on Jews in general'; but this kind of assertion, a common enough one in criticism of the play, cannot account for the fear and shame that Jewish viewers and readers have always felt from the moment of Shylock's entrance to his final exit.[6]

W. H. Auden's essay, 'Brothers and Others', is likewise uneasy about the play in the post-Holocaust period: 'Recent history has made it utterly impossible for the most unsophisticated and ignorant audience to ignore the historical reality of the Jews and think of them as fairy-story bogeys with huge noses and red wigs.' He ventures sombrely, 'I think *The Merchant of Venice* must be classed among Shakespeare's "Unpleasant Plays."'[7]

It is not only the play's critics who find *The Merchant of Venice* problematic; the theatre is also nervous about it. The former artistic director of the Young Vic, David Thacker, who is now resident director at the RSC, remarks, 'If you think that *The Merchant of Venice* is an antisemitic play, the answer is not to change it but not to do it at all.'[8] His direction of the play for the 1993 RSC season may therefore be taken as demonstrating his own attitude towards the play. Other directors are less blithe. In an education pack to accompany his 1990 production of the play for the English Shakespeare Company, Tim Luscombe roundly confronted the issue of racism: 'the question of the play's anti-Semitism is a sensitive one (it's a dangerous subject), and I wanted to be able to say that we had tackled it head-on, and done so in a responsible manner'.[9] Unfortunately, many actors and directors indulge in a kind of special pleading which is motivated by their desire to attribute to the playwright an egalitarian sensibility. In his theatre workshop, *Playing Shakespeare* (which was screened by Channel 4 in 1984), John Barton worked with two distinguished Shylocks, David Suchet and Patrick Stewart. All of them are keen to divorce their image of the Bard from any charges of racism: 'I think one must forget modern anti-Semitism and concentrate on the play as writ' (Suchet); 'The anti-Semitism . . . of the play . . . is a distraction' (Stewart); and perhaps most feebly Barton himself, 'we're not here to talk about anti-Semitism but about character'.[10]

In voicing the assertion that *The Merchant of Venice* is racist one runs the risk of being branded a philistine or the charge that one is 'over-sensitive'. There is an extraordinary reluctance on the part of some literary critics as well as thespians to see the play as anything other than one of Shakespeare's forgiving comedies. Nevill Coghill in the teeth of the play's vicious ending and the court's insistence on the Jew's religious conversion protests that 'Shylock has at least been given his chance of eternal joy. . . . Mercy has triumphed over justice, even if the way of mercy is a hard way.'[11] Even more dangerous than this propensity to romanticise is the insistence that the

present misgivings about the moral standing of the play are somehow anachronistic. Marion D. Perret notes waspishly that '*The
Merchant of Venice* will probably never be produced without someone's complaining about anti-Semitism.'[12] She goes on to castigate
productions (the most notable of which was Jonathan Miller's National Theatre production of 1970) which are designed to emphasise
Jewish suffering:

> Effective as it is, when followed too enthusiastically, this approach
> encourages deliberate distortion of the text. Shakespeare clearly
> did not intend to portray Shylock favorably.... If we assume
> that Shakespeare can be made non-anti-Semitic only by being
> made non-Shakespearean, simple logic suggests that Shakespeare
> is indeed, for whatever reasons, anti-Semitic. Behind the National
> Theatre's adaptation seems to lie the assumption that being un-
> flattering to this particular Jew is tantamount to being prejudiced
> against all Jews.[13]

The problems with this account foreground precisely the assumptions which this book as a whole is designed to challenge. The
production values and ideological accents of the Renaissance theatre are now lost to us. Modern theatre productions are incalculably
different from those which Shakespeare's audience may have experienced. This fact alone makes Perret's stress on Shakespeare's intentionality deeply unrealisable. There is frankly no way we can
ever be sure *what* the playwright intended. As such, a 'distortion of
the text', let alone a 'deliberate distortion of the text', is simply
indeterminable since there is no Shakespearean master-text from
which to measure the apparent deviations of any modern reading
or production. The final sentence reveals the absurd shallowness of
Perret's reading of *The Merchant of Venice* itself for throughout
Shylock is insulted *as a Jew*. In the court scene, for example, while
Antonio is addressed nominally, Shylock is called 'Shylock' on six
occasions while he is addressed as 'Jew' over twenty times. Perret
remarks that 'Shakespeare's play ... was never intended to correct
the injustices of twentieth-century history.'[14] By hypothesising this
bogus intentionality, Perret infuses her reading with a chimera of
historical authenticity. In a separate article, Perret reinforces what
she takes to be the inappropriateness of seeing a four-hundred-
year-old play through the lens of the intervening period, 'Shakespeare [is] innocent of modern history and not responsible for our

preconceptions.'[15] What she fails to realise is that her own critical position is historically situated and embedded within power structures and ideologies which are themselves the result of historical discourses – including the history of racial oppression of the Jewish people. It is not a question of imposing the gas chambers on to the play, it is rather that the play is now encrusted with a knowledge of the Holocaust and that *The Merchant of Venice* and its own cultural history are impossible to separate. As Horst Meller puts it, 'we in Germany, after the genocide perpetrated by the Nazis, will never now be able to watch the staging of the downfall of Shylock from the Rialto ghetto, driven by hatred and thirst for revenge, without being reminded of the fate of the Jews in the Warsaw ghetto and in Auschwitz'.[16]

The Merchant of Venice was an ideal vehicle for the promulgation of Nazi ideology. In September 1939 all playwrights of enemy nationality were banned in the German theatre. Shakespeare, however, on the order of the Ministry of Propaganda, was to be treated as a German.[17] While almost the entire canon was staged during the course of the war the most frequently performed play was, perhaps unsurprisingly, *The Merchant of Venice*. Shortly 'after Kristallnacht in 1938, *The Merchant of Venice* was broadcast for propagandistic ends over the German airwaves'.[18] Productions of the play followed in Lübeck (1938), Aachen (1940), Berlin (1942), Göttingen (1942), and Vienna (1943).[19] According to Werner Habicht, the play was produced approximately fifty times between 1933 and 1944 and productions 'invariably exhibited anti-Semitic and racist interpretations of Shylock'.[20] Moreover, the ending of the play was frequently rewritten to prevent the 'mixed' marriage of Lorenzo and Jessica.

We should note here that the polysemy of Shakespeare's text has enabled the same play to be appropriated and produced by the very victims against whom its Nazi productions were targeted, although usually not without public controversy. Leopold Jessner directed the first Hebrew production of the play at the Habimah Theatre in 1936. One reviewer commented frostily, 'In spite of Jessner's promises in all his speeches that his production was to stress only those points which will suit the Hebrew stage, most of the gentiles appeared almost as decent human beings.'[21] For this reviewer, Shakespeare's Jew stood for the plight of the Jewish race: 'what Shylock symbolizes [is] the humiliation of Israel, for which there is no pardon in the world for ever and ever!'[22] When Yossi Yzraeli staged *The Merchant of Venice* in Tel Aviv in 1972, the difficulty of producing the play was illustrated. Hayim Gamzu wrote, 'It is but natural that we Jews are practically allergic to a typical antisemitic interpretation.'[23] The Nazi enthusiasm for *The Merchant of Venice* and the Jewish reticence towards the play demonstrate the tendency for its anti-Semitism to be reproduced rather than interrogated.

Although an English audience is removed from direct cultural experience of Nazi Germany or Zionist Israel, *The Merchant of Venice* is still a potentially dangerous play; a recent example will illustrate. In a review of the 1984 RSC *Merchant* (directed by John Caird), William Frankel attacked the production on the grounds that its central performance, by Ian McDiarmid, did nothing to challenge the medieval stereotype of Jews as 'comic, villainous and avaricious, cruel and insolent in success, servile in defeat'.[24] Having described the humiliation and embarrassment of reading *The Merchant* as the only Jewish boy in his class, Frankel continues:

> Actors and directors operate in a world which is not entirely populated by the educated and sophisticated. Prejudice, bigotry, discrimination and even persecution have not disappeared. The reproduction, in this real world, of ancient stereotypes should take into account their potential for inciting or reinforcing racial or religious prejudice.
>
> I believe that Mr McDiarmid's Shylock can have that effect, a view which was fortified at Stratford by the approving reception some members of the audience gave to the most virulent passages of the play.[25]

Frankel's criticism led to the subsequent rewriting of the production's programme under the supervision of no less than Sir Kenneth Cork (then chair of the RSC Council). The RSC, like all other theatre companies, commonly inserts errata slips in programmes and will frequently publish a revised edition to include production shots and cast changes where necessary, but it is extremely rare for it to go to the expense of resetting and reprinting an entire programme at the beginning of a run. The amended text included reference to the Holocaust together with a disclaimer that the anti-Semitism of the fifteenth- and sixteenth-century extracts (that it had previously printed) reflected 'the ignorance, prejudice and cruelty of the prevailing opinion in Shakespeare's day'. David Hewson in an article on the controversy pointed out that 'One of those understood to have complained is Mr Cyril Stein, head of Ladbrokes which has sponsored RSC productions in the past.'[26] Whether or not the RSC would have gone to the trouble of composing a new programme had one of its major sponsors not been offended is a question left alarmingly open.

One of the most profound ironies surrounding the RSC *Merchant* concerned McDiarmid's own attitudes. In an interview published before the production opened, he said that his Shylock 'will be just as Jewish as I can make him, although I am not a Jew'.[27] In other words, his performance would rely on the manipulation and recognition of a stereotype of 'Jewishness'. McDiarmid would model his performance on the way in which he saw Jews at that moment, as a type, as a *race*. Although the criticism of McDiarmid did not go unnoticed by the actor – in fact he threatened legal action against Frankel[28] – he later seemed quite complacent about the seriousness of the charge laid against his performance. In a subsequent account of the production he shuffled off any blame on to those offended:

> Regrettably few people coming to the play would be encountering it for the first time. The problem seemed less to do with my 'old luggage' than with theirs. . . . Controversy will never be far away whenever this play is performed. Shylock remains, indisputably, a figure of great energy and passion and like all such figures arouses sharply conflicting emotions perhaps most of all in those who lack his dynamism.[29]

This example shows that racism present in drama exists on two levels – that which is inscribed in plays where characters spit upon Jewish gaberdines and that which surfaces during the reproduction of such plays where actors delineate their characteristics by relying on racial stereotypes. These plays are not merely *about* race but consistently demand during the course of their reproduction that their modern directors negotiate a minefield of contemporary political problems. A reluctance to do so or, even worse, the tendency to ignore such debates as 'irrelevant to the play' marks the most potentially negligent kind of theatre practice.

In 1985 Jean-Marie Maguin recognised the sensitivity aroused by these two plays. He wrote: 'The fierce barrage of criticism which the latest productions of *The Jew of Malta* in Paris, and *The Merchant of Venice* in both Paris and Stratford-upon-Avon in late years – never fiercer than in the 1984 Stratford production of *Merchant* [the production I alluded to above] – makes it unlikely that a company will again dare to attempt a double bill such as the RSC presented in 1965.'[30] Despite Maguin's conviction, in 1987 the RSC staged just such a double bill. Bill Alexander's *Venice* opened in the main house just five weeks before Barry Kyle's *Malta* opened in the Swan next door. The director of the second play expressed his misgivings about the issues raised by its production:

> I read *The Jew of Malta* when I was a student and thought it was unrevivable. I find the whole issue of anti-semitic drama and whether you should revive it very difficult. I've actually directed *The Merchant of Venice* in Israel, so I've been through this discussion at some length. It was quite influential on the thinking I had in *The Jew of Malta*. I couldn't bear the idea of it seeming to be an anti-semitic piece of work.[31]

Like it or not (and Kyle plainly finds it embarrassing), these plays contain the most vehement kinds of racial abuse. Barabas is variously 'an infidel' with 'bottle-nose', Shylock is a Jewish cut-throat dog, continually spat upon. Both are exploited, persecuted, lose their daughters, are finally ruined and, in one case, murdered. However, along with Kyle, the tendency of modern directors has been to exculpate the plays by courting audience sympathy for their protagonists. Barabas and Shylock are turned into victims – Christians into brutal thugs. In Peter Hall's 1989 production, for example, in response to Shylock's good-humoured assent to the bond – he offered Antonio his hand – the merchant spat fully in his face. The tiny frame of Dustin Hoffman was continually surrounded and jostled by thuggish Christians who pulled off his yarmulke and shoved him from one to another. Ian Lavender's Solanio relished the lamentation of Shylock for his lost daughter, impersonating him in a hyperbolic Jewish accent. Leon Lissek's Tubal was spat on across the width of the set but passively walked downstage to join his countryman. Hoffman's charm percolated through his characterisation and made his Shylock a man more sinned against than sinning. His only resistance to the attacks of the Venetians was to raise his hands to protect himself or to gesture submission, coupled with Hoffman's wry half-smile. The catalogue of abuse that Antonio has hurled his way in the past was recounted, quite neutrally, to explain the illogicality of expecting Shylock's help. At 'Hath not a Jew hands, organs, dimensions, senses...', Hoffman's voice was barely a whisper and the pain of social rejection was meekly and passionately suggested.

Whereas many versions of *The Merchant of Venice* attempt to dilute the anti-Semitism of the script by making the Christians just as bad if not worse than the Jew, Tim Luscombe's production for the ESC bravely acknowledged that there is little attractive or sympathetic about Shylock and so his money-lender was a vindictive and calculating operator. Luscombe set the play in the Venice of the late thirties and this allowed him to depict Salerio and Solanio as members of Mussolini's army. The duke in the court room wore the Duce's cap and military uniform (see Plate H). Characters greeted each other with the raised hand of the fascist salute. The growing tension in prewar Italian society was nicely schematised in the programme for us, and Luscombe freely interpolated scenes to eke out the text socially in useful ways. When Shylock told Tubal that he would meet him at the synagogue there followed a scene of the ritual prayer of an assembly of Jews in religious shawls. During the night of the masque, a lone Jew was set upon by Gratiano *et al.* and beaten up. A procession of jeering Venetians walked across the stage with banners depicting the star of David crossed through and holding aloft Jewish effigies. With all of this racist oppression, there was no need to make Shylock into a pathetic figure. Luscombe provoked our sense of indignation on behalf of the members of a social group who find themselves being socially victimised, without compromising the vicious and appalling determination of Shylock to see the personal ruination and brutal execution of the merchant. However understandable it may be to destroy the persecutor, the desire to cut out the heart of a human being can never be morally defended. To make us feel sorry for Shylock is to reduce the rich ambiguities of the play and Luscombe was well aware of this.

Shylock (John Woodvine) was a successful businessman. Sitting behind his desk, he flicked through documents in front of him with a nonchalant and self-satisfied air, to determine the whereabouts of Antonio's ships. Antonio entered and Shylock pronounced, 'How like a fawning publican he looks!' (I. iii. 36). This line, which usually gets a laugh, was damning and icy and Shylock appeared to be less an ironic observer comically chatting about Laban's sheep than a magnificent adversary plotting the personal destruction of a man that, as he tells us, he hates; as he says later, 'since I am a dog, beware my fangs' (III. iii. 7). Woodvine's Shylock was cool even while Antonio walked around his seated figure and sententiously told Bassanio that the devil can cite scripture. But in response to Antonio's question, 'Well, Shylock, shall we be beholding to you?' (I. iii. 100), the Jew lost his temper and slammed his hand down upon the desk. This brief show of passion was quickly controlled as Shylock stood to confront Antonio face to face. The forfeiture was suggested more as a challenge than anything and Antonio leapt into the trap.

Later, as Shylock prepared to leave his house for the business meeting with his clients, he paced worriedly up and down and continually proffered Jessica his keys. As he took stock of the consequences of leaving her with his money, he repeatedly withdrew them and only handed them over after he had given her a stiff talking-to. Luscombe made no concessions by suggesting paternal affection and this had dramatic consequences as Shylock lamented the loss of the ducats and the loss of his daughter together – 'I would my daughter were dead at my foot, and the jewels in her ear' (III. i. 73). Even during Shylock's most pathetic speech, 'Hath not a Jew eyes?' (III. i. 50), Woodvine played the character with defiance. He never wanted sympathy – only justice. Woodvine's Shylock had been dehumanised by the savagery that he had experienced and, as he told Salerio, 'The villainy you teach me I will execute; and it shall go hard but I will better the instruction' (l. 61). This world of callous intolerance was starkly portrayed in Paul Farnsworth's monochrome design. The crimson cloths of the court offered the only instance of colour while all the costumes, even in Belmont, were black and white. Leonard Tucker lit the set with what looked like enormous interrogation lamps, fixed to three scaffold observation towers, and the theatre lanterns were rigged to complement this feeling of starkness.

Hall's and Luscombe's approaches typify a wish to explore the dangerous problems raised by Shakespeare's play. While the former sentimentalised his protagonist, the latter contextualised politically Shylock's vengeful rage. Another option is to downplay the racial issues and this was the solution favoured by David Thacker's 1993 RSC production. Set in the world of eighties yuppiedom complete with compact disc players and mobile 'phones, the play's questions of religion and race seemed irrelevant. Thacker's Venice was London of the big bang and though the financial side of the play made sense in this world of fiscal manoeuvring, the secular setting made the religious contentions seem curiously incongruous: in the stock exchange, Mammon is the only god that counts. Shelagh Keegan's design staged Venice as a postmodern metallic office-block with walkways and ladder-staircases reminiscent of the Pompidou Centre (see Plate I). Shylock sat behind a transparent perspex desk and tapped calculations into a laptop computer as he negotiated the loan. The direction was extremely simple. Before his daughter left him, Shylock was basically good-natured, 'I would be friends with you' (I. iii. 133). As the bond was agreed, the evident absurdity of the fleshy forfeit was treated by all as a joke. The cutting of Shylock's 'If I can catch him once upon the hip . . .' (l. 41) made him considerably less malevolent than the line implies. His tenderness towards a photograph of his (presumably late) wife and his relaxation in a velvet smoking jacket while listening to classical music (which alluded to the civilised intelligence and loneliness of Inspector Morse) made him humane and pitiable. The warped and vicious extremism of the latter half of the play, especially during the trial scene, was entirely due to the elopement of Jessica. As he sought her on the night of the masque his panic became gradually more extreme. He started to run over, through and around the set while masked revellers caught and deflected him. The next time we saw him he had clearly founded his terrible resolve on this familial humiliation. Thacker had made Jessica's elopement the breaking-point for Shylock. This is an entirely defensible interpretation and one that is closely attuned to the play's structure but its elevation occluded the issues of race; this was a family saga rather than a production about prejudice. As Arnold Wesker commented, 'A young audience . . . would not know the Holocaust happened from your production.'[32] Directors of *The Merchant of Venice* can attempt to defuse its anti-Semitism (Hall), explore it in the context of an unmistakably racist environment (Luscombe) or ignore it altogether (Thacker).

Kyles's *Jew of Malta* was another example of an anti-Christian production of an anti-Semitic text. It opposed a witty and adroit Alun Armstrong as Barabas against a ruthless and hard-faced John Carlisle as Ferneze. Moreover this production left us in no doubt who the real villain was. At the opening, Machevill's prologue was spoken from a trapeze in a savage mock-Italian drawl (Plate J). The critics commented on the effect of drawing Machevill up from beneath the stage: Michael Billington described him as 'rising from some Satanic pit', and Irving Wardle wrote of him being 'winched from the infernal regions as a *diabolus ex machina* caressingly describing the havoc to come'.[33] At the end of the play, as the trapeze which had just lowered Barabas into the boiling cauldron was raised from the trapdoor, Ferneze stepped on to it to give his last speech – and at the lines: 'So march away, and let due praise be given / Neither to Fate nor Fortune, but to Heaven' (V. v. 124–5), he transformed himself into Machevill, adopting his black hair and using the accent of the opening prologue.[34] The real Machevill, the production assured us, was not the wicked Jew but the scheming and successful Christian Governor. Read against their own anti-Semitic grain then, it is possible to continue to stage these plays and avoid the charge of racism but this saving of the appearances has not always been possible.

II

By the year of Marlowe's and Shakespeare's birth, Jews had been officially banned from England for over three hundred years. England had excelled in its hostility towards the Jews, expelling, following a series of massacres, the entire Jewish population from its national territory. Before their official expulsion Jews, had been subject to special laws; they had no right of inheritance as they were legally regarded as royal serfs, their money going to the crown upon their death. They were disproportionally taxed; constituting 0.25 per cent of the population in the twelfth century and yet supplying the treasury with 8 per cent of its income.[35] The drama of the Middle Ages repeatedly associates its stock Vice/Jew figure with Satan, and the Jews are held directly responsible for the death of Christ. Chaucer's *Prioress's Tale* is representative. In it a seven-year-old learns to sing the Latin anthem 'Gracious Mother of the Redeemer'. He sings it on his way to school which takes him through the Jewish quarter of town. The Jews (who we are told, entertain in their hearts the wasp-nest of Satan), arrange to have his throat cut and his body thrown into a cesspit. The body continues to sing and is eventually recovered while 'the cursed Jues' are hung, drawn and quartered. The tale is significant not merely in the intensity of its racism but in its subscription to and promotion of medieval stereotypes of Semitic violence. Infanticide and child crucifixion were especially common accusations in the Middle Ages and survive well into the early modern period. Moreover, they were supported by 'documentary' evidence:

In France and many Kingdomes they have used yearly to steale a Christian Boy, and to Crucifie him, fastning him to a Crosse, giuing him Gall and Vinegar, and running him in the end thorow with a Spear, to rub their memories afresh into sweet thoughts of their Crucifying Christ. . . . At *Weissenberg* in *Germany* they Crucified a Boy; at Verona they did it, and Venice also. . . . One *Iohn Matthias Tiberinus*, a Phisitian that lived in *Trent*, writeth that in the Citie *Trent, Anno.* 1475. the Jewes Crucified a Boy there called *Simon*, of twenty moneths old; being taken, they confessed, that one cause was to drink his blood for remedie of their disease.[36]

Although published later than Marlowe's play, such accounts crystallise the popular mythologies from which he assembled the stereotypical Jewish cruelty of Barabas. When Barnadine in *The Jew of Malta* tells Jacomo that he has something 'to exclaim against the Jew', his fellow friar replies, 'What, has he crucified a child?' (III. vi. 46–9). Shylock too persistently talks like a cannibal. As he leaves Jessica he tells her, 'I'll go in hate, to feed upon / The prodigal Christian' (II. v. 14–15) and he later tells Salerio that he will use Antonio's flesh 'To bait fish withal. If it will feed nothing else, it will feed my revenge' (III. i. 44).

Other popular myths find their way through to Marlowe's text. Thomas Calvert writes that 'Sometimes they were accused for poysoning of Wells and Springs to make an end of Christians, sometimes for beggering Christians by excessive Usurie and extortion.'[37] Barabas boasts to Ithamore how he has killed 'sick people groaning under walls' and poisoned wells (II. iii. 177–88). He goes on to characterise his way of living, revelling in its sadism:

Then after that was I an usurer,
And with extorting, cozening, forfeiting,
And tricks belonging unto brokery,
I filled the gaols with bankrouts in a year,
And with young orphans planted hospitals,
And every moon made some or other mad,
And now and then one hang himself for grief,
Pinning upon his breast a long great scroll
How I with interest tormented him.
                                    (ll. 192–200)

The 'interest' with which Barabas torments his victims refers not only to the amounts of profit that result from loan-sharking but the fascination with which the spiteful usurer conducts his affairs. Jews were particularly associated with such sadistic financial dealings. For Henrie Smith the rapacity of usury was simply another symptom of Jewish disobedience:

> The first Vsurers which wee read of, were the Iews, which were forbidden to be vsurers; yet for want of faith and loue, Ezechiel and Nehemiah doe shewe, how the Iewes, euen the Iews which receiued this law from God himselfe, did swarue from it as they did from the rest. First they began to lend vpon vsury to strangers, after they began to lend vpon vsury to their brethren; and now there be no such Vsurers vpon the earth, as the Iewes which were forbidden to be Vsurers: whereby you may see, how the malice of man hath turned mercie into crueltie.[38]

Credit and money-lending were outlawed by the Church. Thomas Lodge is adamant about its immorality and the consequent irreligion of those who pursue it: 'this by the commandement is forbidden to be followed, and therefore irreligious are they that vse it.'[39] Usury was condemned on two counts: first it was unjust because it was contrary to natural law, a type of theft, and secondly because of the Aristotelian belief that money was sterile in itself and therefore unable to reproduce naturally. Aquinas states categorically that to 'take usury for money lent is unjust in itself, because this is to sell what does not exist, and this evidently leads to inequality which is contrary to justice'.[40] In his essay 'Of Usury', Francis Bacon notes the proverbial sterility of money, 'it is against nature for money to beget money'.[41] When Antonio tells Shylock that if he furnishes the loan, he will be lending it to his enemy, he too cites the infertile character of money, 'for when did friendship take / A breed for barren metal of his friend?' (I. iii. 128–9). Above all, moneylending was unnatural: 'contrary to nature and common sense [usury] will make that to engender, whiche beeying without life by no waie can encrease'.[42] Roger Fenton likens the reproduction of money to a prodigious and agonising birth, calling such profits 'the brood of money':

> A woman in trauell . . . doth not sweate and labour to bring foorth with greater anguish of minde, then a debtor compelled to bring home the principall with increase. . . . This vsurious increase of money, which is neither fruitfull by nature, as land and cattell:

nor fit for any other secondarie vse, as to feede, or to cure, or to clothe, or to shelter; but onely to procure such things as haue increase and vse in themselues: that such increase (I say) of so barren a thing, as ... money ... is vnnaturall.[43]

For Francis Meres, the activity of usury is as bad as child abuse. He cites the same two objections, unnaturalness and infertility: 'As *Pederastiae* is vnlawfull, because it is against kinde: so vsurie and encrease by gold and siluer is vnlawful, because against nature; nature hath made them sterill and barren & vsurie makes them procreatiue.'[44] The notion of the usurer selling time which belongs to God is a common one. In his satire 'Against Mandrus the Vsurer', John Davies is appalled by this temporal trade: 'He giueth nought but that which will not stay: / *That's staylesse* Time, *which he doth precious hold, / And sels a little, for no little Gold.*'[45] Money-lending was a mortal sin, but since Jews were supposed to be going to hell anyway, it didn't matter that they dabbled in it; in the words of two of the anti-usurers of the day, '[the usurer's] soule polluted with this vice, and defiled with that damnable synne, [shall] be cast by the iustice of God into euerlasting tormentes'; 'the woord of God abandonneth Vsurie euen to hel'.[46] Fenton relishes the agony of the damned usurer, 'Most wofull is the passage of the Vsurer out of this life; whose death is detestable, whose end is damnation, whose damnation is without end' and Smith notes that the usurer's sin was sufficient to necessitate their forfeiting a proper burial, 'the Cannon law ... dooth depriue him of his Sepulchre, and will not suffer him to be buried, as though hee were worthie to lie in the earth, but to lie in hell'.[47] For Phillip Stubbes, usury was comparable with homicide. In a section headed 'Vusury equall with Murder', he explains:

And good reason, for he that killeth a a [*sic*] man, riddeth him out of his paines at once, but he that taketh vsury is long in butchering his pacient, suffering him by little & little to languish, and sucking out his hart blood, (that is lucre and gaine) comming forth of him. The Usurer killeth not one, but many, both Husband, Wife, Children, seruants, famelie and all, not sparing any.[48]

Philip Caesar considered the usurer as the meeting place of every kind of vice: 'Thei are called wasters, pollers [extortioners], stealers, of holie thynges, Theeues, Murtherers, Idolaters, cousins to fooles, as ill as madde men, because contrary to the nature of thynges thei make that too engender, whiche cannot fructifie.'[49] The sinfulness of usury was connected with the curse of God upon Adam; Bacon explains: 'the usurer breaketh the first law that was made for mankind after the fall, which was, *in sudore vultûs tui comedes panem tuum*; not, *in sudore vultûs alieni*.'[50] For Meres this was another disqualification of usury from legitimate practice: 'Vsurers live on the sweat of other mens browes, and enioy the fruit of other mens labours, agaynst the ordinaunce of God and man.'[51] The distinction between brother and stranger is critical and the biblical text on usury makes just this distinction: 'Thou shalt not lend vpon vsury to thy brother; vsury of money, vsury of victuals, vsury of any thing that is lent vpon vsury. Vnto a stranger thou maiest lend vpon vsury, but vnto thy brother thou shalt not lend vpon vsury' (Deuteronomy 23: 19–20).[52] Stubbes reluctantly concedes that this at least is a Jewish virtue, 'An vsurer is worse than a Jew, for they to this daye, will not take anye Vsurie of their Brethren, according to the lawe of GOD.'[53] Tubal does not charge Shylock. Fenton is not so magnanimous, hypothesising that the limitation of Jewish usury to Gentiles is a consequence of their own overwhelming greed: 'such was the hardness of Jewish hearts, that if they might not haue taken vsurie of strangers, they also would haue made a pray euen of their owne brethren'.[54]

The Jews were the major (although by no means the only) credit brokers in the Renaissance.[55] Merchants, like Shakespeare's Antonio, were continually using Jewish money to back their ventures and in an age burgeoning with financial dealings and trade, credit and usury were vital. Jewish moneylending literally put the capital into capitalism. Walter Cohen accounts for the popular contempt for Jews and usurers with reference to the period as a time of elemental economic change and he notes the 'crisis of the aristocracy' that such change produced: 'Behind [the] fear [of usury] lay the transition to capitalism: the rise of banking; the increasing need for credit in industrial enterprises; and the growing threat of indebtedness facing both aristocratic landlords and, above all, small, independent producers, who could easily decline to working-class status.'[56] For Frank Whigham the contention between Antonio and Shylock occurs 'in a social context where the old feudal hierarchy is being reordered by the pressures of capitalism' and Camille Pierre Laurent recognises the play's setting as significant as a city-state of economic revolution: 'Venice's society is in transition between the feudal, or aristocratic, and the new bourgeois order.'[57] It is within the context of the transitional state of the economic base that we should place the conflict of Antonio, the trade capitalist, and Shylock, the usurer. For Walter Cohen, the play 'may be seen as a special instance of the struggle, widespread in Europe, between Jewish quasifeudal fiscalism and native bourgeois mercantilism. . . . Boh the characterisation and the outcome of *The Merchant of Venice* mark Antonio as the harbinger of modern capitalism. . . . Shylock is . . . an old man with obsolete values trying to arrest the course of history.'[58] Despite the widespread currency of this theory of feudalistic economic organisation yielding, or being forced to yield, to a capitalistic new order, the theory itself may be over-schematic. Although Antonio and Shylock earn their living in very different ways, there is an obvious symbiosis between them and the economic systems they stand for. According to Fenton, usury 'is so twisted into euery trade and commerce, one mouing the other, by this engine, like the wheeles in a clocke, that it seemeth the very frame and course of traffick must needes be altered before this can be reformed'.[59] Trade needs usury to survive and its necessity was grudgingly admitted during the period. Bacon, while he noted that moneylending could jeopardise trade by putting some merchants out of business, regarded it as a necessary evil: 'howsoever usury in some respect hindereth merchandizing, yet in some other it advanceth it; for it is certain that the greatest part of trade is driven by young merchants upon borrowing at interest; so as, if the usurer either call in or keep back his money, there will ensue presently a great stand of trade'.[60] Bacon recognises that usury stimulates trade and moreover that in the capitalistic new world order, it is here to stay: 'to speak of the abolishing of usury is idle. All states have ever had it, in one kind or rate or other. So as that opinion must be sent to Utopia.'[61] Lodge concurs and suggests ironically that it is the very demand of usurers by the state that makes them so unholy, 'their necessarinesse in this world, makes them vnnecessary for God'.[62] Opposed as the leading protagonists seem to be in *The Merchant of Venice*, there is a pronounced interdependence between them which enacts the interdependence of the two economic systems. Stephen Greenblatt notes the subtle semblance between merchant and Jew which is masked by their ostensible hostility: 'The Jew is charged not with racial deviance or religious impiety but with economic and social crime, crime that is committed not only *against* the dominant Christian society but, in less "pure" form, by that society.'[63]

The common pun on *use* and *Jews (iuse)* makes moneylending the trade of this religious and racial group. The argument followed rapidly that because the Jews were supposedly wealthy, they ought to be made to pay more tax. They were taxed on a quarter of their moveable property as opposed to the tenth that everyone else paid. In Venice they were confined to a specific area of the city and forced to take out a permanent lease on that area at a third above the usual rate. In Marlowe's play, Ferneze's decree ensures that racial discrimination forms just such a basis for paying the Turkish tribute: it 'shall all be levied amongst the Jews, and each of them to pay one half of his estate' (I. ii. 70). The perception of Jewish prosperity frequently made them the object of enmity. In particular the association between Jews and faeces was popular. In the poem, 'A new Song, shewing the crueltie of Gernutus, a Jewe, who, lending to a merchant an hundred crowns, would have a pound of his fleshe, because he could not pay him at the time appointed', which pertinently is set in Venice, the Jew is likened first to a pig and subsequently to a pile of manure:

In Venice towne not long agoe
A cruel Jew did dwell,
Which lived all on usurie,
As Italian writers tell.

Gernutus called was the Jew,
Which never thought to dye,
Nor ever yet did any good
To them in streets that lie.

His life was like a barrow hogge,
That liveth many a day,
Yet never once doth any good,
Until men will him slay.

Or like a filthy heap of dung,
That lyeth in a whoard;
Which never can do any good,
Till it be spread abroad.[64]

This association of usurers with faecal matter seems to be a Renaissance commonplace. Meres likens the activity of borrowing to wallowing in a septic tank: 'As he that tumbleth in the mire, becommeth more foule and filthie: so they become more and more indebted, that haue to doe with Vsurers.'[65] He goes on to develop the association, comparing material and faecal costiveness: 'Cholericke men, that will not be purged in time, dayly increase their humor, til dangerously they be diseased: so they that suffer vsury to increase and grow vpon them, and do not discharge themselues of it, doe run into irrecuperable danger & peril.'[66] Robert Fabyan's *Chronicles* (1516) relishes another alarming instance of the association of Jew with excrement:

> In this yere also fell that happe of the Iewe of Tewkysbury which fell into a Gonge [a cesspit] vpon the Satyrday / and wolde not for Reuerence of his Sabot day be pluckyd out whereof herynge the Erle of Gloucetyr that the Iewe dyd so great Reuerence to his Sabbot daye / thought he wolde doo as moche vnto his Holy day which was Sonday / and so kepte hym there tyll Monday / at whiche season he was foundyn dede.[67]

This and similar anecdotes are cited well over a century later by Thomas Calvert, illustrating their common currency. Indeed Calvert provides his readers with a rhyme which the Jew is supposed to have sung on this occasion: '*I honour holy Sabbaths rest, / I will not rise from my foul nest.*' [68] Caesar insists on this faecal association with the aid of an authority: usurers 'are like to vessels full of all stinking carrion, and filthe. For so doeth S. *Brigel* wright of them in this maner: *The wicked are full of ambition, and couetousnesse, which dooe more stincke in the sight of God, and his sainctes, than any filthe in the eyes of men.*'[69] The proverbial smell of the Jew was associated with the bizarre myth according to which Jewish men were said to menstruate. Calvert explains that this is fitting punishment for seeking the blood of Christ: 'This punishment so shamefull they say is, that Jews, men, as well as females, are punished *cursu menstruo sanguinis*, with a very frequent Bloud-fluxe.'[70] Although Calvert recognises the Christian significance of such a curse ('when we see a bloodie Iew [we] remember our bleeding Iesus'), he is unsure whether to believe it, choosing to 'leave it to the learned to judge and determine by writers or Travellers, whether this be true or no, either that they have a monthly Flux of Blood, or a continuall mal-odoriferous breath'.[71] In his characteristically conciliatory way, Sir Thomas Browne refutes the charge that gives the blunt title to his essay, 'That Iews stinke': 'Now the ground that begat or propagated this assertion, might be the distasteful aversness of the Christian from the Jew, upon the villany of that fact, which made them abominable and stink in the nostrils of all Men. Which real practise, and metaphorical expression, did after proceed into a literal construction; but was a fraudulent illation.'[72] Although, as Browne points out, the myth has its origins in the metaphors of hate, the very existence of his essay demonstrates a common belief in its veracity; as he puts it, 'how dangerous it is in sensible things to use metaphorical expressions unto the people, and what absurd conceits they will swallow in their literals'.[73] The putative impurity of the Jews provided a pretext with which, exactly as in the case of Hitler's Germany, to justify their annihilation. In Leicester, for example, Simon de Montfort was granted the earldom in August 1231. His charter of 1253 reads, 'Know . . . that I, for the good of my soul, and the souls of my ancestors have granted . . . that no Jew or Jewess, in my time or in the time of any of my heirs to the end of the world, shall within the liberty of the town of Leicester, inhabit or remain or obtain a residence.'[74] This kind of malicious victimisation brought about a whole string of thirteenth-century Jewish massacres at places including York, King's Lynn and Stamford. After 1217 Jews were compelled to wear the yellow badge and by 1282 only one synagogue remained in London. Having twice petitioned to leave England, they were finally expelled in 1290 not to be re-admitted until 1655 when Cromwell allowed new Jewish settlement.[75]

III

It is frequently argued that because there was no open Jewish community to form the target of anti-Semitism at the time when Marlowe and Shakespeare wrote, *The Jew of Malta* and *The Merchant of Venice* cannot be racist. Not only does this ignore the causal relationship between anti-Semitic propaganda and anti-Semitic violence, but it overlooks the importance of the titles of the plays themselves. Marlowe's other major plays centre dramatically on a main character and their titles coincide with their central protagonists: *Tamburlaine, Dr Faustus, Edward II*. This play is not called *Barabas*, because Marlowe is much more interested in exploiting a stereotype of Jewishness than exploring an individual. The title page of the 1633 Quarto edition actually calls the play *The Famous Tragedy of the Rich Ievv of Malta*. This preference for labelling Barabas a Jew before portraying him as a fully characterised individual is borne out by the play. Machevill says that he is come 'to present the tragedy of a Jew' (Prologue. 30) but never names him. When Barabas instructs the merchant to pay the customs duties with his credit, he describes himself as the Jew of Malta before giving his name: 'Go tell 'em the Jew of Malta sent thee, man: / Tush, who amongst 'em knows not Barabas?' (I. i. 66–7). Abigail identifies herself to the Abbess as 'The hopeless daughter of a hapless Jew / The Jew of Malta, wretched Barabas' (I. ii. 316–17). Repeatedly throughout the play, Barabas is a rich Jew *before* he is man, merchant, bourgeois figure or father. Even when he is named, it is after the person for whom Christ most immediately died, the criminal who was pardoned leaving Christ to be crucified in his place – a fact of which, as the note by Richard Baines protests, Marlowe was gleefully aware since he is alleged to have held the opinion 'That Christ deserved better to die than Barabbas and that the Jews made a good choice though Barabbas were both a thief and a murderer.'[76] The choice of character name underlines the charge of deicide levelled at all Jews in Marlowe's time.

Shakespeare's title is similarly intriguing. Despite the widespread contempt for usury and the anti-Semitism that it frequently spawned, *The Merchant of Venice*, as we have seen, is not infrequently considered to be a comedy – albeit a problem comedy. This certainly seems to have been the case in the Renaissance. The quarto editions describe the play in their running-titles as 'a comical history' while the First Folio includes it with the comedies. In 1598 Francis Meres had grouped the play with other more straightforwardly recognisable comedies such as 'his *Gentlemen of Verona*, his *Errors*, his *Loues labors lost* [and the tantalising] *Loue labours wonne*'.[77] I have written in Chapter 2 of the conspiratorial or consensual nature of the titles of Shakespeare's comedies. Shakespeare's tragedies, which are essentially about the isolation of an individual, the impossibility of his (Shakespeare is usually only interested in male protagonists) integration into his community, have titles that foreground a single individual against a usually hostile social group: *Hamlet*, *Othello*, *King Lear*, *Macbeth*. *The Merchant of Venice* is a curious exception. It appears to offer a single protagonist and isolate him/her against the background of a city – a fixed and identifiable social group. But who is the merchant? Antonio, whose mercantile success and failure form the rise-and-fall structure of the play, or Shylock to whose fiscal passions the play pays such close attention, or even Portia who, when she intervenes in the court, displays an acute awareness of Venetian economic and legal structures? The drama never tells us and perhaps this is why the play which has traditionally been labelled a comedy with its bald racism, homophobia and threat to cut out lumps of living flesh, sits so uneasily in this category; the text stages 'a rebellion against the expectations of its own title'.[78] In her programme note for Peter Hall's production Barbara Everett roundly states that 'The Merchant of the play's title is Antonio . . . '. If this is the case, one wonders why Shakespeare (of whose titles over half consist of names) did not entitle the play after its protagonist. Moreover, this misgiving was given particular emphasis by Peter Hall's *Merchant*, because what it rightly urged us to recognise was that *all* the characters are in their own ways business adventurers: Antonio, Bassanio, Shylock and Portia. When Gobbo shifted his allegiance from Shylock to Bassanio, he swaggered on in his new livery; everyone in this Venice aspired to be upwardly mobile. When the play is first mentioned in the Stationers' Register on 22 July 1598, it appears as *a booke of the Marchaunt of Venyce or otherwise called the Iewe of Venyce*. The fact that the play has two alternative titles perhaps indicates that we are required to puzzle, rather more than Everett suggests, over the identity of its protagonist. It also acknowledges its debt to Marlowe's play and it is to the nature of this debt that I now wish to turn.

Although the precise quantification of this debt is impossible to determine, it is generally acknowledged that Shakespeare's play stems from that of Marlowe.[79] Shakespeare may even have acted in *The Jew of Malta* in the early 1590s and this would certainly account for its extraordinary influence on *The Merchant*.[80] Traditional criticism sees Marlowe as John the Baptist to the Shakespearean Messiah but although there is little doubt that the Bard's eventual achievements outshine those of his prophet, it should be remembered that by the year of his death (1593), Marlowe had effectively appropriated and interpreted blank verse and fully realised the extent of its dramatic potentialities (as the closing speeches of *Dr Faustus* illustrate).

In terms of plot, *The Jew of Malta* and *The Merchant of Venice* are indeed alike; in each an isolated Jew exists within a morally dubious Christian society and the plays explore, through the interrelated themes of wealth, political power and geographical range, the tensions thrown up by such a relationship. In each case the Jew is accompanied by a servant who either leaves him (Gobbo) or betrays him (Ithamore). Both Jews' families are represented by a single daughter and in both cases the desire of this daughter to marry 'out' causes a rift between generations. The final downfall takes place in the teeth of political triumph. Barabas has been given the governorship of Malta and victory over Ferneze, while the duke and Portia have granted Shylock's legal suit. Barabas is physically destroyed, while Shylock's humiliation, confiscation of his property and compulsory religious conversion are represented as a fate worse than death (IV. i. 369–72).

The differences between the plays may appear even more spectacular. Structurally, for instance, Marlowe's play has neither an alternative setting that corresponds to Shakespeare's Belmont nor any subplot corresponding to the confusion over the rings. But more important is the difference between the dramaturgies of the plays signified in the alternative titles of Shakespeare's play: *The Iewe of Venyce / The Marchaunt of Venyce*. Near the beginning of Marlowe's play, Barabas describes his fleet:

> I hope my ships
> I sent for Egypt and the bordering isles
> Are gotten up by Nilus' winding banks;
> Mine argosy from Alexandria,
> Loaden with spice and silks, now under sail,
> Are smoothly gliding down by Candy shore
> To Malta, through our Mediterranean sea.
> (I. i. 41–7)

The Jew of Malta and the merchant of Malta are the same person but in Shakespeare's play the argosies that come 'From Tripolis, from Mexico, and England, / From Lisbon, Barbary, and India' (III. ii. 270–1) do not belong to Shylock. If Everett is right that the eponymous merchant is Antonio (and most of the play's commentators agree with her), then Shakespeare has refocused the structure of Marlowe's play and the actions of the Jew become contingent upon those of his society as a whole. Barabas is largely successful in maintaining his autonomy; he has no loyalties and therefore has no friends. He divides his enemies and enflames their mutual hatred, turning Turk against Christian and betraying Christian to Turk. He repeatedly resorts to role-playing, disguising himself as a French lute player, feigning death, pretending to lament his loss of wealth (when in fact he has already taken the precaution of hiding coins under a floor-board in preparation for such a seizure) and publicly scorning his daughter's mock-apostasy to enable her to recover his booty. Moreover, Barabas is quite prepared to betray the trust of his fellow Jews. Debating their corporate action in the face of their unreasonable financial burden, Barabas assures them, 'If anything shall there concern our state, / Assure yourselves I'll look (*Aside.*) unto myself' (I. i. 170–1). On the one hand, Barabas is identified by others as a Jew. In terms of his self-identification, however, he is without racial obligation. He is convinced of his personal superiority: 'Barabas is . . . framed of finer mould than common men' (I. ii. 219–20) and he informs the audience that 'Howe'er the world go, I'll make sure for one' (I. i. 184). Barabas displays a selective loyalty unashamedly articulated and ruthless in its self-interest. Shylock, by contrast, is solidly and faithfully Jewish. Although he does not have the money himself he is confident that 'Tubal, a wealthy Hebrew of my tribe, / Will furnish me' (I. iii. 52–3).

The fundamental difference between the plays emerges in the attitude towards religious faith in Venice and Malta. In Bill Alexander's 1987 version of *The Merchant*, Antonio was dragged into the courtroom with his arms outstretched on a horizontal plank. Shylock (Antony Sher, see Plate K) washed his hands, chanted ritualistically and put on a religious shawl. The scene was plainly meant to allude to the Pharisees demanding the death of Christ. In any case, Shylock was about to perform a holy sacrifice rather than a murder. This version of the courtroom scene certainly fits with the seriousness with which Shylock regards his religion. James C. Bulman points out that Sher's performance, especially in the trial scene, was suggestive of 'fundamentalist' religions unassimilated by and arousing the moral opprobrium of the West:

> Sher's Shylock invoked the image of such alien and often misunderstood peoples, ignorance of whose traditions and values all too readily has led to racial prejudice. His behaviour at the trial played on audiences' fears of religious fanaticism, the blood ritual recalling not Judaism, but the vengeful outbursts of an ayatollah bent on destroying the Great Satan – and settling for the heart of Salman Rushdie.[81]

Shylock is certainly firm in his religious observance as Barabas would never be. He tells Bassanio that he will not eat pork and furthermore that he must forgo Christian company during the most sacramental phases of his daily life: 'I will not eat with you, drink with you, nor pray with you' (I. iii. 32). He is, as we have seen, loyal to other Jews, and desirous that Jessica should marry one. He is familiar with the Old Testament and cites the story of Jacob tending Laban's sheep to Antonio. In the courtroom scene, Shylock imbues his 'bond' with the vehemence of religiosity: 'And by our holy Sabbath have I sworn / To have the due and forfeit of my bond' (IV. i. 36–7).[82]

In contrast, Barabas's pursuit of his religion is conducted in line with Machevill's opinion expressed in the prologue: 'I count religion but a childish toy, / And hold there is no sin but ignorance' (ll. 14–15). In *The Prince*, Machiavelli had insisted upon the cultivation, in the absence of religious conviction, of a religious persona:

> it is not necessary for a prince to have all of the above mentioned qualities [wisdom, goodness, piety, honour], but it is very necessary for him to appear to have them. Furthermore, I shall be so bold as to assert this: that having them and practising them at all times is harmful; and appearing to have them is useful; for instance, to seem merciful, faithful, humane, trustworthy, religious. . . . And it is essential to understand this: that a prince, and especially a new prince, cannot observe all those things for which men are considered good, for in order to maintain the state he is often obliged to act against his promise, against charity, against humanity, and against religion.[83]

Barabas tells his daughter that it is morally acceptable to disguise herself as a nun 'for religion / Hides many mischiefs from suspicion' (I. ii. 280–1). Everybody on Malta works out their intricate machinations under the guise of religious protestation. Ferneze justifies the burden of the tax on the grounds that the guilt of the Jews has somehow brought it about in the first place: 'through our sufferance of your hateful lives / (Who stand accursed in the sight of Heaven) / These taxes and afflictions are befallen' (I. ii. 63–5). The running smut about the lewd behaviour of the nuns and the friars, which is confirmed when Barnadine laments that Abigail has died a virgin (III. vi. 41), makes a mockery of the celibacy of Catholic orders. Elsewhere the ironies of religious hypocrisy are even more trenchant. Ithamore remarks that 'To undo a Jew is charity, and not sin' (IV. iv. 85) and Barabas tells Abigail that 'It's no sin to deceive a Christian' (II. iii. 311). Paradoxically neither of them seems aware of the religious vocabulary that they are using. Again, Ferneze tells Barabas that the impounding of his goods will have the effect of sparing those of his countrymen 'we take particularly thine / To save the ruin of a multitude: / And better one want for a common good / Than many perish for a private man' (I. ii. 97–100). This is a reworking of the advice of Caiaphas who urges the Pharisees to recognise that 'it is expedient for us, that one man should die for the people, and that the whole nation perish not' (John 11: 50).

As religion is transmuted into a smokescreen for political manipulation, so relationships, both familial and marital, mask a sinister interest in financial viability. The notion of maintaining a Jewish lineage is, as we would expect, of greater importance to Shylock than Barabas. Jessica's father is plainly worried about the bad influence of witnessing Christian over-indulgence. As he leaves her on the night of the masque, he warns her to

> Lock up my doors, and when you hear the drum,
> And the vile squealing of the wry-neck'd fife,
> Clamber not you up to the casements then,
> Nor thrust your head into the public street
> To gaze on Christian fools with varnish'd faces.
>   (II. v. 28–32)

His contempt for Christian foppery is clear as is his desire to keep her away from the licence of carnival. The family tradition is crucial to Shylock and his daughter's virginity is its prerequisite. Shylock voices his paternal frustration in the courtroom: 'I have a daughter— / Would any of the stock of Barrabas / Had been her husband, rather than a Christian!' (IV. i. 290–2). Barabas challenges his daughter rather more abrasively, 'Are there not Jews enow in Malta, / But thou must dote upon a Christian?' (II. iii. 360–1). Semitic marriage is intended to promulgate the race and the choice of a Jewish husband is the father's prerogative; the apparent lottery of Portia's betrothal would never do. The reproductive potency of the Jews contrasts sharply with the familial chaos of the Christians. When, more through luck than design, Bassanio ends up with Portia (and Gratiano with Nerissa, which is contingent on the success of Bassanio's choice of casket), the union is instantly ruptured by the necessity of returning to Venice to the aid of Antonio:

First go with me to church and call me wife,
And then away to Venice to your friend;
For never shall you lie by Portia's side
With an unquiet soul . . . .
My maid Nerissa and myself meantime
Will live as maids and widows.

(III. ii. 305–11)

The subsequent confusion over the rings and the mock infideli-
ties of Portia and Nerissa, who claim to have slept with the lawyer
and his assistant, shroud with comic complexity and dilute with
levity the Christian sacrament of marriage. Problems of love rather
than lineage dog these romantic ventures. Shylock's conception of
marriage seems much more profound: the immortality of his race
is what counts. Relating the story from Genesis, in which Jacob
induced the conception of spotted lambs by placing coloured rods
in front of the 'woolly breeders', Shylock concludes, 'thrift is bless-
ing if men steal it not' (I. iii. 85). Antonio asks him the point of the
anecdote: 'Was this inserted to make interest good? / Or is your
gold and silver ewes and rams?' (ll. 89–90) Shylock replies sagely,
'I cannot tell; I make it breed as fast.' The use/iues association is
implicit, here overlaid with another homonym – ewes: Shylock means
that his familial and financial potency is assured. This mercenary
attitude to familial relationships is not monopolised by Shylock.
Bassanio understands the monetary advantages of marrying Portia.
He tells Antonio quite unashamedly that through marrying her,
he will 'get clear of all the debts I owe' (I. i. 134) and his description of her beauty is ruthlessly materialistic: 'her sunny locks /
Hang on her temples like a golden fleece . . . / And many Jasons come in
quest of her' (ll. 169–72). Later Gratiano tactlessly blurts out this
pastoral acquisitiveness in front of their new wives: 'We are the
Jasons, we have won the fleece' (III. ii. 243). It is in the light of this
ovine metaphor that we should understand Antonio's reference to
himself as a 'tainted wether of the flock' (IV. i. 114). The unmarried
and conventionally homosexual merchant images himself as a castrated ram.[84] It is thus no surprise that Shylock's anecdote, in which
siring offspring is a guarantee of economic and social advancement,
is incomprehensible to Antonio. Far from viewing money with its
Aristotelian associations of sterility and barrenness, Shylock regards
it as teeming. Moreover, its fecundity is not unrelated to his own
sexual prowess. It is Antonio, in Shylock's scheme of things, that

is sterile in his homosexuality: the merchant is not a fecund ewe-surer, but an impotent wether.

As well as Portia, Jessica is a sound proposition. When she deserts her father, Shylock laments the loss of his fortune as much as the loss of his daughter: 'Two thousand ducats in that, and other precious, precious jewels. I would my daughter were dead at my foot, and the jewels in her ear; would she were hears'd at my foot and the ducats in her coffin!' (III. i. 74). Jessica has stolen not only his ducats, but his 'two stones, two rich and precious stones' (II. viii. 20). She has taken his jewels but also, as she is his only heir, she has deprived him of his lineage; she has metaphorically castrated him – *stones* was the Renaissance slang for 'testicles'.[85] Children and money are interchangeable commodities for the patriarch and as she 'gild[s]' herself (II. vi. 49) so she gelds her father.[86] Gratiano literalises this vocabulary of emasculation when he threatens to 'mar the young clerk's pen' (V. i. 237) for sleeping with Nerissa and, as he wishes that the judge's clerk 'were gelt that had it, for my part' (l. 144), he identifies sexual transgression as the ultimate cause of symbolic castration. Shylock's money, his jewels, his daughter and metaphorically his sexual potency are lost; but more serious than all of these is the disqualification from Jewish worship. According to Deuteronomy 23: 1, 'Hee that is wounded in the stones, or hath his priuie member cut off, shall not enter into the Congregation of the LORD.' Ultimately then his daughter's betrayal is a religious one.

The physical and emotional are bonded to the financial. Portia tells her new husband, 'Since you are dear bought, I will love you dear' (III. ii. 315), and Antonio associates his money with the physicality of his love, telling Bassanio, 'My purse, my person, my extremest means, / Lie all unlock'd to your occasions' (I. i. 138–9).[87] It is Portia's portion (the Renaissance term for a dowry)[88] which attracts Bassanio to her and which is offered in lieu of his friend's life. Her whole estate is surrendered to him as is her body – Belmont, or the 'beautiful mountain' of the *mons veneris* – in Portia's equivalent of Antonio's purse / person analogy: 'Myself, and what is mine, to you and yours / Is now converted' (III. ii. 167–8).[89]

In the fiercely materialistic world of Marlowe's play, value is em*bodied*: slaves have their price written on their backs. When Abigail rescues her father's coins, his rapturous jubilation oscillates between daughter and money: 'Oh girl, oh gold, oh beauty, oh my bliss!' (II. i. 53). Later, Barabas tells Lodowick that his daughter will be a diamond for his delectation and possession. Personal integrity is continually reified, every man – and even more so, woman – has his / her price. In the course of his mock conversion, Barabas describes himself as 'a covetous wretch, / That would for lucre's sake have sold my soul' (IV. i. 52–3). Later, when Dr Faustus finally does part with his soul, a written credit note has replaced hard cash.

IV

If they're black, send them back; if they're yids, kill their kids.[90]

At its extreme the voracious materialism of the English Renaissance, which we have seen shadowed in these plays, expresses the aspirations of an age which is beginning to find its capitalistic feet. These plays are situated on the faultline between an economy of ready cash and credit balances; they dramatise what James Shapiro has recently called 'a cultural identity crisis'.[91] The anti-Semitism that they contain is symptomatic of their particular historical position and the economic revolution taking place at the time of their composition. Their prejudice is thus, mercifully, historically specific. Yet, despite their historical distance, both plays continue to resonate in a period which operates according to such ghoulish formulae as 'separate development' and 'ethnic cleansing'. In the same way as those of twenties and thirties Germany, current economic and social problems are expressing themselves in popular racism. Now, more than ever, it is time to divest the Marlovian and Shakespearean texts of their complacent and commonplace defences. As spectators, critics and students of these plays, it is our responsibility to ensure that their continued dissemination is accompanied by an awareness of their historical specificity and their racist potentialities.

Notes

1. Adolf Hitler, *Mein Kampf,* trans. Ralph Manheim (1973), p. 113.
2. Walter Benjamin, *Illuminations,* trans. Harry Zohn, ed. Hannah Arendt (1973), p. 258.
3. *Is Shakespeare Still Our Contemporary?* ed. John Elsom (1989), pp. 143–4.
4. Cited by Morton Cohen in 'Shylock through the looking glass', *The Guardian,* 4 August 1989.

5.   D. M. Cohen, 'The Jew and Shylock', *Shakespeare Quarterly*, 31 (1980), 53–63, p. 53.
6.   Ibid., p. 53.
7.   W. H. Auden, *The Dyer's Hand and Other Essays* (1963), pp. 223, 221.
8.   *Is Shakespeare Still Our Contemporary?*, p. 179. When Thacker produced *The Two Gentlemen of Verona* for the RSC in 1991–2, he cut the play's anti-Semitism by excising the following lines: 'A Jew would have wept to have seen our parting' (II. iii. 9); 'thou art an Hebrew, a Jew, and not worth the name of a Christian' (II. v. 44).
9.   Tim Luscombe, *The Merchant of Venice and Volpone, Background Notes* (1990), p. 2.
10.   John Barton, *Playing Shakespeare* (1984), pp. 170–1.
11.   Nevill Coghill, 'The Basis of Shakespearean Comedy', *Essays and Studies*, 3 (1950), 1–28, p. 23. David Suchet agrees, 'Shylock himself is perhaps the first Jew in literature to have the chance of his soul being saved' (*Playing Shakespeare*, p. 170).
12.   Marion D. Perret, 'Shakespeare and Anti-Semitism', in *Shakespeare on Television: An Anthology of Essays and Reviews*, ed. J. C. Bulman and H. R. Coursen (1983), 156–68, p. 167.
13.   Ibid., p. 167.
14.   Ibid., p. 167.
15.   Marion D. Perret, 'Shakespeare's Jew: Preconception and Performance', *Shakespeare Studies*, 20 (1988), 261–8, pp. 265–6.
16.   Horst Meller, 'A Pound of Flesh and the Economics of Christian Grace: Shakespeare's *Merchant of Venice*', in *Essays on Shakespeare in Honour of A. A. Ansari*, ed. T. R. Sharma (Meerut, 1986), 150–74, p. 154.
17.   Werner Habicht, 'Shakespeare and Theatre Politics in the Third Reich', in *The Play Out of Context: Transferring Plays from Culture to Culture*, ed. Hanna Scolnicov and Peter Holland (Cambridge, 1989), 110–20, p. 113.
18.   James Shapiro, *Shakespeare and the Jews* (Southampton, 1992), p. 23.
19.   Maria Verch, '*The Merchant of Venice* on the German Stage since 1945', *Theatre History Studies*, 1985, 84–94, p. 91.
20.   Habicht, 'Shakespeare and Theatre Politics', p. 116.
21.   Cited by Avraham Oz, 'Transformations of Authenticity: *The Merchant of Venice* in Israel 1936–1980', *Shakespeare Jahrbuch*, 1983, 165–77, pp. 168–9.
22.   Ibid., p. 169.
23.   Ibid., p. 175.
24.   William Frankel, *The Times*, 17 April 1984.
25.   Ibid.
26.   David Hewson, *The Times*, 4 May 1984.
27.   Ian McDiarmid, *The Times*, 9 April 1984.
28.   This threat was withdrawn after *The Times* published a reply from McDiarmid on its letters page. *The Times*, 1 May 1984; see also the *Jewish Chronicle*, 4 May 1984.
29.   McDiarmid, 'Shylock in *The Merchant of Venice*', in *Players of Shakespeare 2*, ed. Russell Jackson and Robert Smallwood (Cambridge, 1988), 45–54, pp. 47–54.

30. Jean-Marie Maguin, 'The Jew of Malta: Marlowe's Ideological Stance and the Play-World's Ethos', *Cahiers Elisabéthains*, 27 (1985), 17–26, p. 17.
31. *This Golden Round: The Royal Shakespeare Company at the Swan*, ed. Ronnie Mulryne and Margaret Shewring (Stratford-upon-Avon, 1989), p. 75.
32. *The Guardian*, 13 April 1994.
33. Michael Billington, *The Guardian*, 16 July 1987; Irving Wardle, *The Times*, 15 July 1987.
34. All references to *The Jew of Malta* are from the edition by Peter J. Smith (1994).
35. Toby Lelyveld, *Shylock on the Stage* (1961), p. 5.
36. Thomas Calvert, *A Diatriba of the Iews Estate* (York, 1648), pp. 18–19, 31.
37. Ibid., p. 18.
38. Henrie Smith, *The Sermons of Master Henrie Smith, gathered into one volume* (1592), p. 165.
39. Thomas Lodge, *An Alarvm against Vsurers. Containing tryed experiences against worldly abuses* (1584), F iii^r.
40. Aquinas, *Summa Theologica*, trans. fathers of the English Dominican Province, second edn, 22 vols (1920), X, 330–1.
41. Francis Bacon, *Essays*, introduced by Michael J. Hawkins (1973), p. 123.
42. Philip Caesar, *A General Discovse Against the damnable sect of Vsurers* (1578), p. 5^v.
43. Roger Fenton, *A Treatise of Vsurie* (1611), pp. 6–7.
44. Francis Meres, *Palladis Tamia* (1598), Tt 2^r.
45. John Davies, *The Scourge of Folly* (1611), pp. 71–2.
46. Caesar, *General Discovse*, p. 2^v; Phillip Stubbes, *The Anatomy of Abuses* (1583), K vii^r.
47. Fenton, *Treatise*, p. 55; Smith, *Sermons*, pp. 186–7.
48. Stubbes, *Anatomy*, K vii^r. The image of the usurer sucking out the heart of the victim anticipates Shylock's demand to have 'A pound of flesh, to be ... cut off / Nearest the merchant's heart' (IV. i. 227–8).
49. Caesar, *Discovse*, p. 3^v.
50. Bacon, *Essays*, p. 123.
51. Meres, *Palladis Tamia*, Tt 2^v.
52. Henrie Smith also notes Exodus 22 and Leviticus 25 as biblical texts outlawing usury (*Sermons*, pp. 168). Among the humanist sources regularly cited against usury were Plato, Aristotle, Cato, Seneca, Pliny, Plutarch (see, for example, Fenton, *Treatise*, pp. 66–7).
53. Stubbes, *Anatomy*, K viii^v.
54. Fenton, *Treatise*, p. 45.
55. Fenton cites S. Bernard, 'if the Iewes were any where wanting, Christian Vsurers did play the Iewes worse then themselues', ibid., p. 52.
56. Walter Cohen, 'The Merchant of Venice and the Possibilities of Historical Criticism', *ELH*, 49 (1982), 765–89, pp. 767–8.
57. Frank Whigham, 'Ideology and Class Conduct in *The Merchant of Venice*', *Renaissance Drama*, 10 (1979), 93–115, p. 103; Camille Pierre

Laurent, 'Dog, Fiend and Christian, or Shylock's Conversion', *Cahiers Elisabéthains*, 26 (1984), 15–27, p. 17.

58. Cohen, '*The Merchant of Venice* and the Problems of Historical Criticism', p. 771.
59. Fenton, *Treatise*, p. 2.
60. Bacon, *Essays*, p. 124.
61. Ibid., p. 124.
62. Lodge, *Alarvm*, E ii^v.
63. Stephen J. Greenblatt, *Learning to Curse: Essays in Early Modern Culture* (1990), p. 41.
64. *Percy's Reliques of Ancient English Poetry*, ed. Ernest Rhys, 2 vols (n.d.), I, 202–3.
65. Meres, *Palladis Tamia*, Tt 2^v.
66. Ibid., Tt 2^v.
67. Robert Fabyan, *Chronicles*, 2 vols (1516), II, fol. xxxii^r.
68. Calvert, *Diatriba*, pp. 41–2. 'In the reign of *Henry* the third, a Iew fell into a Jakes at Tewkesbury in *England*, to whom it being offered to draw him out, it being Saturday, (the Iews Sabbath) he refused, lest he should pollute the holinesse of the day. The thing comming to the chiefe Lord of the Countrey, he commanded they should let him lie the next day too, for the honour of the Lords Day, the Christians Sabbath, lest he should prophane it; so by abiding in it that day also, he perished. . . . The like was the lot of a Iew at *Meidenburg* in *Germany*, that sat two dayes together in so uncomfortable a place, the one day for the honour of their Sabbath, the other for the Christians pleasure, to give honour to ours.' Ibid., pp. 41–2.
69. Caesar, *Discovse*, p. 4^r.
70. Calvert, *Diatriba*, p. 20.
71. Ibid., p. 31.
72. Sir Thomas Browne, *Works*, ed. Sir Geoffrey Keynes, 4 vols (1964), II, 301.
73. Ibid., p. 301.
74. Cited by Colin Richmond, 'Englishness and Medieval Anglo-Jewry', in *The Jewish Heritage in British History: Englishness and Jewishness*, ed. Tony Kushner (1992), 42–59, p. 48. Ironically, modern Leicester 'boasts' a street, a concert hall and, most recently, a new university named after this brutal anti-Semite.
75. In fact, despite the expulsion order, there was certainly a rump Jewish population, though its size remains a matter of conjecture. The number was swollen by *Marranos*, Jews who had fled from the Inquisition. The size of the Jewish population is difficult to determine, since they usually professed to being Christian and only secretly observed Jewish ritual.
76. The Baines note is conveniently available in *Christopher Marlowe, Complete Poems and Plays*, ed. E. D. Pendry and J. C. Maxwell (1976), p. 513.
77. Meres, *Palladis Tamia*, Oo 2^r.
78. Kiernan Ryan, *Shakespeare* (1989), p. 21.
79. Maurice Charney, 'Jessica's Turquoise Ring and Abigail's Poisoned

Porridge: Shakespeare and Marlowe as Rivals and Imitators', *Renaissance Drama*, 10, (1979), 33–44, p. 43.

80. James Shapiro, '"Which is *The Merchant* here and which *The Jew*?": Shakespeare and the Economics of Influence', *Shakespeare Studies*, 20 (1988), 269–79, p. 270.

81. James C. Bulman, *The Merchant of Venice: Shakespeare in Performance* (Manchester and New York, 1991), p. 121.

82. 'Due' appears in the trial scene four times. It is most likely an unfortunate pun drawing together Shylock's religion and his ruthless litigiousness. Note especially 'Three thousand ducats, due unto the Jew' (IV. i. 411).

83. Niccolò Machiavelli, *The Prince*, ed. Peter Bondanella (Oxford, 1984), p. 59.

84. On Antonio's homophobic homosexuality, see Seymour Kleinburg, '*The Merchant of Venice*: The Homosexual as Anti-Semite in Nascent Capitalism', in *Literary Visions of Homosexuality*, ed. Stuart Kellogg (New York, 1983), 113–26, p. 120.

85. Other examples of this usage occur in Shakespeare's plays. In *The Merry Wives of Windsor*, Caius tells Simple in advance of the duel that he 'will cut all his [Hugh's] two stones' (I. iv. 107). In the RSC 1992 production of the play, this meaning was made explicit as Caius placed his sword between Simple's legs and withdrew it on the line. In *Romeo and Juliet*, as the nurse reminisces about the fall of the baby Juliet, she remarks that she had a 'bump [on her brow] as big as a cockerel's stone' (I. iii. 53).

86. See Sonnet 20. 6 for another instance of the *gild / geld* pun.

87. The formulation 'purse and person' is undoubtedly sexual. When Falstaff is reprimanded for exploiting Quickly financially and sexually, the Lord Chief Justice sternly remarks, 'You have, as it appears to me, practised upon the easy-yielding spirit of this woman, and made her serve your uses both in purse and in person' (*II Henry IV*, II. i. 115). Compare also with Barabas as he makes Ithamore his heir: 'My purse, my coffer, and myself is thine' (III. iv. 94).

88. Ann Jennalie Cook, *Making a Match: Courtship in Shakespeare and his Society* (Princeton, 1991), p. 121.

89. Lawrence Normand, 'Reading the Body in *The Merchant of Venice*', *Textual Practice*, 5 (1991), 55–73, p. 70.

90. Demonstration chant of the British National Party. Quoted in *The Independent on Sunday*, 2 August 1992.

91. Shapiro, *Shakespeare and the Jews*, p. 8.

8

Playing with Boys: Homoeroticism and All-Male Companies in Shakespearean Drama

Rance: Was the girl killed before or after you took her clothes off?

Prentice: He wasn't a girl. He was a man.

Mrs Prentice: He was wearing a dress.

Prentice: He was a man for all that.

Rance: Women wear dresses, Prentice, not men. I won't be a party to the wanton destruction of a fine old tradition.[1]

Come, gentle Ganymede, and play with me[2]

I

Shakespeare's privileged position at the centre of our culture is beyond contention. Homosexuality, however, is far from dominant and is subject always to the hegemonic pressures of heterosexuality. The Local Government Act of 1988 is an instance of this state-sponsored oppression of 'deviant' sexualities. Under Section 28 of the act, a local authority may not 'intentionally promote homosexuality or publish material with the intention of promoting homosexuality'. There is an obvious tension between the desire of the State to erect its cultural totems around the figure of the Bard and the suggestion that Renaissance theatre, in its wholesale transvestism, utilised a form of dramatic representation which (according to its contemporary opponents) promoted homosexuality. Indeed in his enthusiasm for dressing boys as girls and having them pretend to be boys, Shakespeare seems to be somewhat vague about the 'correct' identification of the two sexes and deliberately to

182

undermine the heterosexual erotic practice founded upon it. Perish the thought that Shakespeare himself might be liable for prosecution under Section 28!

At stake in any discussion of Renaissance representations of homoeroticism are ideological questions about 'High Culture' reified in the figure of the playwright. As Simon Shepherd notes, 'Discussion of homosexuality in Shakspeer seems to be motivated not by an interest in Renaissance sexuality but by Shakespaire's national status. Criticism's task is to discover a fitting sexuality for the National Bard.'[3] The most obvious symptom of this appropriation of Shakespeare for a heterosexually ordered establishment is a critical embarrassment in the face of textual and dramatic practices which are homoerotic. Gwyn Williams's *Person and Persona* is typical of this: 'It could have been his nearness to a homosexual experience, coupled with acquaintanceship with homosexuals, which gave Shakespeare the sympathy he shows for them in his works.'[4] This is literary criticism at its most blinkered and offensive. Firstly, it is spuriously based on the sexual orientation of Shakespeare himself – a personal quality which is entirely unknowable. Secondly, by stating that Shakespeare is 'near' a homosexual experience, it implies that he retains some distance and thus remains 'untainted' by it. Thirdly, by showing sympathy 'for *them* in his works' both Bard and critic are placed safely on the other side of the divide extending their indulgent compassion to *those* poor queers. The normative suggestion has all the clumsy intentionality of the statement: 'Some of Shakespeare's best friends were gay!' Later in his discussion of Antonio in *The Merchant of Venice*, Williams compounds his critical discomfiture: 'Like the other Antonio [in *Twelfth Night*], he has nothing effeminate about him, and his only fault in our eyes may be his early anti-semitism.'[5] The logic of the grammar implies first that it is a 'fault' to be 'effeminate' and moreover that effeminacy equals homosexuality. If Williams is dismissive of homosexuality in this way it should come as no surprise that his attitude towards anti-Semitism is less than rigorous. Antonio is guilty, according to Williams, of this prejudice early in the play but the suggestion is that we should acquit him as he has reformed his ways. I would offer as a counter-example the overwhelming injustice of the final court scene. No one here, least of all Antonio, has repented of their early anti-Semitism; the state's final 'justice' is founded upon it. The outstanding assumption of criticism like that of Williams is that, simply, heterosexuality is a better state of affairs, a superior condition to homosexuality. In the wake of Freud it is not unusual to conceptualise the process of maturation as a 'development' from narcissism and same-sex eroticism to adult heterosexuality. In short, homoerotic experience is eclipsed and occluded by an erotic practice predicated on the successful reproduction of the social order as prescribed in state apparatuses such as the church, education (Section 28) and the media.

The consequence of this for literary criticism and more especially for a discussion of Renaissance erotic practices as realised in the drama of the period is that any homoerotic features of early modern texts are edited to provide a prescriptive version of a social organisation hospitable to the morality of market capitalism – what Joseph A. Porter calls 'the canonisation of heterosexuality'.[6] It is with an awareness of as well as a hostility to the political ramifications of this crude reductionism that this chapter attempts to explore the complexities of the representation of homoerotic relationships on the Renaissance and the modern stages and to consider the dramaturgical consequences of the playing of female characters by young males.

II

The recency of the publication of a handful of books on Renaissance homosexuality is testament to the non-canonicity of the subject.[7] In fact, some commentators, in the wake of Foucault's work on the history of sexuality, assert the improbability of the existence of homosexuality in any recognisable form at all in this period. Simon Shepherd contends that 'Elizabethan culture had no conception of "homosexuality" as a positive form of sexuality in its own right.'[8] Christopher Hill is even more emphatic: 'There was no homo-sexual subculture' in sixteenth- and seventeenth-century England.[9] And Alan Bray, whose groundbreaking socio-historical study opened up the territory as a site of debate warns against the inapposite application of modern sexual terminology to a period as historically distant as the Renaissance: 'To talk of an individual in this period as being or not being "a homosexual" is an anachronism and ruinously misleading. . . . the terms in which we now speak of homosexuality cannot readily be translated into those of the sixteenth and seventeenth centuries.'[10] Bray's study maintains that the molly houses of the late seventeenth and early eighteenth centuries were the first indication of an emergent homosexual culture. Bray is not suggesting that homoeroticism *per se* did not previously exist, rather that a perception of it as being a constituent of a distinct and distinctly 'other' kind of erotic modality was not available to the Renaissance. However, despite the widespread currency of the proposal that the early modern period was unable to recognise and certainly reluctant to prosecute homosexuality, a reading of the literature of the period demonstrates that homoerotic sentiments were neither as rare nor as invisible as this thesis might suggest.[11] Richard Barnfield's 'The Teares of an affectionate Shepheard sicke for Loue or The Complaint of *Daphnis* for the Loue of *Ganimede*' is unabashed in its homoerotic promise:

> If it be sinne to loue a sweet-fac'd Boy,
> (Whose amber locks trust vp in golden tramels
> Dangle adowne his louely cheekes with ioy,
> When pearle and flowers his faire haire enamels)
> If it be sinne to loue a louely Lad;
> Oh then sinne I, for whom my soule is sad.[12]

Despite the vehemence of this poetry, Bray is most reluctant to acknowledge that it constitutes an example of homosexual writing. He maintains that 'These poems have a good deal of charm . . . but there is no reason to think that they are [anything but] literary exercises. . . . It was not about homosexuality.'[13] In support of this somewhat surprising assertion, Bray notes that Barnfield's commonplace book contains erotic writing which is 'both robustly pornographic and entirely heterosexual'.[14] Whether or not Barnfield's other writing is heterosexual, the assertion that 'The Teares of an affectionate Shepherd' is homoerotic (irrespective of its being a literary imitation of Vergil's second eclogue)[15] seems undeniable. It may well be that the comparative obscurity of Barnfield's work is itself a symptom of the heterosexist bias of literary commentators and the institutions that support them.[16] Joseph Pequigney in his analysis of Shakespeare's *Sonnets* is incensed by the effective censorship that Barnfield has suffered at the hands of a heterosexist literary establishment. Of Barnfield's *Certain Sonnets* he notes dryly:

> One might have thought that the other Elizabethan sequence that also treats of love for a youthful master-mistress would have received attention – even particular attention – in the vast output

of the Shakespearean commentators. Instead, Barnfield is a dirty little skeleton to be kept in the closet, while insistent and exaggerated claims are advanced for the concept of 'Renaissance friendship'.[17]

Barnfield is not alone in constituting a counter-example to the assertion that homosexuality was unrecognisable in the Renaissance. John Donne's cynical 'Satire I' mentions intercourse with 'thy plump muddy whore, or prostitute boy' (1. 40) and in 'Elegy XI' which warns his mistress not to follow him on his foreign journey in the guise of a page, he notes that her male disguise would incite 'Th' indifferent Italian [to] haunt thee, with such lust and hideous rage / As Lot's fair guests were vexed' (ll. 38–40). Ben Jonson is caustic about the sexual intemperance of his poetic equivalent of Sir Epicure Mammon, the wonderfully named Sir Voluptuous Beast who disports himself with partners female, male and animal!

> While Beast instructs his faire, and innocent wife,
> In the past pleasures of his sensuall life,
> Telling the motions of each petticote,
> *And how his Ganimede mov'd*, and how his goate,
> And now, her (hourely) her own cucqueane makes,
> In varied shapes, which for his lust shee takes:
> What doth he else, but say, leave to be chast,
> Just wife, and, to change me, make womans hast.[18]

In his play about the cross-gendering of male and female, *Epicoene*, Jonson has Truewit comment in a quite unanimated way on the life-style of Clerimont with 'his mistress abroad and his ingle at home'.[19] Everard Guilpin's *Skialetheia* contains ribald poems about Pollio with his 'ingles face' and 'fatte buttocke' and it goes on to satirise Licus, 'VVho is at euery play, and euery night / Sups with his *Ingles*'.[20]

Instances of homosexuality in Shakespeare's work include the relationships of Coriolanus and Aufidius, Antonio and Bassanio, Antonio and Sebastian, and Othello and Iago.[21] As we have seen in Chapter 6 Mercutio's ribald language games and his jealous attitude towards women manifest a form of repressed homoerotic desire for Romeo. In *King Lear*, the Fool laments the proverbial inconstancy of male lovers, 'He's mad that trusts in the tameness of a wolf, a horse's health, a boy's love, or a whore's oath' (III. vi. 18)

while Thersites is less than complimentary about the intimacy between Achilles and Patroclus:

> *Ther.*: Prithee, be silent, boy; I profit not by thy talk; thou art
> said to be Achilles' male varlet.
> *Patr.*: Male varlet, you rogue! What's that?
> *Ther.*: Why, his masculine whore.
>
> (*Troilus and Cressida*, V. i. 13–16)

In assuming the name of Jove's cup-bearer and toy-boy, Rosalind
is explicitly foregrounding the homoerotic dimensions of her relationship with Orlando: the 'implicit associations of Ganymede [are]
with girlish male beauty, transvestism, androgyny, and homosexuality'.[22] In the case of *As You Like It*, the very setting is a signifier of
the play's homoerotic interest. The Forest of Arden is a version of
pastoral and carries with it pastoral's impression as a place of
homoerotic activity: this is a male society. When Eve appears, she
does so as a slut in the shape of Audrey whose sole purpose is to
provide Touchstone with sexual relief. Celia's pseudonym, Aliena,
although adopted with the intention of reflecting her exile from
court, in fact describes the position of all women in Arden. In *As
You Like It* females appear as destructive sexual forces – as Phoebe
the spiteful shepherdess or in the guise of a fatal snake ('Who
with *her* head . . .' IV. iii. 108, my emphasis) or a predatory lioness
'with udders all drawn dry' (l. 113). The only 'woman' who in-
trudes significantly is named in accordance with homoerotic principles; Ganymede is less a woman than a homoerotic/androgynous
genius of the place. This means that Orlando is in a position to
rehearse the heterosexual formulae required of a marital relationship without breaking the fundamental masculine ethos of the
forest society.

While the relationship between Ganymede and Orlando is something of a game (at least for Orlando), that between Cesario and
Orsino is one of erotic attraction on both sides. Valentine remarks
(possibly with a touch of pique) that 'If the Duke continue these
favours towards you, Cesario, you are like to be much advanc'd: he
hath known you but three days, and already you are no stranger'
(I. iv. 1). The intimate scenes between master and servant allow the
fantasy of homoerotic attraction to take place while ensuring that
the final outcome is one in accordance with the requirements of the
comic genre as the couple arrange to be married at the end. Unlike

Ganymede though, Cesario does not remove his disguise because the marriage and the assumption of female identity that it requires, are deferred beyond the end of the play. Unlike Rosalind, we never see Viola in her 'woman's weeds' (V. i. 265). *Twelfth Night* ends without the purgation of homosexuality that takes place in the multiple marriages dignified by Hymen's blessings at the end of *As You Like It*. Indeed even after Cesario has assured everyone that she is Viola, Orsino still seems to think of her as his page, addressing her as 'boy' and 'Cesario'.

To these examples of homoeroticism in Shakespearean drama, we might also add the obvious Marlovian instances, Gaveston, Spenser and the King in *Edward II*, Ganymede and Jove from *Dido* and the impassioned Neptune in *Hero and Leander*. Perhaps the most significant homoerotic text of the period is Shakespeare's sonnet sequence. These examples suggest that Bray's contention – that homosexuality was unrecognisable in the Renaissance – needs refining. Although the word *homosexual* is an invention of the late nineteenth century (the *OED* dates its first use as 1892), the concept was not as exceptional in the literature and culture of the Renaissance as Bray implies.

In an article published eight years after his influential book, Bray maintains the absence of a distinct homosexual culture from the early modern period ('Elizabethan society was one which lacked the idea of a distinct homosexual minority'); but this essay is less strident in its assertion that homoerotic activity was unrecognisable.[23] Bray investigates the discourse of 'friendship' in the period and alerts us to the possibility of labelling male friendship erroneously as homosexuality. He notes a 'surprising affinity' between the concepts of friendship and sodomy and the potential for a modern misreading of the one for the other: 'the public signs of a male friendship – open to all the world to see – could be read in a different and sodomitical light from the one intended'.[24] As an example of this, Bray instances the company of Gaveston and Edward in Marlowe's *Edward II*. He writes, 'the passionate language and the embraces we see between these two men have ready parallels in Elizabethan England in the daily conventions of friendship without being signs of a sodomitical relationship'.[25] Although he later observes (in a surprisingly judgemental way) that 'there are in the relationship . . . dark suggestions of sodomy', the desire to read this as a mere acquaintance seems, at best, obdurate.[26] Bray's argument highlights the difficulty of disengaging the discourses of friendship

from those of homoeroticism and ironically this contention is enough
to undermine his confidence that the two can be separated at all. In
the case of Montaigne's essay 'Of friendship', for example, the
concept is certainly underpinned by an erotic interest. Montaigne
notes that women are incapable of sustaining a relationship of such
intensity as that of male sociality and then goes on to suggest
that a homosocial relationship can only be intensified by physical
intimacy:

> the ordinary sufficiency of women cannot answer this conference
> and communication, the nurse of this sacred bond: nor seeme
> their mindes strong enough to endure the pulling of a knot so
> hard, so fast, and durable. And truly, if without that, such a
> genuine and voluntarie acquaintance might be contracted, where
> not only mindes had this entire jovissance, but also bodies, a
> share of the alliance, and where a man might wholly be engaged:
> It is certaine, that friendship would thereby be more compleat
> and full.[27]

If the difficulty in delineating friendship from homosexuality is
there, might taking advantage of such indeterminacy not be a deliberate strategy of the writer? Thomas Stehling, in his discussion of
medieval homoerotic poetry, notes that the convention of friendship may have functioned as a vehicle through which to voice the
lineaments of homoerotic desire: 'Love poems between men elab-
orated other poetic conventions; most frequently they infused the
heat of passion into conventional expressions of friendship.'[28]
Homoeroticism is thus encoded into a language of friendship, voicing allegorically an emotion which, if openly expressed, could have
been severely punished. This is almost certainly the way to understand Montaigne's essay and may also provide useful insights into
the Barnfield poems as well.

One negative effect of Bray's over-cautious reluctance to concede
the existence of homosexuality in the early modern period is that
homosexuality itself is censored into silence; it remains a love that
dare not speak its name. In the case of Shakespeare for example, the
Bard is offered up as a 'full-blooded heterosexual' and the *Sonnets*
are consigned to the realms of aberration or, even worse, presented
as a neutered allegorical exploration of Platonic friendship. Peter
Erickson rejects this obfuscation of male relationships: 'As applied
to male ties in the plays, the terms *spiritual* and *Platonic* are ethereal

and bland to the point of distorting the rich material with which we must come to grips.'[29] Undoubtedly the Renaissance was permeated with a variety of sexual practices of which male same-sex eroticism was merely another type. Although, as noted above, the period lacked the word *homosexual*, it certainly had no shortage of recently coined verbal equivalents, *ganymede* (1591), *ingle* (1592), *catamite* (1593), and so on. Bray's work is important in alerting us to the differences between modern and early modern ways of thinking about sexuality and in its sustained stress on the historicising of social practice. His work is a useful corrective to the sloppy inaccuracies represented by a transcendental category of 'the homosexual'. An example of the woeful inadequacy of such a concept is A. L. Rowse's description of the personality of Milton:

> The young Milton was a pretty boy, after a feminine fashion: the 'Lady of Christ's'. . . . Milton belonged to a recognisable feminine type who would not accept it; one has known such examples. The effect often is to over-emphasise their masculinity; it leads to a discernible psychological strain, repression, the sharpening of the senses and faculties that goes with that, the finer edge, the acridity and liability to bitterness. It is all there in Milton – a world away from William Shakespeare, the completely released, normal, masculine heterosexual.[30]

This kind of normative and moralistic criticism is flawed by its ahistorical acceptance of modes of sexual behaviour. [31] Rowse's writing should function as a warning of what happens when definitions of erotic practice are discussed without reference to the sexual epistemology of a period which has altered significantly. Yet, at the same time, the reluctance to acknowledge a homosexuality – evident in the above literary examples – that at least resembles our own, seems perversely to refuse the possibility of making sense of the sexual past. Though there cannot be transhistorical sexual categories and thus no hetero- or homosexuality outside of each sociohistorical place, the loose identification of varying forms of sexual behaviour allows one to describe and discuss interrelationships between dominant ideologies and social forms including those based upon a recognition and subsequent oppression of so-called deviant sexualities.

The instancing of homoerotic writings from the Renaissance is not the only way of countering Bray's reluctance to acknowledge a discourse of homosexuality in the early modern period. Perhaps the best way of illustrating the seriousness with which the matter was considered is to turn our attention to the numerous contemporary condemnations of 'aberrant' sexualities. These are voiced in any number of prose denunciations of lewdness and immorality and are often linked with attacks on the theatre.

III

Thomas Beard's *The Theatre of Gods Iudgements* contains a typical example of the horror of homosexuality which is commonplace in Renaissance conduct books. In a chapter entitled 'Of effeminate persons, Sodomites, and other such like monsters', Beard cites a series of examples of homosexuals and transvestites that have received their come-uppance:

> *Sardanapalus* King of Assyria, was so lasciuious and effeminate, that to the end to set forth his beauty, hee shamed not to paint his face with ointments, and to attire his body with the habites and ornaments of women, and on that manner to sit and lie continually amongst whores, & with them to commit all manner of filthinesse and villany: wherefore being thought vnworthy to beare rule ouer men, first *Arbaces* his lieutenant rebelled, then the Medes and Babylonians reuolted, and iontly made warre vpon him, till they vanquished and put him to flight: and in his flight he returned to a tower in his pallace, which (mooued with griefe and despaire) he set on fire, and was consumed therein.[32]

The moral is clear: sexual indulgence, transvestism and self-gratification render the ruler unsuitable and deserving of death. There is something strangely Marlovian about this particular exemplar. Sardanapalus is a cross between the narcissistic Edward and the grandiose and exotic Tamburlaine. The climax of the story, set in the flaming tower, also has a Marlovian intensity about it. The lesson of the importance of moral probity in the ruler was a Renaissance commonplace. When Malcolm 'tests' Macduff with his boast that 'there's no bottom, none, / In my voluptuousness' (*Macbeth*, IV. iii. 60–1), Macduff replies that Malcolm is not only not fit to govern but not fit to live (l. 103). Rulers thus serve as particularly effective examples of providential punishment for sexual misdemeanours:

two vnworthy Emperors, *Commodus* and *Heliogabalus*, who laying aside all Emperiall grauitie, shewed themselues oftentimes publikely in womans attire; an act as in nature monstrous, so very dishonest and ignominious . . . these cursed monsters ranne too much out of frame in their vnbridled lusts and affections.[33]

As we might expect, their end is nothing if not sensational, the former being poisoned and strangled 'when that would take no effect', and 'the other . . . slaine in a iakes where he hid himselfe, and his body (drawne like carrion through the streets) found no better sepulchre but the dunghill'.[34] In these examples, the Elizabethan reader is insulated from the horror by the removal in time and space – these are ancient and oriental rulers. But Beard is eager to point out the relevance of these tales; for him nothing much has changed since God took the law into his own hands and destroyed those two Biblical dens of iniquity; even after the destruction of 'those abominable wretches of Sodome and Gomorrah . . . there are [still] too many such monsters in the world, so mightily is it corrupted and depraued'.[35] Occasionally this depravity was attributed to the general turpitude of Catholicism: 'Pope *Iulius* the third, whose custome was to promote none to Ecclesiasticall liuings, save onely his buggerers: amongst whome was one *Innocent*, whome this holy father . . . would needs make Cardinall: nay, the vnsatiable and monstrous lust of this beastly and stinking goat was so extraordinary that he could not abstaine from many Cardinals themselues.'[36] The 'stinking goat' leads Beard quite naturally to an instance of bestiality. It is worth reminding ourselves that anal intercourse and bestiality were both legally termed 'sodomy' and that there seems to have been little to choose between them.

> It is not for nothing that the law of God forbiddeth to lie with a beast, and denounceth death against them that commit this foule sinne: for there haue been such monsters in the world at sometimes. . . . *Crathes* a sheepheard, that accompanied carnally with a shee goat, but the Buck finding him sleeping, offended and prouoked with this strange action, ran at him so furiously with his hornes, that hee left him dead vpon the ground. God . . . emploid . . . this bucke about his seruice in executing iust vengeance vpon a wicked varlet.[37]

The importance of this extraordinary tale for our discussion of homosexuality is to illustrate that all kinds of 'errant' sexualities

from transvestism to caprine or ovine indiscretions, homoeroticism
to incest were grouped together. All were seen to represent a departure from the sacramental ideal of heterosexual monogamy and
thus all were culpable. Fundamentally the sodomite was constructed
discursively outside the structure of married monogamy as an example of the Renaissance nightmare of the inversion of the order of
things. Such behaviour was literally anti-social and was thus the
object of legislative power. Dressing in women's clothing, bestiality, homosexual intercourse and pederasty were an affront to an
age which valued the conceptions of divine order and natural
harmony. Bray writes forcefully: 'What sodomy and buggery
represented . . . was . . . the disorder in sexual relations that, in principle at least, could break out anywhere.'[38] It is in the context of the
conception of homosexuality as this terrible inversion of God's
proper scheme of things that we should pick up the recurrent
term 'monster'. The title of Beard's chapter was 'Of effeminate
persons, Sodomites, and other such like monsters'. Commodus and
Heliogabalus's transvestism was 'an act . . . monstrous', while the
inhabitants of Sodom and Gomorrah were 'monsters'. The prelates
were possessed of a 'monstrous lust' and those with a predilection
for bestial intercourse are also labelled monsters. The term, like
'sodomy', covers a multitude of sins and William Rankins employs
it in his condemnation of sexual intemperance and theatrical indulgence when he published in 1587 his *Mirrovr of Monsters: Wherein
is plainely described the manifold vices, & sported enormities, that are
caused by the infectious sight of Playes, with the description of the subtile
slights of Sathan, making them his instruments.* The tract clearly holds
actors responsible for corruption in the state. Near the beginning
Rankins describes them in the following vituperative terms:

> What men are these? (naie rather monsters) that thus corrupt so
> sweete a soile: such are they, as in outward shew seeme painted
> sepulchers, but digge vp their deeds, and finde nothing but a
> masse of rotten bones.
>   Some terme them Comedians, othersome Players, manie
> Pleasers, but I Monsters, and why Monsters? Bicause vnder col-
> our of humanitie they present nothing but prodigious vanitie.[39]

As if we could have missed the point, a marginal note harangues
us, '*They are monsters.*' For William Prynne, transvestites, such as
the infamous

Male-priests of Venus, the Roman Galli or Cinœde, the passive Sodo-
mites in Florida, Gayra and Peru; who clothing themselves sometimes,
not always in womans apparell . . . are for this, recorded to posterity,
as the very monsters of nature, and the shame, the scum of men. If men
in womens apparel be thus execrable unto Pagans, how much
more detestable should they bee to Christians who are taught not
onely by the light of nature, but of the *Gospel too*, to hate such
beastly male-monsters in the shapes of women?[40]

Phillip Stubbes condemns all transvestism whether or not it is
part of a dramatic entertainment, citing as his authority Deuteronomy 22: 5: 'The woman shall not weare that which pertaineth
vnto a man, neither shall a man put on a womans garment: for all
that doe so, are abomination vnto the LORD thy God.' Stubbes continues with the standard exegesis: 'Our Apparell was giuen vs as a
sign distinctiue to discern betwixt sex and sex, and therefore one to
weare the Apparel of another sex, is to participate with the same,
and to adulterate the veritie of his owne kinde. Wherefore these
[transvestites] may not improperly be called *Hermaphroditi*, that is,
Monsters of bothe kindes, half women, half men.'[41] The notion of
clothes as a 'sign' of sex appears in Stephen Gosson's *Playes Con-*
futed in five Actions published the preceding year. Gosson again
bases his condemnation of transvestism on divine commandments:

The Law of God very straightly forbids men to put on womens
garments, garments are set downe for signes distinctiue between
sexe & sexe, to take vnto vs those garments that are manifest
signes of another sexe, is to falsifie, forge, and adulterate, contrarie
to the expresse rule of the worde of God. Which forbiddeth it by
threatning a curse vnto the same. . . . in Stage Playes for a boy to
put on the attyre, the gesture, the passions of a woman . . . is by
outwarde signes to shewe them selues otherwise then they are.[42]

It would seem that once again, as with Mercutio's distortion of
linguistic signs which we have witnessed above (see Chapter 6),
that the law of the father is being undermined by 'refusing the
signs', this time sartorial ones. The anxieties over cross-dressing
illustrate the Renaissance apprehension about dress which is inappropriate to the wearer either in terms of class or sex.[43] John Williams
attributed monstrous transvestites directly to the work of Satan:
God 'had diuided male and female, but the deuill hath ioyn'd them,

that *mulier formosa*, is now become, *mulier monstrosa superne*, halfe man halfe woman'.[44] William Harrison's *The Description of England* (1587) notes that so much cross-dressing is taking place in respect of both sexes that 'women become men and men [are] transformed into monsters'.[45] John Rainoldes is clear about stage homoeroticism resultant from boy actors: 'Those monsters of nature, which *burning in their lust one toward an other, men with men worke filthines,* are as infamous, as *Sodome*: not the doers onelie, but the sufferers also.'[46] The furious insistence on the monstrous is symptomatic of a fear of the illusionistic properties of disguise and playing.

At stake in the various contentions over cross-dressing and boy actors was a complex and critical question to do with the mimetic particularities of drama: that is, did the players actually *become* the characters they were playing on-stage? Rankins is in no doubt that they did:

> Of which sort of men in the chief place, may be placed Players, when they take vpon them the persons of heathen men, imagining themselues (to vaineglory in the wrath of God) to be the men whose persons they present. . . . No doubt but there is amongst them can play *Iudas*, as naturally as if he were the very man that betrayed Christ, & verily think that the visarde of godly learning, is so far from good liuing, that vnder these pretended collours, these godlesse men crucifie Christ a newe.[47]

For Prynne, theatrical transmutation undermined essential aspects of masculinity: 'our men-woman Actors are most effeminate, both in apparell, body, words and workes'.[48] The possible metamorphosis of the player was all the more dangerous in the case of boy actors performing female roles because, according to some of the commentators, boys and women were naturally alike. Rosalind notes this affinity when she tells Orlando how she has acted as a mock-fiancé(e) in the past; of one of Ganymede's apparent former clients s/he tells him:

> He was to imagine me his love, his mistress; and I set him every day to woo me; at which time would I, being but a moonish youth, grieve, be effeminate, changeable, longing and liking, proud, fantastical, apish, shallow, inconstant, full of tears, full of smiles; for every passion something and for no passion truly anything, *as boys and women are for the most part cattle of this colour.*
>
> (III. ii. 373–7, my emphasis)

The capricious youth has a lot in common with woman who according to the misogynist mythologies of the period, was characterised by inconstancy and instability: 'Frailty, thy name is woman!' (*Hamlet*, I. ii. 146). As far as the opponents of the theatre were concerned, this affinity made the youths particularly vulnerable to a kind of transsexual identity crisis. In fact it is important to recognise that the similarity between women and boys and their mutual disparity from men had always underpinned a discourse of homosexual desire. Thomas Stehling points out that homoerotic poetry frequently 'makes male beauty a category of female beauty. Nobody here is tall, dark, and handsome; instead we find only fair, pretty boys.'[49] The correspondence between boys and women was not merely the result of theatrical activity. Stephen Orgel notes that up to the age of about seven years, male children were treated exactly the same as females and that they acquired their manhood when they were 'breeched' – put into breeches – 'a formal move . . . into the world of men [and] traditionally the occasion for a significant family ceremony'.[50] Manhood is a condition into which boys grow and from which women are always excluded. Boys and women begin in a comparable state and it is this similarity which threatens to facilitate the monstrous transmutation of the boy actor into the woman that he plays. Indeed this is exactly the situation of Ganymede who is transformed into the woman that she plays for Orlando's benefit.

According to the anti-theatrical propagandists then, acting is not a form of disciplined pretence but a kind of dramatic transubstantiation; to *act* immorally on-stage is to *be* immoral in real life. It is not disbelief but identity itself which is suspended, or rather unfixed as the player is required to abnegate his own self and exchange his person for a persona. Laura Levine writes, 'It is not that the actor himself has the power to shape identity, but that the part is actually constitutive and shapes the man [or, we should add, boy] who plays it.'[51] The iniquity of playing is thus not a function of any collaborative self-delusion by company and audience, it is the factual metamorphosis of the actor into the character and this transformation is an insult to the God that shaped the actor's identity in the first place. It is no accident that the transfiguration of Bottom into an ass takes place within the context of a dramatic rehearsal. The mutation is symptomatic of the theatre's ultimate possibilities and dangers in a play which alludes parodically to one of the period's most widely-known classical texts which explores the subject of physical transformation and shape-shifting – Ovid's *Metamorphoses*. Prynne is possibly alluding to this very source when he remarks upon the degradation of playing:

> I may . . . condemne these Play-house Vizards, vestments, images and disguises, which during their usage in outward appearance offer a kinde of violence to Gods owne Image and mens humane shapes, *metamorphosing* them into those idolatrous, those bruitish formes, in which God never made them.[52]

The very physicality of the performer is at stake. Rankins remarks: 'men doo then transforme that glorious image of Christ, into the brutish shape of a rude beast, when the temple of our bodies which should be consecrate vnto him, is made a *stage* of stinking stuffe, a den for theeues, and a habitation for insatiate *monsters*'.[53] The actor's body is a 'stage of stinking stuffe', a place of corporeal corruption and mortal degradation – a site, in short, fit only 'for insatiate monsters'. Shakespeare seems cognisant of the word as signifying particularly bodily uncertainty. As Stephano struggles to make sense of the bizarre corporeality of Caliban and Trinculo beneath a gaberdine, he ponders, 'Four legs and two voices; a most delicate monster!' (II. ii. 83). But it is in Shakespeare's employment of the term to refer to the sexual confusion of his transvestite characters that Rankins's concerns are most obviously highlighted. As Viola, disguised as Cesario, realises that Olivia has fallen for her, she laments her deceptive physicality which has not only cheated the Countess but has prevented her own confession of love to Orsino:

> My master loves her dearly,
> And I, poor *monster*, fond as much on him;
> And she, mistaken, seems to dote on me.
> What will become of this? As I am man,
> My state is desperate for my master's love;
> As I am woman – now alas the day! –
> What thriftless sighs shall poor Olivia breathe!
> (II. ii. 31–7, my emphasis)

Viola is both man and woman here transfixed in her own transvestism – a boy actor, playing a girl, performing a boy. Her brother's later admission of identity is a double-take at this 'monstrous' duality as he explains to Olivia that 'You are betroth'd both to a maid and man' (V. i. 255) – to the play's own 'master-mistress'.

IV

It is with a sense of the vehemence of the opposition to cross-dressing in the period that we should approach Stephen Greenblatt's enormously influential essay on the subject of Renaissance (homo) sexuality, 'Fiction and Friction'. Based on the writings of Renaissance medicine and gynaecology, and on several bizarre accounts of sexual transmutation, Greenblatt attempts to demonstrate that femaleness was perceived as simply a partially formed maleness and that sexual homology constructed woman as a genitally interiorised man.

> At least since the time of Galen it had been widely thought that both males and females contained both male and female elements. . . . since Galen it had been believed that the male and female sexual organs were altogether comparable, indeed mirror images of each other. . . . In the sixteenth and seventeenth centuries, physicians and laymen of sharply divergent schools agreed that male and female sexual organs were fully homologous.[54]

The implications of this fascinating thesis are enormous for the present discussion for if women were basically semi-realised men, then all difference between homo- and heteroeroticism disappears. As Greenblatt mischievously puts it, 'One consequence of this conceptual scheme – "For that which man hath apparent without, that women have hid within" – is an apparent homoeroticism in all sexuality.'[55] The obvious response to this argument is that if men and women were seen to be essentially the same, then why did the anti-theatrical polemicists of the period become so anxious about cross-dressing? If men and women are thought to be identically endowed, though configured differently, the objections of Rankins, Prynne *et al.* would make no sense.

I would like to complicate the issue further by engaging with Greenblatt on two other counts. Firstly the cavalier assertion that the theory of genital homology was sponsored by 'physicians and laymen of sharply divergent schools' is at odds with other evidence. Ian MacLean charts the breakdown of the scientific certitude in genital homology instancing the 'Parisian Doctor André Du Laurens [who] writes a very coherent account of [the] medical dispute in 1593, concluding against comparability'.[56] MacLean goes on to assert that 'By 1600, in nearly all medical circles . . . one sex is no longer thought to be an incomplete version of the other. Indeed, far from being described as an inferior organ, the uterus now evokes admiration and eulogy for its remarkable rôle in procreation.'[57] Key sections of Greenblatt's evidence are drawn from editions of Galen, Ambroise Paré, and Henri Estienne which were published in 1536, 1573, and 1579 respectively. Yet the conclusions he draws from them are cited in an attempt to explain the sexual situation of Shakespeare's heroines, who were created well over half a century after the publication of the first of these. The challenges to the homological theory were in fact occurring at precisely the time of the composition of Shakespeare's plays. For example, Thomas Vicary in his *The Anatomie of the Body of Man*, published in 1586, likens the clitoris to the penis. But by 1615, Helkiah Crooke is pointing out the differences between clitoris and penis when he notes that the former 'hath no passage for the emission of seed; but the virile member is long and hath a passage for seed'.[58]

Moreover, Greenblatt's choice of medical authorities is mostly continental yet he employs them in an effort to explain the transvestism of the English theatre. Ironically, European continental theatre was not transvestite, as the surprised Thomas Coryate observed during his travels in Venice in 1608: 'Here I obserued certaine things that I neuer saw before. For I saw women acte, a thing that I neuer saw before, though I haue heard that it hath beene sometimes vsed in London' and William Prynne notes this foreign tendency, though less enthusiastically – 'they have now their female-Players in Italy, and other forraigne parts, and as they had such *French-women Actors*, in a Play not long since personated in *Black-friers Play-house*, to which there was a great resort'.[59] Greenblatt's central thesis, then, is undermined both by the abundant and fierce treatises of the antitheatre lobby which certainly indicate that the theory of genital homology was not universally accepted, and by his anachronistic and inapposite selection of primary sources.[60]

Secondly, we ought to note that 'Fiction and Friction' is of a piece with the new historicist propensity to analyse forms of sociality within a framework which serves to promulgate the very power structures under scrutiny and that, as a direct consequence of its argument, oppositional voices and subversive strategies surrounding issues of sexuality are utterly disempowered. This tendency has been reproved by materialist critics and is perhaps the clearest division between American new historicism and English cultural materialism. In her introduction to *The Matter of Difference*, for example, Valerie Wayne castigates what she calls 'the depoliticising tendencies of some new historical practice' and 'its apolitical and recuperative effects'.[61] In the case of 'Fiction and Friction', one might be tempted to ask, if all men and women are really men, then what hope for feminism?

Although Greenblatt does overlook the severity of the anti-theatrical polemicists in his effort to support his thesis that in essence, there was no transformation going on when boys dressed as girls, and though his argument is flawed in the ways described above, it is not the case either that invective towards dramatic transvestism was universally shared. While Gosson, Rankins, Prynne and others worried about the transformation of boys into monstrous parodies of women, the professional thespians seemed interested in demonstrating the error of their opponents' ways. Of these, the most notable is Thomas Heywood, whose *An Apology for Actors* was published in 1612. Obviously, the pamphlet's success was important to the industry and various poets and playwrights indicated their support for it by prefixing the essay with eulogistic poems. John Webster, for example, notes that far from theatre being a place of vice and iniquity, it is an instrument for moral direction, displaying the evils of the past for the instruction of the present, 'Who dead would not be acted by their will / It seems such men have acted their liues ill.'[62] In another introductory poem, 'To my approued good friend M Thomas Heywood', John Taylor ingeniously proposes that if the play's moral import is being overlooked by its puritan opponents, then the fault lies not in the drama, but in them:

> A Play's a true transparant Christall mirror,
> To shew good minds their mirth, the bad their terror . . .
> For Playes are good or bad as they are vs'd,
> And best inuentions often are abus'd.[63]

With this sentiment, Heywood himself concurs, 'Playes are in vse as they are vnderstood, / Spectators eyes may make them bad or good.'[64] In line with this stress on the hermeneutic duty of the spectator, Heywood emphasises the allegorical import of the Scriptures when he tackles the tricky subject of transvestism:

> Yea (but say some) you ought not to confound the habits of either sex, as to let your boyes weare the attires of virgins, &c. To which I answere: The Scriptures are not alwayes to be expounded meerely, according to the letter . . . but they ought exactly to be

conferred with the purpose they handle. To do as Sodomites did, vse preposterous lusts in preposterous habits, is in that text flatly and seuerely forbidden: nor can I imagine any man that hath in him any taste or relish of Christianity, to be guilty of so abhorred a sinne. Besides, it is not probable, that Playes were meant in that text, because we read not of any Playes knowne in that time that *Deuteronomie* was writ, among the Children of Israel.[65]

For Heywood, there is never any danger of the parable of trans-vestite drama turning into truth: 'To see our youths attired in the habit of women, who knowes not what their intents be? who can-not distinguish them by their names, assuredly knowing they are but to represent such a Lady, at such a tyme appoynted?'[66] Of course, such a prolific playwright as Heywood, reliant on theatre for his livelihood, is unlikely to bite the hand that feeds him. Even so, a reading of the drama of the period with its plethora of jokes and double-takes dependent upon cross-dressing, suggests that the au-dience were unlikely to have been seduced by theatrical convention and to have mistaken the boy actors for the women that they played. William Gager, like Heywood, clearly differentiates between sodomitic acts and theatrical representation: 'it doth not beseeme them to folow wemens maners: in the common course of life, to the perverting of the law of nature, honestie, and comelines; or for any evill purpose; yet a boy, by way of representation onely, may, not indecently, imitate maydenlie or womanlie demeanour'.[67] For the most part, accounts of audience experience are well able to separate life and art. When Thomas Coryate saw the Venetian women play-ers he was impressed: 'they performed it with as good a grace, action, gesture and whatsoeuer conuenient for a Player, as euer I saw any masculine Actor'.[68] The fact that these female actors were considered to have performed women's roles as well as the boys back home, implies that Coryate for one was under no illusion when attending the English theatre. Boy actors must have been accepted as a convention, otherwise the effect of so many of the stage jokes would have been lost.

When Christopher Sly 'recognises' his long-lost wife (who is of course a page) and suggests that they make up for fifteen years' sexual inactivity, the page has hastily to grope for an excuse:

Sly: Madam, undress you, and come now to bed.
Page: Thrice noble lord, let me entreat of you

To pardon me yet for a night or two;
Or, if not so, until the sun be set.
For your physicians have expressly charg'd,
In peril to incur your former malady,
That I should yet absent me from your bed.
                                    (Induction. II. 114–21)

There is surely a double-take here as the page in woman's clothing is *seen to be* a confidence trick in which the audience share at the expense of the gullible drunk. The paradox is that a Renaissance audience was prepared daily to accept plays in which this cross-dressed pretence occurred as a matter of course. The effect of this scene is to foreground the conventions of Elizabethan theatre and to alert the audience to the ludicrous nature of misapprehending theatre as life. Sly mistakes the boy for a girl for the same reason that he mistakes himself for a lord: he is a fool. *Hamlet* offers another transparent example of the self-consciousness of the playwright in using boy actors. As he greets the players, the prince notes that the boy who played the female roles has grown in height and is sporting the first signs of a beard, 'O, my old friend! Thy face is valanc'd since I saw thee last; com'st thou to beard me in Denmark? – What, my young lady and mistress!' (II. ii. 418). He continues lightly, 'Pray God, your voice, like a piece of uncurrent gold be not crack'd within the ring' (l. 420). These stagey jokes staged can only have been designed to be apprehended; they are not secret signatures for the reading *cognoscenti* since, in Shakespeare's day, there were none.

Not all contemporary critics agree, however, that Shakespeare wanted deliberately to expose the boy beneath the gown. Robert Kimbrough, for example, protests that 'a speech assigned by Shakespeare to a woman in disguise as a boy can work in the theatre *only* if the audience knows and accepts that the speaker is really a woman. . . . We do Shakespeare a disservice not to accept his women as women.'[69] Kimbrough's mistake is that he considers the Renaissance theatre to be illusionist in the first place. In writing of Rosalind, he betrays an attitude to drama which is simply anachronistic: 'In consciously using her disguise to act in a way that society will not allow a woman to act, she is more her real, essential self – or can move more easily to discovery and revelation of that essential self.'[70] The point is, that there is no 'essential self', only performances of it, as rendered by each actor (male or female) who takes the role. A theatre without the modern technical sophistication – set, lights, sound and so on – is of necessity a theatre of self-consciousness.[71] In the light of Shakespeare's deliberate, even heavy-handed, gender jokes, Kimbrough's essentialist protestations should not be accepted uncritically.

Perhaps the most obvious example of Shakespeare's theatrical reflexiveness towards boy actors comes late in *Antony and Cleopatra*. As the Egyptian Queen laments the theatricalisation of her reign, she anticipates the humiliation of being portrayed by a male youth: 'I shall see / Some squeaking Cleopatra boy my greatness / I' th' posture of a whore' (V. ii. 218–20). The *OED* defines the verb *boy* as follows: 'To represent (a woman's part) on the stage, as boys did before the Restoration', and illustrates with instances from 1568 and 1573 as well as this particular example. This is Shakespeare at his most self-consciously representational, reminding his audience in the very teeth of Cleopatra's fear that she will be parodied by a boy, that she is being parodied by a boy. As I remarked above in Chapter 4, nowhere do we *see* the goddess on her barge; nowhere is there a pretence at 'reality'. It is as though Shakespeare's boy actor needs to remind us that the play we are watching is an illusion, that Cleopatra's majesty is too great to represent other than symbolically, just as the Chorus insists on the fallacy of the battle of Agincourt we 'witness' in *Henry V*. Members of a Renaissance audience were never required to forgo a knowledge that they could not help but possess – that they were at a play and that these actors were precisely that whether they impersonated kings, villains or women. For all the disapproval of the polemicists, there was no more chance of mistaking a boy for a girl than there is confusing Kenneth Branagh with Hamlet or mistaking Judi Dench for Volumnia.

Shakespeare's otherwise misogynist canon can be neatly appropriated for feminism by suggesting that the playwright is deconstructing the essentialism of binary opposites based on the category of fe/male. Marianne L. Novy's rather sentimental *Love's Argument* is typical of this approach: 'If boys can play women and the characters that we think of as women can play boys, this reminds us doubly that gender can be seen as a role rather than as [a] biological given.'[72] This is also the view of Juliet Stevenson, the actress who played Rosalind in the 1985 RSC production of *As You Like It*: 'I'd always suspected that there's a much more dangerous play in *As You Like It*. A subversive play, one that challenges notions of gender, that asks questions about the boundaries and qualities of our "male" and "female" natures.'[73] Paradoxically, the playing of female characters by women on the modern stage may have actually served to shut down this aspect of the plays' feminism. The self-conscious ironies of the various transvestite boy-heroines further pretending to be boys or of having Sly's wife played by a boy who is a page pretending to be a woman, must inevitably be invalidated when the parts of female characters are taken by female actors. The effect is to thin the complexity of the transsexual motif – for *boy posing as girl posing as boy* we now have to read simply, *girl posing as boy*. Cleopatra's remark, 'I have nothing / Of woman in me' (V. ii. 237–8), exposes the constructedness of gendered representation which could in turn be read as a feminist strategy, but without the double-take at the boy beneath the costume the moment can only be seen as transcending sexual identity rather than problematising its limits. Ironically, the arrival of female actors in the theatre has eroded dramatic polysemy and served to weaken the apparent radicalism with which, according to critics like Novy, Shakespeare's works challenge sexual stereotyping.

The humanist desire to find in Shakespeare a proto-feminism is misplaced when it is reliant upon what Kathleen McLuskie has called 'psychological realist modes of interpretation'.[74] Rather than functioning to highlight issues of feminism, Shakespeare's boy actor serves as a basis for the interrogation of issues surrounding homoeroticism. This is because, quite simply, in a large number of the plays, especially the comedies, the wooing takes place between two men both diegetically (Ganymede and Orlando) and extra-diegetically (the boy playing Rosalind and the boy playing Orlando). There is then an exact equivalence between the two kinds of playing in my title; erotic engagement at the level of the story is paralleled by same-sex performance at the level of the storytelling and it is in this context that the otherwise extreme claim of the theatrical opponents – that the audience are vulnerable to an erosion of their heterosexuality – needs to be read.

In *Still Harping on Daughters*, Lisa Jardine was one of the first commentators to investigate the question of Shakespeare's boy actors specifically in relation to the modes of eroticism that they aroused. She contends that the erotic interest of the audience towards the boy actor 'hovers somewhere between the heterosexual and the homosexual'.[75] Jardine is right but for the wrong reasons. She is correct to assume that the boy actor was a focus of homoerotic interest but she is wrong in as much as she adduces her argument almost exclusively from the views of the Puritan opponents who can hardly have been expected to write about the theatre in an objective or reasonable way. When they imply that the theatre is a den of iniquity, we should not always assume, as Jardine does, that they were telling the truth – propagandists rarely do.[76] There is, however, ample evidence from the plays themselves to demonstrate the overlap between boy actors and erotic motivation. This is primarily the result of the equivalence between the same-sex eroticism in the play – Ganymede/Orlando, Cesario/Orsino, etc. and the all-maleness of the company performing the play. As Jardine puts it, 'Wherever Shakespeare's female characters . . . draw attention to their own androgyny . . . the resulting eroticism is to be associated with their *maleness* rather than with their femaleness.'[77] Despite Jardine's telling analysis, she shows herself to be hostile to the boy actor himself. At one point, she refers to him as 'Ganymede . . . the boy-actor mincing and lisping his way through his "woman's part".'[78] It is unfortunate that in her desire to address what she takes to be the sexism of an exclusively male acting company, Jardine begins to sound homophobic.[79]

She is not alone and this homophobia is itself symptomatic of the difficulty of separating out performance and erotic arousal, playing and playing. James L. Hill offers another example of this antipathy towards Shakespeare's boy actors, arguing that they were not accomplished and were certainly not to be trusted with major parts.[80] The article is a bizarre attempt to belittle the female roles in an effort to demonstrate that Shakespeare himself was aware of the shortcomings of his young actors and so deliberately reduced the dramatic demands he made upon them. The essay is predicated throughout upon a prejudice against the boy actors. For Hill, they are just not manly enough: 'The demands upon the actor playing Lear are so infinitely beyond those made upon the boy playing Ophelia that there is little point in comparing them.'[81] The implication – that Shakespeare's women are easier to play than his men – is entirely unsound; one could easily counter-argue by noting that Beatrice or Paulina are more demanding roles than Osric or Fabian. Underpinning Hill's whole essay is the assumption that the boy actor is an impaired performer, not up to playing a masculine role, liable to be 'overwhelmed by its dramatic demands'.[82] Though mistaken, the article demonstrates that questions of performance and potency in both dramatic and sexual senses are immanently connected. Hill never attempts to refute the suggestion that boy actors formed the focus of homoerotic attention; instead, he simply criticises them as performers in a manner which, like Jardine's, smacks of homophobia.

V

Parts for women in classical drama are fewer than those for men and all-male companies must assume a responsibility for further disenfranchising women in the profession. There is a pressure to perform Shakespeare's plays with male and female parts taken by actors of the 'right' sex. Productions as a Renaissance audience would have seen them, in this respect, are not common. In 1991–92, however, Declan Donnellan directed an all-male version of *As You Like It* for the theatre company of which he is artistic director, Cheek by Jowl. The testament to the success of the 'female' performances – Tom Hollander as Celia and Adrian Lester as Rosalind – was the rapid cessation of audience embarrassment following their first entrance. The risks were high: Donnellan required the two actors to perform the court scenes in full-length dresses, beads, lipstick, earrings and with piping voices; moreover, both of them utilised a glib giggling which did little to intensify the emotional tension between the characters. In this early part of the play, the production ran the risk of losing the story under the novelty of transvestism. It may well be that it flirted deliberately with this possibility but the care with which Donnellan had prepared us for their cross-dressing suggested that this was probably not the case. At the beginning, the full company assembled on-stage in a standard uniform of black trousers and collarless shirts. One of the actors stepped forward and announced, 'All the world's a stage, / And all the men [*whole company except two move across stage right*] and women [*Hollander and Lester move down-stage left*] merely players.'

The relationship of the 'women' was infused with comic lightness. In her attempts to console the isolated and dejected Rosalind, Celia would lift her friend's skirt and kiss her calves. There was a playfulness and a clear homoeroticism about the gesture which was sharpened by Celia's passionate defence of Senior's daughter in the face of her father's brutality: 'we still have slept together, / Rose at an instant . . .' (I. iii. 69–70). Jardine's contention that 'whenever

Shakespeare's female characters ... draw attention to their own androgyny ... the resulting eroticism is to be associated with their *maleness* rather than with their femaleness' was clearly demonstrated by this relationship. The actors, though playing women, were visibly *male* (their dresses were sheer and there was no bosom padding) and the intimation of a primary erotic relationship between them was consequently more heavily suggestive of male homosexuality than lesbianism. As Orlando wooed Ganymede, Hollander's Celia movingly looked on in a mixture of jealousy and pathetic resignation. The frustration was pointed up in her reprimand, 'You have simply misus'd our sex in your love-prate' (I. i. 181). Rosalind's response – 'O coz, coz, coz, my pretty little coz ...' – was an attempt to calm her but also an acknowledgement that Orlando had come between them. Again, the nature of the attraction was an ambiguous mixture of male homoeroticism and heterosexuality.

Lester's Ganymede was a combination of bravado and brittle emotional instability, one minute cooing, the next shouting, the next indulgently fantasising. At one point, as Joe Dixon's ostentatiously gay Jaques made to kiss the boy, Ganymede demonstrated her 'true' (female) sex by taking his hand and placing it on her breast. Of course the fact that the actor was male doubled the irony with which Jaques met this peculiarly androgynous figure. All of the boy / girl / boy / girl gender-bending was dramatically immanent. By the time Sam Graham's Phoebe and Richard Cant's Audrey entered, there was a playful self-consciousness about the cross-dressing. This allowed the foul Audrey to enter subsequently for the wedding in a tiny bright yellow mini-dress.

Donnellan, at the final moment, shocked the audience out of the comic comfort of Arden. As the couples lined up to be married, each bride knelt down-stage of her partner. Rosalind entered to provide the solution to the marital riddle. She lifted her veil and told Orlando, 'To you I give myself, for I am yours' (V. iv. 110). Orlando, with a look of utter shock, staggered back and shoved her from him, darting up-stage. Rejected, Rosalind had no option but to throw herself, weeping, on her father, 'To you I give myself, for I am yours.' In this reversal of addressees (in the text Rosalind speaks to her father first), the lines became failed and then successful attempts to submit herself to male authority figures. Orlando visually recanted and walked down-stage to reclaim his wife but the damage had been done and the effect was to question the firmness of such a union. The presence of Jaques, looking on in a mixture of cynicism and superciliousness, did little to set these misgivings to rest and, despite the cheerful dancing at the end, a sour flavour remained.

The force of this closing sequence was to imply that Orlando was unable to face *as a woman* the boy he had been wooing – he was clearly embarrassed that his male confidant turned out to be his future wife and that the love that Ganymede had protested during their courtship was nothing less than a homosexual version of the erotic discourse in which he had been training. The extraordinary achievement of this production was that, in casting male actors, all of this ambiguity was obvious to the audience in a way that it could not have been to Orlando. Despite the final unveiling of Ganymede as Rosalind, the actual presence of the boy actor tended to reinforce the homoerotic element of the relationship and, although Orlando was seeing this for the first time, he was seeing it in reverse (Plate L). For him the character he had met in the forest was transformed from man into a woman; for us s/he had never been anything else but a man.

While Donnellan's *As You Like It* raised issues of homoeroticism through its casting of male actors and its careful exploitation of them in dramatic situations, such as the unveiling of Rosalind, Sam Mendes's *Troilus and Cressida* for the RSC's 1990–91 season emphasised the degraded nature of all sexual relationships irrespective of their orientation. *Troilus and Cressida* contains the most explicitly homosexual relationship in the canon but it is also a play engaged with the relationships between men and women and in particular with the issue of female fidelity. It is worth reminding ourselves that while Hermione, Desdemona, Innogen and Hero are assumed to be unfaithful, only Cressida is. This idea of betrayal set the tone for a production which despised human sexuality with all the vehemence of Thersites: 'Lechery, lechery! Still wars and lechery! Nothing else holds fashion. A burning devil take them!' (V. ii. 192). It was thus entirely fitting and symptomatic of the production as a whole that the face that launched a thousand ships, the woman at the centre of the most epic of all wars, the ultimate goddess of physical desire, was a tired and lewd vamp with something of Fenella Fielding's coarse sexuality in *Carry On Screaming*. Sally Dexter's Helen of Troy was brought down-stage on the shoulders of four semi-naked servants, wrapped in gold material like a present. Paris unwrapped her and the irony was apparent. A curly black wig, a tight red dress with a heaving décolleté and make-up that was so thickly and badly applied that it caused a mixture of revulsion and embarrassment (Plate M). Pandarus's song degenerated into a series of absurd sexual grunts, accompanied by phallic thrusts, and Helen licked him and groaned in lascivious appreciation. Mendes in this brilliantly directed central scene emptied the epic tale of all its grandiose pretensions. Instead of the mythical Helen, he offered us the woman to which Diomedes attributes the destruction around him: 'For every false drop in her bawdy veins / A Grecian's life hath sunk; for every scruple / Of her contaminated carrion weight / A Trojan hath been slain' (IV. i. 71–4). The production's attitude to human relationships was infused throughout with a caustic nihilism.

Much of the sexual deviousness of the production was placed in Norman Rodway's pimpish Pandarus. Dressed in blazer and panama, Rodway was a swanky combination of humorous do-gooder and camp voyeur. His admiration for Troilus was close to fantasy and he relished his physical details like his cloven chin with such abandon that it was clear that Cressida was not the only one attracted to him. Throughout Pandarus was the source of much kissing and patting on bottoms, flirtation and *double entendre*. He was entirely nonchalant about sexual morality, with a tired indifference towards the enormity of the consequences of marital infidelity: 'The ravish'd Helen, Menelaus' queen, / With wanton Paris sleeps [*pause, shrugs shoulders*] – and *that's* the quarrel' (Prologue. 10). There was a prevailing atmosphere of enervation and listlessness towards the possibility of forming human relationships, signalled most clearly in the *ennui* of Achilles.

Ciaran Hinds's Achilles was a disaffected new-romantic. In black leather boots and trousers, buckles and straps and with black string vest, slicked-back hair and designer stubble, he looked like something out of early-eighties glam rock (Plate N). Hinds sometimes assumed a black leather maxi coat which swept after him as he exited with a self-dramatising and androgynous flourish. When he welcomed Hector to the Greek lines he draped himself from a ladder up-stage and whispered a smouldering *Willkommen* in the manner of Emcee from *Cabaret*. The allusion to the musical, with its sordidness and degradation, was entirely appropriate in a world where 'Nothing [is] but lechery [and] All [are] incontinent varlets!' (V. i. 95). Mendes's production, permeated throughout by an onanistic lethargy, illustrated the play's indifference towards the identity, or even sex, of the object desired. *Troilus and Cressida* demonstrates a fundamental ambiguity towards different kinds of sexuality and a complete refusal to simplify desire and the afflictions caused by it.

VI

> He remembered Ophelia. All those nights stripping the wrecked garlands and crumpled white dress from his body, the wrong body, he had been in such trouble, his hands not his hands, the only words in his head her chilly plaints, his hair not his hair, prickling ghoststruck under the mat of long blonde hair he lifted off, nightly.[83]

When Tim Luscombe's London Gay Theatre Company declared that they intended to perform Shakespeare with a homoerotic emphasis, they were vilified by the tabloid press. *The Sun* responded with characteristic boorishness. Its article on the subject, headed 'All's Well That Bends Well: Trendy Theatre Gay-Writes want to do King Queer', featured a top ten of re-written Shakespearean titles including: 'Mince-summer Night's Queen', 'Tight-ass Andronicus', 'Julius Teaser' and 'The Fairy Wives of Windsor'.[84] Predictably *The Sun*'s stable-mate, *The Daily Star*, ran almost an identical story. Its headline read: 'Hail, Good Sir – What a Gay Play' and the article continued with manifest hyperbole, 'Lecherous Henry VIII will be turning in his grave as his six wives are transformed into RENT BOYS.'[85] It also contained a list of play titles which included 'Butch Ado About Nothing' and 'As Hugh Likes It'. As if to distance their own readers from this depraved version of the Bard, both stories appeared on page 3 alongside 'Curvey Kirsten' and Gayner Goodman. The latter model was described as touring with a theatre group – 'Let's hope our London beauty studies her lines. After all, everyone else does.' Press attention to the London Gay Theatre Company was, fortunately, not limited to the tabloids. A front-page piece in *The Independent* had raised the issue the previous day and *The Times* noted the controversy in its editorial which, however, included the surreal assertion that 'Shakespeare is a misty ocean in which elephants can swim and lambs can paddle'![86] For *The Times* the embarrassment of the controversy could be laid to rest with the aid of the transcendental affirmation that the plays 'can survive the quirks and obsessions of their contemporary directors. . . . Never mind the bias of directors. Go for the words, and find whatever you want there, with pleasure. The old fellow is a manifesto for all seasons.'[87] In contrast to this essentialising faith in the plays' textual authority, Luscombe is unashamed about his theatrical appropriation of this powerful cultural totem. He sees the necessity of gay Shakespearean production as an antidote to the limitations of traditional theatre:

> Because one feels excluded from so much of society one also feels excluded from an appreciation of Shakespeare because all the plays one sees of Shakespeare, or at least nearly all the productions one sees of Shakespeare, are 'heterosexualist' . . . and . . . as a gay director, working with a gay company, I feel like grabbing him back to redress the balance.[88]

The cultural struggle for the possession of Shakespeare is on – Luscombe's *Hamlet* will contravene Section 28 if presented in a publicly subsidised theatre – and an informed awareness of the issues surrounding the various modalities of sexuality in the early modern period as well as those raised by the dramatic practice of male transvestism can serve only to broaden and complicate, in a positive way, the parameters of such a struggle. Shakespeare, if justly deployed, constitutes one of the most empowering tools for undoing pernicious and destructive prejudice. In its fidelity to the dramaturgical procedures of Shakespeare's time and in its self-conscious complication of erotic practices, playing with boys (as Cheek by Jowl demonstrated), may contribute to the development of a society in which the cultural construction of the Bard as a 'normal' heterosexual, is perceived to be an ideological mythology.

Notes

1. Joe Orton, *What the Butler Saw*, in *The Complete Plays*, ed. John Lahr (1976), p. 429.
2. Christopher Marlowe, *Dido Queen of Carthage*, in *Complete Plays and Poems*, ed. E. D. Pendry and J. C. Maxwell (1976), p. 193.
3. Simon Shepherd, 'Shakespeare's private drawer: Shakespeare and homosexuality', in *The Shakespeare Myth*, ed. Graham Holderness (Manchester, 1988), 96–110, p. 97.
4. Gwyn Williams, *Person and Persona: Studies in Shakespeare* (Cardiff, 1981), p. 132.

5. Ibid., p. 136.
6. Joseph A. Porter, 'Marlowe, Shakespeare, and the Canonisation of Heterosexuality', *The South Atlantic Quarterly*, 88 (1989), 127–47.
7. Alan Bray, *Homosexuality in Renaissance England*, second edn (1988); Gregory W. Bredbeck, *Sodomy and Interpretation: Marlowe to Milton* (1991); Bruce R. Smith, *Homosexual Desire in Shakespeare's England: A Cultural Poetics* (1991); Jonathan Goldberg, *Sodometries: Renaissance Texts, Modern Sexualities* (Stanford, California, 1992).
8. Simon Shepherd, *Marlowe and the Politics of the English Theatre* (Brighton, 1986), p. 199.
9. Christopher Hill, *The Collected Essays*, 3 vols (Brighton, 1985–86), III, 230.
10. Bray, *Homosexuality*, pp. 16–17.
11. 'During the . . . sixty-eight year period [of Elizabeth's and James's reigns] there was but one conviction for sodomy' (Smith, *Homosexual Desire*, p. 48).
12. Richard Barnfield, *Poems 1594–1598*, ed. Edward Arber (Birmingham, 1883), p. 5.
13. Bray, *Homosexuality*, p. 61.
14. Ibid., p. 61. Smith casts doubts over the authorship of the commonplace book (*Homosexual Desire*, pp. 112–13).
15. For the homoerotic model of the second eclogue, see Byrne R. S. Fone, 'The Other Eden: Arcadia and the Homosexual Imagination', in *Literary Visions of Homosexuality*, ed. Stuart Kellogg (New York, 1983), 13–34. See also Bredbeck, *Sodomy and Interpretation*, pp. 200ff; Smith, *Homosexual Desire*, esp. Chapter 3; Goldberg, *Sodometries*, Chapter 3.
16. A symptom of this discrimination is the extent to which Barnfield is under-represented in anthologies of the period. In *The Penguin Book of Elizabethan Verse*, ed. Edward Lucie-Smith (Harmondsworth, 1965) only three poems appear, none of which is homoerotic. In *Poems of the Elizabethan Age*, ed. Geoffrey G. Hiller (1977) Barnfield is completely absent. David Norbrook's *Penguin Book of Renaissance Verse 1509–1659*, ed. H. R. Woudhuysen (Harmondsworth, 1992), contains only two sonnets. The poet fares best in Emrys Jones's *The New Oxford Book of Sixteenth Century Verse* (Oxford, 1991) which reprints 'The Affectionate Shepherd'.
17. Joseph Pequigney, *Such is my Love: A Study of Shakespeare's Sonnets* (1985), p. 65.
18. *Poems of Ben Jonson*, ed. George Burke Johnston (1960), first published 1954, p. 16, my emphasis.
19. *Epicoene or The Silent Woman*, ed. L. A. Beaurline (1967) I. i. 24. The *OED* rather frostily glosses *ingle* as 'A boy-favourite (in bad sense)'.
20. Everard Guilpin, *Skialetheia or A shadowe of Truth, in certaine Epigrams and Satyres* (1598), A 8ʳ, B 1ᵛ.
21. See for example, *Coriolanus*, IV. v. 115–27; *Twelfth Night*, III. iii. 4–13, and the extremely intense form of 'marriage' ritual that Othello and Iago undertake together, III. iii. 469–86.
22. James M. Saslow, *Ganymede in the Renaissance: Homosexuality in Art and Society* (1986), p. 83.

23. Alan Bray, 'Homosexuality and the Signs of Male Friendship in Eliza-bethan England', *History Workshop*, 29 (1990), 1–19, p. 2.
24. Ibid., pp. 4, 13.
25. Ibid., p. 9.
26. Ibid., p. 9.
27. Michel Montaigne, *The Essayes*, trans. John Florio, 3 vols (1904), I, 219.
28. Thomas Stehling, 'To Love a Medieval Boy', in *Literary Visions of Homosexuality*, ed. Stuart Kellogg (New York, 1983), 151–70, p. 157.
29. Peter Erickson, *Patriarchal Structures in Shakespeare's Drama* (1985), pp. 6–7.
30. A. L. Rowse, *Milton: The Puritan* (1977), p. 21.
31. Rowse seems to have a monopoly on superficiality in relation to the study of sexuality in history. In an extraordinary interview published in *The Sunday Times* under the title 'Rowse to the rescue of the hetero Bard', he says, 'You must remember William Shakespeare was 100% hetero, dear, while any number of people insisted that he was homo. Well, I wouldn't care tuppence if he was – Marlowe was 100% homo, only interested in the boys, but William Shakespeare was a strongly sexed *hetero*.' (24 February 1991)
32. Thomas Beard, *The Theatre of Gods Iudgements* (1597), p. 359. Sardanapalus was obviously a proverbial example of lewdness. Thomas Heywood's *Apology for Actors* (1612) remarks that 'Sardanapalus [is played as a moral lesson] against luxury' (F 3ᵛ).
33. Ibid., p. 360. William Prynne also condemns Heliogabalus and Sardanapalus in *Histrio-mastix. The Players Scovrge or Actors Tragaedie* (1633), pp. 199–200, 882.
34. Beard, *Theatre*, p. 360.
35. Ibid., p. 361, misnumbered p. 359.
36. Ibid., p. 361, misnumbered p. 359. Both Bray and Hill note that the sensationalism surrounding the trial and execution of the Earl of Castlehaven for rape and sodomy in 1631 was in part a result of his Catholicism (*Homosexuality*, p. 49; 'Male Homosexuality', p. 227). See also Smith, *Homosexual Desire*, p. 52.
37. Ibid., p. 362.
38. Bray, *Homosexuality*, p. 25.
39. William Rankins, *Mirrovr of Monsters* (1587), B iiʳ.
40. Prynne, *Histrio-mastix*, p. 200.
41. Phillip Stubbes, *The Anatomie of Abuses* (1583), F vᵛ. The Biblical au-thority is also cited by John Rainoldes, *Th'Overthrow of Stage-Playes* (Oxford, 1599), p. 82. It is also cited *ad nauseam* by Prynne, *Histrio-mastix*, pp. 179, 200, 207, 212, 884, 886 and so on.
42. Stephen Gosson, *Playes Confuted in fiue Actions* (1582), E 3ᵛ-E 5ʳ.
43. See Chapter 2 for a discussion of Renaissance fashion and also Lisa Jardine, *Still Harping on Daughters: Women and Drama in the Age of Shakespeare*, second edn (1989), especially Chapter 5.
44. John Williams, *A Sermon of Apparell* (1620), p. 7.
45. William Harrison, *The Description of England* (1587), ed. G. Edelen (Ithaca, 1968), p. 147.
46. Rainoldes, *Th'Overthrow*, p. 44.

47. Rankins, *Mirrovr*, G i^v.
48. Prynne, *Histrio-mastix*, p. 187.
49. Stehling, 'To Love a Medieval Boy', p. 156.
50. Stephen Orgel, 'Nobody's Perfect: Or Why Did the English Stage Take Boys for Women?', *The South Atlantic Quarterly*, 88 (1989), 7–29, p. 11.
51. Laura Levine, 'Men in Women's Clothing: Anti-theatricality and Effeminization from 1579 to 1642', *Criticism*, 28 (1986), 121–43, p. 125.
52. Prynne, *Histrio-mastix*, p. 893, my emphasis.
53. Rankins, *Mirrovr*, B ii^v, my emphases.
54. Stephen Greenblatt, *Shakespearean Negotiations* (Oxford, 1988), 66–93, pp. 78–9.
55. Ibid., p. 92.
56. Ian MacLean, *The Renaissance Notion of Woman* (Cambridge, 1980), p. 33.
57. Ibid., p. 33.
58. Cited by Thomas Laqueur, 'Orgasm, Generation, and the Politics of Reproductive Biology', in *The Making of the Modern Body*, ed. Catherine Gallagher and Thomas Laqueur (1987), 1–41, p. 15.
59. Thomas Coryate, *Coryats Crudities* (1611), p. 247; Prynne, *Histrio-mastix*, pp. 214–15.
60. For more generalised criticism on Greenblatt's methodology in 'Fiction and Friction', see Joel Fineman, 'The History of the Anecdote: Fiction and Fiction', in *The New Historicism*, ed. H. Aram Veeser (1989), 49–76.
61. *The Matter of Difference: Materialist Feminist Criticism of Shakespeare*, ed. Valerie Wayne (1991), pp. 11, 4.
62. Heywood, *An Apology for Actors* (1612), A 6^v. As Hamlet tells Polonius, the players 'are the abstract and brief chronicles of the time; after your death you were better have a bad epitaph than their ill report while you live' (II. ii. 520).
63. Ibid., A 7^v.
64. Ibid., F 2^v.
65. Ibid., C 3^r.
66. Ibid., C 3^v.
67. Cited by his opponent, Rainoldes, *Th'Overthrow*, p. 103.
68. Coryate, *Coryats Crudities*, p. 247.
69. Robert Kimbrough, 'Androgyny Seen through Shakespeare's Disguise', *Shakespeare Quarterly*, 33 (1982), 17–33, p. 17.
70. Ibid., p. 25.
71. See Anne Righter, *Shakespeare and the Idea of the Play* (Harmondsworth, 1967), first published 1962.
72. Marianne L. Novy, *Love's Argument: Gender Relations in Shakespeare* (1984), pp. 193–200.
73. Quoted in *Clamorous Voices: Shakespeare's Women Today*, ed. Carol Rutter (1988), p. 97.
74. Kathleen McLuskie, 'The Act, the Role, and the Actor: Boy Actresses on the Elizabethan Stage', *New Theatre Quarterly*, 3 (1987), 120–30, p. 128.

75. Jardine, *Still Harping*, p. 11.
76. In this respect I disagree with Colin MacCabe who writes, 'I would argue that the Puritan attacks on the theatre are perhaps the best introduction to understanding what Elizabethan theatre was actually like' ('Abusing self and others: puritan accounts of the Shakespearian stage', *Critical Quarterly*, 30 (1988), 3–17, p. 4). Only Gosson seems to have had any first-hand experience of the theatre (see MacCabe, p. 6).
77. Jardine, *Still Harping*, p. 20.
78. Ibid., p. 20.
79. Goldberg attacks Jardine who, he maintains, 'slips perilously from explaining the attitudes of antitheatrical polemicists to adopting them' (*Sodometries*, p. 112).
80. James L. Hill, '"What are they Children?" Shakespeare's Tragic Women and the Boy Actors', *Studies in English Literature*, 26 (1986), 235–58.
81. Ibid., p. 242.
82. Ibid., p. 251.
83. A. S. Byatt, *The Virgin in the Garden* (Harmondsworth, 1981), first published 1978, p. 60.
84. *The Sun*, 11 January 1992. Ironically, while the paper asserted that 'Bard buffs were aghast last night, fearing productions like Antonia and Cleopatra and even Macbent', it continued with the misplaced assertion that 'Coriolanus would be alright' – presumably the author had overlooked the possible joke on *anus*. In a piece of correspondence, Luscombe informed me that *As You Like It* and *Coriolanus* were in fact the two plays he would most like to direct (27 October 1992).
85. *The Daily Star*, 11 January 1992.
86. *The Independent*, 10 January 1992; *The Times*, 11 January 1992.
87. Ibid.
88. Correspondence with the author, 27 October 1992.

9

Shakemyth:
The Fabrication of
Shakespearean Culture

I

At the end of Edward Bond's play *Bingo*, first performed in 1973, William Shakespeare takes an overdose. The play ends with the Bard convulsing on the floor and his daughter, Judith, ransacking his bed for the final version of his will. Bond's Shakespeare is a corrupt businessman who colludes with the system of enclosure which evicts the poor and persecutes the dispossessed. In a scene earlier in the play, he drinks himself unconscious in the presence of his candid and truculent contemporary, Ben Jonson. He is tired: 'Time goes. I'm surprised how old I've got.' In reply to Jonson's questions about the meaning of *The Winter's Tale* and his present writings, Shakespeare can only respond with negative utterances.

> *Jons.:*   What are you writing?
> *Shak.:*   Nothing.
> *[They drink]*
> *Jons.:*   Not writing?
> *Shak.:*   No.
> *Jons.:*   Why not?
> *Shak.:*   Nothing to say.
> *Jons.:*   Doesn't stop others. Written out?
> *Shak.:*   Yes.
> *[They drink]*
> *Jons.:*   Now, what are you writing?
> *Shak.:*   Nothing.[1]

In the preface to the play, Bond discusses the historical changes he made to some of the dates and personages in Shakespeare's biography:

I made all these changes for dramatic convenience. To recreate in an audience the impact scattered events had on someone's life you often have to concentrate them. I mention all this because I want to protect the play from petty criticism. It is based on the material historical facts so far as they're known, and on psychological truth so far as I know it. . . . Of course, I can't insist that my description of Shakespeare's death is true. I'm like a man who looks down from a bridge at the place where an accident has happened. The road is wet, there's a skid-mark, the car's wrecked, and a dead man lies by the road in a pool of blood. I can only put the various things together and say what probably happened. Orthodox critics usually assume that Shakespeare would have driven a car so well that he'd never have an accident.[2]

Bond confesses that he is not in the business of constructing anything like a biographical study and in his departure from historical veracity for the sake of dramatic effect, he has the precedent of Shakespeare's own work.[3] The reason why Bond is so determined to protect his play from the charge of historical inaccuracy or, as he calls it, petty criticism, is that, for Bond, Shakespeare is not a person but a site of competing theories about the role of the artist in society and the interconnections between history and literature: 'Part of the play is about the relationship between any writer and his society.'[4] For Gary O'Connor, who reviewed the play at the Royal Court in 1974 (in which the celebrated Shakespearean actor, Sir John Gielgud, played the Bard), Shakespeare, as Bond's play portrayed him, was the victim of a terrible smear campaign. Bond's progress, he wrote, 'as a playwright is from the direct, cold-blooded infanticide of *Saved*, to the more refined literary assassination of *King Lear* (a mythological figure of English culture), and now, in *Bingo*, the more abstract assassination of Shakespeare's reputation (a writer who lived a blameless life, happened to be gifted with genius, and probably believed in original sin)'.[5] For O'Connor, Bond's work constitutes an attack not merely on the person of the Bard but, as if that was not bad enough, on the Bard's greatest play, *King Lear*. Bond's version of the play, *Lear* (first performed in 1971) is particularly violent. Bond admitted that the play was full of what he called, 'aggro-effects' and he claimed such devices corresponded to the *Verfremdungseffekt* in the plays of Brecht. They needed to be all the more shocking than instances of Brecht's alienation effect, however, because these have become politically etiolated:

Alienation is vulnerable to the audience's decision about it. Sometimes it is necessary to emotionally commit the audience – which is why I have aggro-effects. Without this the V-effect can deteriorate into an aesthetic style. Brecht then becomes 'our Brecht' in the same sloppy, patriotic way that Shakespeare becomes 'our Shakespeare'. I've seen good German audiences in the stalls chewing their chocolates in time with Brecht's music – and they were most certainly not seeing the world in a new way. . . . Brecht is no more of a writer for all time than Shakespeare is.[6]

In *Lear* and in *Bingo*, Bond is concerned to prevent Shakespeare becoming 'our Shakespeare'. As he says, he finds this sloppy and patriotic. O'Connor's unsubstantiated assumptions that Shakespeare lived a 'blameless life', and his curiously inapposite claim that he 'probably believed in original sin', not to mention the casual attribution of 'genius' to him is precisely the kind of sloppiness to which Bond (and Brecht before him) is so vehemently opposed. The kinds of cultural assumptions that underpin O'Connor's admiration of Shakespeare, make him one of those 'Orthodox critics' who, in Bond's words, 'usually assume that Shakespeare would have driven a car so well that he'd never have an accident.'

I want to dismantle the values inscribed at the centre of the theoretical position of these 'Orthodox critics', to lay bare the issues surrounding the processes by which Shakespeare has become 'our Shakespeare' and to account for the unwritten assumption that the plays of the Renaissance, and especially those of Shakespeare, constitute the Formula-1 of literary driving. Bond's driving metaphor is a useful one in terms of pedagogy. The degree that students pursue has to be conducted in compliance with a highway code, according to which some literary practices are 'safer' than others while still others are downright dangerous. Ultimately though, like the golden rule of driving on the left, the selection of Shakespeare as our literary Aston Martin is arbitrary. We could, as long as we all did it at the same moment, cross the central reservation and drive from that moment on, on the right. There is nothing more *inherently* valuable in the writings of Shakespeare than there is right in driving on the left. Although the canon of Shakespeare's writings, his range of genres and his variety of styles is greater (in the sense of 'larger') than that of say, Marlowe, that does not necessarily mean that it is greater (in the sense of 'better'). Shakespeare has become the ultimate driving machine, not because he is intrinsically superior to Marlowe or anyone else, but because he is revered as such. Although this reverence started early it has not always been as powerful as at present. Indeed Shakespeare has been deliberately engineered as both a theatrical and educational vehicle for specific social, cultural and political purposes. In both the dramatic and auto-matic senses, Shakespeare is the product of a particular kind of workshop.

For the purposes of this chapter, I am going to differentiate between Shakespeare, the Renaissance dramatist and theatre entrepreneur, and what I am going to call Shakemyth, which is the complex of cultural ideas surrounding the plays, the social institutions through which they are represented and the mythologised persona of Shakespeare. It is clear that while O'Connor is apparently referring to the playwright, he is really drawing on the shared cultural assumptions about Shakemyth. Ideas about universality, that the plays say something to all people at all times, that the playwright is in some mysterious way Everyman, are central to the construction of Shakemyth. For Christopher Hampton this 'essentially mythical and fixed order of things . . . is . . . nothing but a mystifying absurdity'.[7] According to their prevalent analyses, the plays deal with aspects of 'human nature' which apparently have gone unchanged for the last four hundred years and show no sign of changing.[8] People are dangerously reduced in this scheme of things to static essential characteristics. They comprise jealousy, goodness, hypocrisy, nobility, frivolity, self-deceit, love, courage, malevolence and so on. According to the principles of Shakemyth, the plays of Shakespeare are, above all else, *relevant* and they are about *us*. Shakespeare, according to the famous study by Jan Kott, is 'our contemporary' and any suggestion that the plays might be fruitfully approached by our becoming one of Shakespeare's contemporaries is anathema to many thespians.[9] 'Shakespeare himself was a theatre practitioner,' they tell you angrily, 'and you academics always pick him to pieces instead of allowing him to live and breathe!' Perhaps the most offensive and shallow example of this insular arrogance is that of Charles Marowitz who begins his *Recycling Shakespeare* with the sentence, 'This book is directed at two enemies – the academics and the traditionalists.'[10] Repeatedly Marowitz insists on his empirical theatrical wisdom, distinguishing it from fusty scholarship: 'Unlike the views of scholars or critics, mine have evolved from hands-on experiences with several of Shakespeare's plays.'[11] One of his chapters is headed 'Free Shakespeare! Jail

Scholars!' and Marowitz is insistent about the ineptitude or sheer laziness of academics who consistently fail to emerge from their carpeted studies: 'The professors never have to get on their feet at all.'[12] Marowitz continues to reproduce the most callow and ignorant stereotypes about ivory-tower academics, challenging what he asserts is their sheltered naivety with his own hard-nosed expertise based on years of theatrical experience. In this posturing assault, he succeeds only in calling into question his own intelligence:

> In Academe, wanking is a full-time job, and teaching others how to wank, a sign of intellectual respectability. The yardstick of successful wanking, if you are a professor or lecturer, is the number of periodicals which will allow you to wank for them in public; if you are a critic, the number of books devoted to wanking which will be circulated to other members of the cult, and the amount of notoriety your wanks will incite – compared to the wanks of older and more knowledgeable hands. The crowning success of a wanker is not so much to have his wanks bound and circulated but to transfer them into the minds of non-wankers (directors) who are dealing practically with material which the wanker deals with only pornographically.[13]

Thespians and academics rarely get on and their mutual enmity, fuelled by this kind of vituperative attack, can only surrender the plays even further to an ideology which seeks to depoliticise Shakespeare both academically and theatrically. It further compromises the institutions of theatre and education themselves.

According to Kott, man is basically violent and lustful for power. As he writes in his appendix, miserably entitled 'Shakespeare – Cruel and True', the playwright 'gave an inner awareness to passion; cruelty ceased to be merely physical. Shakespeare discovered the moral hell.'[14] Human existence is degrading and there is little hope of anything getting better. Peter Hall, who became director of the RSC in 1960, admitted to driving his productions very much under the influence of this book. Both he and his successor, Trevor Nunn, directed Shakespeare's plays (and formulated the character of the RSC as a result) in line with Kott's dark pessimism. As Alan Sinfield has shown, both disdained the drama's potential to be politically interventionist. Following the turmoil of 1968, Hall expressed his despair for 'a new generation who want to shout down all opposing opinions' while Trevor Nunn explained that 'In most of our work now we are concerned with the human personalities of a king or queen rather than with their public roles.'[15] Shakemyth deals not with the tragedy of state but with the psychological collapse of individuals, not with social revolution but with the passions of characters and experiences that are supposed to be recognisable by each and every one of us. It is this rejection of an engaged political position that transforms Shakespeare into Shakemyth. Humanity is entirely corrupt, as Kott seeks to prove, and there is very little that we can do about it. Moreover, since we are experiencing apparently the same passions, disappointments and frustrations as Hamlet *et al.*, the plays illustrate the futility of political intervention: something is rotten but the rottenness, according to Shakemyth, is not confined to Denmark.

In the prelude to his play *Saved*, Bond exposes this kind of apolitical nihilism for what it is – a deeply reactionary position:

> The idea that human beings are necessarily violent is a political device, the modern equivalent of the doctrine of original sin. For a long time this doctrine helped to enforce acceptance of the existing social order. For reasons the church could not explain everyone was born to eternal pain after death unless the church saved them. It carefully monopolised all the sacraments which were the only means to salvation. [16]

Shakemyth promotes the idea that the plays glimpse this depressing reality and that the reason they are powerful is precisely because they express humanity's powerlessness. So overwhelming is this idea, that when directors or playwrights dare to suggest that Shakespeare is political they are hounded for so doing. O'Connor's reaction to *Lear* is typical of this. Nakedly political and interventionist productions, like those of the confrontational director Michael Bogdanov, are charged with travestying Shakespeare. In the best tradition of Orton's Edna Welthorpe, Mrs A. N. Butler wrote to the then Minister for the Arts, Richard Luce, to complain about the English Shakespeare Company's post-Falklands history cycle (which opened in 1986):

Dear Mr Luce
I wish to protest in the strongest possible terms about the performances being given by the English Shakespeare Company. . . . I do beg you to send someone to view this subversive and indecent production before further harm is done. The leaflet is advertising

for school parties, but in my opinion no children should be allowed near it – they would come away with an extraordinarily muddled view of history, and the impression that it is all right for British soldiers to shoot prisoners in the back, rob the dead, use foul language and behave like hooligans – and that in fact this is what the British army does. How dare the producers equate the heroes of Agincourt with football hooligans? And why should they be allowed to destroy our culture by knocking down our historical heroes? This is just a travesty of Shakespeare misused as a vehicle for modern pornography. . . . I strongly object, personally, to any part of my taxes being used to fund such an obscene and degrading performance. . . . I do believe Mrs Thatcher's aim is to uphold our cultural values, and so I do hope that better control can be exercised over what is funded by taxpayers' money through the Arts Council.[17]

One extraordinary thing about this letter is the assumption that if the plays were done 'straight' they would be historically accurate as though the playwright was a writer of documentaries rather than dramas. According to Shakemyth, politics, especially those of a confrontational nature, do not belong in the theatre.

What has happened, according to Bond, to the oppositional state of Brecht, is that he has become appropriated by the *status quo*. Shorn of his politics, his alienation effect has now been reduced to a mere aesthetic. Shakespeare too has suffered a similar fate though recently a breed of young directors has emerged who are suspicious about Shakemyth. They include Tim Luscombe who directed the ESC *Merchant of Venice* in a way which pointed up rather than tried to sanitise, the play's anti-Semitic content, and Simon Usher who, although possessed of a tragic despondency, does engage with contemporary issues, especially to do with sexual and gender politics.[18] It is significant that both of these directors work mostly away from the mainstream: the large theatre establishments seem to produce Shakemyth rather than Shakespeare. Indeed Bond has clashed with both institutions (the RSC and the National Theatre) and now prefers to see his work produced by youth and community or even student companies.[19] He has noted the political paralysis of the larger theatres: 'Great national institutions – national theatres, national galleries and so on – promote culture but also control and repress it. They make the whole of society a ghetto.'[20] Of the RSC itself, Bond mischievously remarked:

The standard of work is catastrophic. 'RSC' is a sort of aftershave they spray on everything. It must be good also for upholstery. The plays – Shakespeare's or others – are not examined at all. They are made to work with an all purpose costume, wig, lighting rig, music (well actually two tunes: the anthem and the 'naughty one') and even an emotion which comes with a volume control to increase the intensity. It all works together like a flyblown orgy – the music, the lights, the costumes, the wigs all reach a climax together.[21]

Of course some political statements (that is, the right ones or more precisely statements of the Right) are permissible in the theatre provided they validate established social institutions or state-sponsored aspirations. Olivier's film of *Henry V* which went into production in 1942 and was funded by the Ministry of Information, dedicated as it is to the forces of the Second World War, is an obvious example of the political appropriation of Shakespeare.[22] The only acceptable theatrical politics, according to Shakemyth, are those that maintain the hegemony of the dominant culture, yet this is a paradoxical state of affairs considering we are talking not about literature but *drama*.

In *Marxism and Literature*, Raymond Williams contends that Literature 'did not emerge earlier than the eighteenth century and was not fully developed until the nineteenth century'.[23] In this sense Shakespeare's works are pre-literary. Moreover, the plays are profoundly *un*literary in another way. They are, as this book has insisted throughout, *dramatic texts*, performance pieces and, like other performance arts (music, dance, opera etc.), they exist solely at the moment of their performance. They are not like novels, pieces of sculpture or paintings which can be read and re-read, read backwards, interrupted, slowed down, speeded up by the reader/viewer. All plays are mediated to us by a director, designer, lighting designer, actors, stage managers, production managers, producers, theatre architects, programme compilers and so on. The reception of the play will be affected by the reviewers, censorship, technical possibilities of the space, ticket price, time of performance, publishing rights, etc. Indeed, whether or not we ever get the chance to see the play is a decision taken by Arts Council drama officers and regional arts development officers. Drama is socially produced; Shakespeare can never be anything other than Social Shakespeare. Even a small-scale production presented in a studio theatre may easily involve over a hundred people: nowhere is the death of the author more apparent than in drama.

One facile solution to the embarrassing problem that Shakespeare's plays are not really Literature (and it is a solution that thespians and academics alike are guilty of), is simply to ignore it. The polysemic nature of dramatic representation is comfortably fossilised when one says, 'Shakespeare is the greatest poet of the English language.' If we treat the plays as poetry we can turn them into Literature. T. S. Eliot was perhaps the most extreme example of this, asserting that all the plays formed 'one poem'.[24] In English departments we fetishise the text, decoding it in an absolute way rather than interpreting it as it changes from production to production. But in the study of a playwright we ignore the institutions of the theatre at our peril. Studies of the plays, like Tillyard's *Elizabethan World Picture* (1943) and *Shakespeare's History Plays* (1944) promote the idea of the playwright as spokes*man* for ideas of hierarchy and political stasis. Like the theatre, conservative criticism is happier with Shakemyth than Shakespeare. The *literary* virtues that critics like Tillyard and Traversi value are wholeness, unity, textual and human coherence. Traversi, for instance, challenged the political contextualisation of Shakespeare's history plays as a distraction:

> The increased attention now given to the background of the plays in terms of contemporary political thought . . . has not been without dangers of its own. There is a very real risk that erudition, in relating these plays to their period, may end by obscuring their true individuality, the personal contribution by which they live as works of art.[25]

In his introduction to *Coriolanus*, published three years later, John Dover Wilson is similarly horrified by the imputation that Shakespeare might be inflected in any political way whatsoever:

> Inasmuch as its main theme or rather its political shell or envelope bears an accidental resemblance to the political controversies that dominate the modern world, the play is often read, and sometimes produced, as if it were a political pamphlet. . . . In *Coriolanus*, as in his other plays, Shakespeare is interested in dramatic art and nothing else.[26]

Political knowledge is a dangerous thing and critical accounts and productions which foreground contemporary ideological issues spoil these 'living works of art'. Over twenty years later, Wilson's apparently apolitical reading was appropriated by the chancellor, Nigel Lawson, who, citing the same play, asserted Shakespeare's Conservative credentials: '*Coriolanus* [is] written from a Tory point of view. . . . Man doesn't change. Or man's nature doesn't change. The same problems are there in different forms.'[27] Lawson offers this Hobbesian instance of the presumption of man's iniquity in order to naturalise the necessity of a rigorous social hierarchy.[28] By purporting to step outside of history, Lawson naturalises his own historically contingent position.

Coriolanus can be read as an index of the political engagement (or lack of it) of the major English theatre companies. Terry Hands' and John Barton's 1989 RSC version was reviewed by Michael Ratcliffe under the title 'Keeping politics out of Shakespeare'.[29] Ratcliffe identified a tendency of the production to gravitate towards its charismatic hero (played by Charles Dance) at the expense of any wider social comment: 'After 10 years of one-party government in Britain and against the momentous events of autumn 1989, the new production has nothing to say about the nature of political responsibility or the covenant of power and leadership between the rulers and the ruled.'[30] Michael Coveney shared this disappointment: 'Even with the acceptable face of mob democracy baring its teeth in Eastern Europe at the end of this astonishing year, the Royal Shakespeare Company . . . cannot make *Coriolanus* sound like a play that really matters.'[31] Charles Osborne, on the other hand, saw the virtue of this political apathy, voicing the values of Shakemyth:

> Too many productions present the play as an example of Shakespeare's political conservatism. There have also been perverse stagings (among them Brecht's adaptation) which – by suppressing certain scenes and lines – have attempted to turn it into a piece of left-wing polemic. It is to the credit of the new production . . . that it follows neither of these paths. . . . [Hands and Barton] remain faithful to Shakespeare.[32]

The charge of politicised infidelity is by now a familiar one. For the Renaissance Theatre Company's production in 1992, Tim Supple recruited a mob of over fifty amateur performers. He rehearsed them over the preceding ten weeks and had drilled them with a military precision. They whirred around Kenneth Branagh's

Coriolanus whom they hoisted up on a ladder; they divided before the tribunes and closed ranks around them, splitting and reuniting with amoebic fluency. At the end of the production, Aufidius faced up-stage and defied the Roman warrior who was brought down-stage, as at the beginning, on the top of a ladder. At an instant, the ladder was lowered and the plebes rushed in. These moments were the high points of this *Coriolanus*: massive realisations of mob power and the terrible potential for inhuman violence. In comparison, Branagh's Coriolanus was disappointing: indignant rather than defiant, blustering rather than lofty. In black biker's boots, black leather trousers and naked under a silver breast-plate with greased-back hair he looked like a science-fiction hero (see Plate O). This *Coriolanus* was a triumph of sabre-rattling but although it was full of images of a mighty and unruly populace, it was a version that buried the political beneath the epic. When David Thacker directed the play for the RSC in 1994, despite setting it in post-revolutionary France, the production, with its clear prioritisation of Toby Stephens's central performance, yet again avoided any sustained political engagement. This Coriolanus was a Napoleonic despot screaming his way through social confrontations and the accent was firmly on his personal determination rather than any kind of political complexity: 'the vague period shift does not work with great resonance. . . . The drama, therefore, focuses unrelentingly upon Coriolanus.'[33] Despite Fran Thompson's explicit design which included blood-spattered banners draped round the theatre reading 'Liberty', 'Equality' and 'Fraternity' as well as a huge version of Delacroix's painting of Liberty up-stage of a half-demolished wall (the Bastille?), the playing was firmly focused on the psychology of Coriolanus himself; there seemed little wider context. The critics were not seduced by the design's overt composition: Michael Billington wrote simply, 'Thacker irons out the political complexities' and, while John Stokes conceded that the setting was potent, he was baffled about its politics: 'the principles underlying Thacker's iconographically powerful production are politically imprecise'.[34] While the RSC's star system makes the play vulnerable to the lead actor taking precedence over the play as a whole (as happened with Dance and Stephens), Supple's production seemed distracted by mob violence and lost sight of the political intrigues of the play. As Ralph Berry writes: 'the essential underlying feature of the modern *Coriolanus* in England is its disengagement from politics. . . . Directors prefer to give the title-role actor his head.'[35]

A notable exception to this tendency was Michael Bogdanov's 1990 production for the ESC. Bogdanov seems at his best when he is dramatising an issue from contemporary politics and, for this *Coriolanus*, he chose the disintegration of Eastern communism and the ousting of the old order. As the cast assembled under full house-lights, bearing a banner reading 'Demokratie' (which plainly alluded in the style of its graphics to the Solidarity logo), the topicality of the revolutionary struggle was enforced. The play's Rome had become an amalgam of Poland, Romania, East Germany and Czechoslovakia; its setting (BC 494), 1989–90. As the house-lights dimmed they were replaced by search-lights, sirens and tear-gas. Protesters sang about bread as riot police waded into their midst. Michael Pennington's Coriolanus had not merely to confront the plebes but the theatre audience which was peppered with members of the cast variously cheering and heckling. The scenes before the people were staged as press conferences: live microphones, papers, jugs and glasses helped create a 'newsy' atmosphere (see Plate P). These scenes took place under full house-lights and they served both to rupture the mimesis of the production and to foreground Bogdanov's political awareness. As he remarked in rehearsal, 'What we have in Europe now, daily, in ten or fifteen places, is in essence the situation we have in *Coriolanus*. People jockeying for power, new regimes taking over, wars starting somewhere else and having to be dealt with, alongside a political situation that changes daily at home.'[36] *Coriolanus* seems unavoidably political, yet Bogdanov's engaged version was the exception rather than the rule.

II

Education is the other major ideological state apparatus through which the values of Shakemyth are promoted. In particular the discipline of 'Eng. Lit.' is constructed around the central figure of Shakespeare and takes its value from him. It is Touchstone in *As You Like It* who remarks that 'the truest poetry is the most feigning' (III. iii. 17) and Shakespeare is the true touchstone of Literature. Shakespeare's poetry is true – true for all time and for all *men* – but, as is the case in the large national theatre institutions, it is the most feigning because, when transformed in the alembic of cultural mediation into Shakemyth, it protests its political neutrality while ensuring the continued promulgation of a politically interested kind of social organisation. As is all too apparent, the State is intrusively engaged in the formulation of educational programmes through the National Curriculum which has eroded schools' autonomy. A consultative paper published by the government in 1989 entitled *English for Ages 5 to 16: Proposals of the Secretary of State for Education and Science*, asserted the centrality of the Bard in its grand scheme of things: 'Many teachers believe that Shakespeare's work conveys universal values, and that his language expresses rich and subtle meanings beyond that of any other English writer. . . . almost everyone agrees that his work should be represented in a National Curriculum.'[37] Thus, as Lesley Aers notes, while Shakespeare is only compulsory at Level Seven and above, he is still mentioned by name for examinations as low as Level Three.[38] Following the midsummer examinations at GCSE in 1992 the Secretary of State for Education, John Patten, suggested that record achievements were the result neither of the success of teachers and administrators nor simple hard work by schoolchildren faced now as never before with the overwhelming possibility of unemployment unless they are high-achievers; rather Patten attacked an exam which, he alleged, had gone soft on academic standards. In an attempt to restore what he considered to be the correct degree of difficulty, a return as he put it, to 'real education', Patten ordered that all 14-year-olds must face tests on *A Midsummer Night's Dream*, *Romeo and Juliet* or *Julius Cæsar*. Nigel de Gruchy, leader of the National Association of Schoolmasters and Union of Women Teachers, responded, 'It is extremely limiting and dictatorship of the curriculum. It will be fine for some pupils, hard work for some and disastrous for others.'[39] This cultural totalitarianism runs the risk of alienating not only teachers but the pupils that they are forced to force through these texts. The decree is based on the equation of Shakespeare with High Culture which is apparently beneficial to the national constitution. At the 1992 Tory party conference, Patten savaged an examination board which had used a hamburger advert in one of its questions. Whatever next?, he asked, 'Chaucer with chips? Milton with mayonnaise? I want William Shakespeare in our classrooms, not Ronald McDonald.'[40] The Secretary of State was echoed by the Prime Minister in his address to the Tory Women's Conference in June 1993: 'People say there is too much jargon in education – so let me give you some of my own: Knowledge. Discipline. Tables. Sums. Dates. Shakespeare.'[41]

From its inception the standardisation of literature revolved around the teaching of Shakespeare. As early as 1921, the Newbolt Report spelt out the unavoidable presence of the Bard, 'Shakespeare is an inevitable and necessary part of school activity because he is . . . our greatest English writer.'[42] The report goes on to express a powerful nostalgia for the Elizabethan period as a lost Golden Age of literary creativity and social harmony. It was an organic society, which was apparently ordered, happy and secure: 'It was no inglorious time of our history that Englishmen delighted altogether in dance and song and drama, nor were these pleasures the privilege of a few or a class.'[43] The fact that this was the period in which subversive dramatists could find themselves thrown into prison (as happened to Ben Jonson), the period in which actors were little more than vagrants, the period in which capital punishment could take the form of public disembowelling, is glossed over in this image of indulgent merriemaking.[44] This is the England not of Shakespeare but of Shakemyth.

The nationalism implicit in Newbolt's statement that Shakespeare is 'our greatest English writer' is commonplace in criticism of the first half of this century. F. R. Leavis, in one of his usual lamentations on the degraded nature of modern society, noted that Shakespeare had written at a period when, unlike that of his own time, 'national culture [was] rooted in the soil.'[45] This organicist ideal finds its explicit formulation in the suggestion that the language of the Bard is English at its most glorious; merely reading the plays aloud will teach children 'correct' or 'standard English'. Moreover there is a thinly veiled but potent myth of cultural ascendancy attached to this linguistic legitimacy. In his 1991 Shakespeare Birthday lecture, the Prince of Wales noted the world-wide superiority of the Bard: 'Shakespeare's message is the universal, timeless one, yet clad in the garments of his time. He is not *our* poet, but the world's. Yet his roots are ours, his language is ours, his culture ours.' Of course, English is now only one of the languages that British society speaks. Charles's monologism unwittingly articulates a chilling hegemonic assumption which demonstrates that it is not just Caliban who is forced to learn the grammar of the ruling classes.

Despite the cultural prejudice of Conservative policy on the teaching of Shakespeare and the intention to limit Shakespearean study to a mere three plays, the playwright is represented widely in Higher Education. In a random sample of prospectuses for entry to various institutions of higher education, 70 per cent specified at least one whole course on Shakespeare. To qualify for entry into Higher

Education to study English, however, it is usually necessary to obtain an English 'A' level and, in most cases, a major proportion of the examination (usually one whole paper) is dedicated to Shakespeare. The con trick of English, to students who have come through that particular exam, ought by now to be plain. On the one hand, teachers and lecturers will offer students *carte blanche* to formulate their own opinions. Expressions like, 'Your interpretations are as valid as mine', or 'I don't know the answers any more than you do' will be familiar to undergraduates; varieties of interpretation are supposed to be equally valid. Poststructuralist relativism divests English lecturers of the authority assumed by Leavis and the Scrutineers. Yet, while protesting their ignorance, the same lecturers are editing student editions and writing critical books, setting and marking examination papers. All interpretations are equal, but some are more equal than others. Bernard Bergonzi takes this to be an act of bad faith:

> it is disingenuous for academics to pretend that they can participate in . . . discussion on terms of complete equality with their students, for there are questions of power and authority involved; at the end of the day, grades and marks, assessing and examining, come into the picture. Students do not forget these overshadowing realities even if academics, caught up in the euphoria of a 'really lively discussion', sometimes do.[46]

Lecturers protest too much that there are no right answers and yet, there is something that the examiners know, that the study guides know and that the exam papers are designed to elicit and, if students read the study guides and are successful in the exams, they too will have been initiated into its mysteries.

III

While the institutions of theatre and education have been discussed separately, it is necessary to point out that they enjoy a symbiotic relationship. Course contents in Higher Education are influenced by local, and therefore affordable, theatre productions. Conversely, while they would never admit it, theatres are guided in their programming by 'A' level syllabuses. Study days and outreach events attached to productions generate a large student box-office while proselytising for a future audience. Shakespeare, because of the education market, is generally good business. In 1991 the Sheffield Crucible replaced *The Revenger's Tragedy* with *As You Like It* in their autumn programme because, in the words of Mark Brickman, the theatre's unusually candid artistic director, 'all the indications suggest a fairly chilly autumn, and frankly we'd be taking a bit of a flyer with a play which doesn't really exist in the public's consciousness. We don't want to find at Christmas that we've come a financial cropper.'[47] 'Public consciousness' may be translated more accurately as the demands of education and because of the limited demands of the National Curriculum, theatregoers may find their choice of Shakespeare limited to just three plays.

What then is the place of Shakespeare in our culture, our education, our theatre? If Shakemyth is so deeply entrenched and so ideologically unsound, why do we continue to teach Shakespeare? If examination papers are simply a test of conformity to the values of Shakemyth, why bother to set and mark them? Shakespeare is not infrequently represented as the immovable epitome of reactionary culture, the representation of white, male, middle-class power. Shakespeare is apparently 'difficult' and texts from the early modern period too distant to be 'relevant'. But this is an approach which generates a vicious circle of low expectations. Under the kind of syllabus that this brings about, students graduate with degrees in English, having read nothing written before 1800. This kind of problem is acute in the former polytechnics because they have traditionally stressed vocational skills. Moreover, more time is spent on basic writing and language work than in the universities, which squeezes the timetable still further.

Those academics keen to see the back of courses in Renaissance literature confuse Shakespeare and Shakemyth. The way forward is not to ditch Shakespeare or even Shakemyth, but to unravel it, to expose its apparent disinterestedness as profoundly ideological. *Every* version of Shakespeare is a *version*; neither closer to nor further from the ever-elusive truth than any other. Shakemyth will not go away any more than Shakespeare will, but a clear distinction between the two and an understanding of their relationship will enable us to appreciate the ideological and cultural fraud of Shakemyth. The most dangerous procedure would be to abandon the plays altogether, to give up performing and teaching them, for if we cease working with them we surrender them to the insidious mythology of Shakemyth. They will remain totems of Englishness,

of human nature, essential and universal, unchangeable and therefore rigidly orthodox. 'The fossils of lies are all we have to base
truth on.'[48]

In the preface to *The Fool*, Bond explains the fallacious permanence of human nature: 'We don't have a fixed nature in the way
other animals do. We have a "gap" left by our freedom from the
captive nature of other animals, from the tight control of instincts.
The gap is filled by culture. Human nature is in fact human culture.'[49] If we accept this equivalence of nature and culture we may
change the former by deconstructing the latter. To explode Shakemyth is therefore not simply to reform an aspect of our theatre, our
educational system or Eng. Lit. but because of the centrality of
Shakemyth in all of these it is to interrogate radically the foundations on which Shakemyth is constructed and thus to revolutionise
our culture.

Notes

1. Edward Bond, *Plays: Three* (1987), pp. 43–4.
2. Ibid., pp. 3–4.
3. As is well-known, Shakespeare substantially reduced the age of
   Hotspur to effect a dramatic contrast with Hal in *I Henry IV* and he
   increased the age of Queen Isabel in *Richard II* to enable him to construct a romantic sympathy at the couple's enforced separation.
4. Bond, *Plays: Three*, p. 4.
5. *Plays and Players*, September 1974, p. 26.
6. Edward Bond, 'On Brecht: a Letter to Peter Holland', *Theatre Quarterly*, 8 (1978–79), pp. 34–5. Compare: 'Since Brecht's time capitalism
   has become adept at weaving alienation and empathy into one self-
   negating experience' (Bond, *The War Plays* (1992), p. 329).
7. Christopher Hampton, *The Ideology of the Text* (Milton Keynes, 1990),
   p. 29.
8. On the importance of 'human nature' to traditional critics of tragedy
   and especially A. C. Bradley, see Chapter 3.
9. Jan Kott, *Shakespeare Our Contemporary*, trans. Boleslaw Taborski, second edn (1967).
10. Charles Marowitz, *Recycling Shakespeare* (1991), p. ix.
11. Ibid., p. ix.
12. Ibid., p. 72.
13. Ibid., p. 73.
14. Kott, *Shakespeare Our Contemporary*, p. 282.
15. Cited by Alan Sinfield, 'Royal Shakespeare: theatre and the making
    of ideology', in *Political Shakespeare: New Essays in Cultural Materialism*,

ed. Jonathan Dollimore and Alan Sinfield (Manchester, 1985), 158–81, p. 169.

16. Bond, *Plays: One* (1977), p. 10.

17. Cited by Michael Bogdanov and Michael Pennington, *The English Shakespeare Company: The Story of the Wars of the Roses, 1986–1989* (1990), pp. 301–3.

18. For an account of an example of Usher's compelling work, see my review of his *Winter's Tale*, *Cahiers Elisabéthains*, 39 (1991), pp. 84–6. His 1990 *Pericles* (Leicester Haymarket Studio) was a sustained attempt to tackle the incestuous elements of the play rather than downplay them as is more usually the case.

19. For example, *Jackets II* which was produced by the Outreach department of the Leicester Haymarket as a community tour in 1989 having been premiered by students at the University of Lancaster. '[O]ften when schools and colleges perform my plays the approach is understood as if it were self-evident and does not need to be theorized. Youthful energy and imagination make the play theatrical, and the youthful need to understand the world makes the philosophical consequences clear. Professional theatres and players have more acting skills, more elaborate equipment and often use more strenuous treatment, but they cannot compensate for the lack of social truth' (Bond, *The War Plays*, p. 330).

20. *The War Plays*, p. 260. Recently Bond said of the RSC version of his *War Plays*, 'I only sat through [it] because they gave me a complimentary ticket. If I'd had to pay I would have asked for my money back.' For Bond, the children of a school in Milton Keynes performed 'way beyond the abilities of the RSC' (*The Guardian*, 15 October 1992). Bond wrote of the article itself, 'It fitted me into a category of disaffected, posturing, embittered writers – and I'm not. . . . I . . . find always a growing interest in what happens and in writing about it' (correspondence with the author, 31 October 1992).

21. Correspondence with the author, 28 December 1992.

22. See Graham Holderness, 'Agincourt 1944: Readings in the Shakespeare Myth', *Literature and History*, 10 (1984), 24–45. On Branagh's version, see Holderness, ' "What ish my nation?": Shakespeare and national identities', *Textual Practice*, 5 (1991), 74–93.

23. Raymond Williams, *Marxism and Literature* (Oxford, 1977), p. 46.

24. T. S. Eliot, *Selected Prose* (Harmondsworth, 1953), p. 102.

25. Derek Traversi, *Shakespeare: From Richard II to Henry V* (1957), p. 1.

26. *Coriolanus*, ed. John Dover Wilson (Cambridge, 1960), p. xxi.

27. *The Guardian*, 5 September 1983.

28. Rosalind King has remarked upon the Tory appropriation of the national Bard, 'It has been a long-standing aim of the Conservative Party to make our greatest national poet a paid-up member. Quotations from *Henry V* made out of context have become a predictable feature of Tory conferences' (*The Guardian*, 6 October 1992).

29. Michael Ratcliffe, *The Observer*, 10 December 1989.

30. Ibid.

31. Michael Coveney, *The Financial Times*, 7 December 1989. Irving Wardle

noted Hands's abiding reluctance to tackle the politics of *Coriolanus*: 'Terry Hands's last production of the piece side-stepped political issues altogether' (*The Times*, 7 December 1989).

32. Charles Osborne, *Daily Telegraph*, 7 December 1989. Bond has noted the conservative press's disdain for Brecht: 'They keep burying him – the *Sunday Times* was doing it again just recently. Someone who has to be buried so often is very much alive' ('On Brecht', p. 34).

33. Nicholas de Jongh, *Evening Standard*, 25 May 1994.

34. Michael Billington, *The Guardian*, 26 May 1994; John Stokes, *The Times Literary Supplement*, 3 June 1994.

35. Ralph Berry, *Shakespeare in Performance* (1993), p. 55.

36. *Background Pack to Coriolanus and The Winter's Tale* (1990), p. 24.

37. Cited by Thomas Healy, *New Latitudes: Theory and English Renaissance Literature* (1992), p. 38.

38. Lesley Aers, 'Shakespeare in the National Curriculum', in *Shakespeare in the Changing Curriculum*, ed. Lesley Aers and Nigel Wheale (1991), 30–9, p. 33.

39. *The Guardian*, 9 September 1992. *Stage Write* (the journal of the National Theatre) published the results of a survey of teachers in Spring 1993. This showed that '92% are greatly disturbed at the prospect of Key Stage 3 paper and pencil tests on Shakespeare.'

40. *The Guardian*, 8 October 1992. Patten continued in a tone which was a mixture of provocation and threat, 'I have a message for those exam boards. Listen very carefully. I will say this only once. Get your act together.'

41. *The Guardian*, 22 January 1994. Patten lost his job in the cabinet reshuffle of July 1994. Since his appointment as Secretary of State he had alienated the teaching unions over compulsory testing in schools and opting out and was widely perceived to have been a disastrous Minister for Education.

42. See Derek Longhurst, 'Not for all time, but for an Age: an approach to Shakespeare studies', in *Re-Reading English*, ed. Peter Widdowson (1982), 150–63, p. 150.

43. Newbolt Report, ibid., p. 151.

44. The Vagrancy Act of 1598 made unlicensed performances punishable by death.

45. F. R. Leavis, *For Continuity* (Cambridge, 1933), p. 216.

46. Bernard Bergonzi, *Exploding English: Criticism, Theory, Culture* (Oxford, 1990), pp. 147–8.

47. *The Guardian*, 12 July 1991.

48. Bond, *The War Plays*, p. 338.

49. Bond, *Plays: Three*, p. 72.

Index